Tkinter GUI Programming by Example

D1594908

Learn to create modern GUIs using Tkinter by building
real-world projects in Python

David Love

BIRMINGHAM - MUMBAI

Tkinter GUI Programming by Example

Copyright © 2018 Packt Publishing

Commissioning Editor: Aaron Lazar
Acquisition Editor: Denim Pinto
Content Development Editor: Anugraha Arunagiri
Technical Editor: Subhalaxmi Nadar
Copy Editor: Safis Editing
Project Coordinator: Ulhas Kambali
Proofreader: Safis Editing
Indexer: Aishwarya Gangawane
Graphics: Tania Dutta
Production Coordinator: Arvindkumar Gupta

First published: April 2018

Production reference: 1240418

Published by Packt Publishing Ltd.
Livery Place
35 Livery Street
Birmingham
B3 2PB, UK.

ISBN 978-1-78862-748-1

www.packtpub.com

`mapt.io`

Mapt is an online digital library that gives you full access to over 5,000 books and videos, as well as industry leading tools to help you plan your personal development and advance your career. For more information, please visit our website.

Why subscribe?

- Spend less time learning and more time coding with practical eBooks and Videos from over 4,000 industry professionals

- Improve your learning with Skill Plans built especially for you

- Get a free eBook or video every month

- Mapt is fully searchable

- Copy and paste, print, and bookmark content

PacktPub.com

Did you know that Packt offers eBook versions of every book published, with PDF and ePub files available? You can upgrade to the eBook version at `www.PacktPub.com` and as a print book customer, you are entitled to a discount on the eBook copy. Get in touch with us at `service@packtpub.com` for more details.

At `www.PacktPub.com`, you can also read a collection of free technical articles, sign up for a range of free newsletters, and receive exclusive discounts and offers on Packt books and eBooks.

Contributors

About the author

David Love is a web developer from Kent, England. He has worked on a multitude of different systems over his career. Programming languages in his arsenal include Python, PHP, and JavaScript. He is well-trained in Linux server management and its relevant technologies, including MySQL, PostgreSQL, NGINX, and supervisor.

David has written an e-book called *Tkinter By Example*, which is available for free under a Creative Commons licenses and maintains an ever-growing blog post named *The Tkinter Cookbook*, full of small examples on how to perform some specific tasks.

About the reviewer

Erik S. Rapert is a programmer and a twin who loves Linux and video games. He lives in Dallas with his wife, who is also a software engineer. Erik has a wide range of experience, which includes creating blinking LEDs using Arduino, building small desktop apps using Python and Tkinter, web development with PHP or Ruby, and developing cutting-edge virtual reality using C++. He has used a very broad range of programming languages, but Python is one of his favorites.

Thank you William C. Slater for teaching me how to write software. Thank you Andrew Closson for being a teacher. Thank you Ashley N. Tharp for being you.

Packt is searching for authors like you

If you're interested in becoming an author for Packt, please visit `authors.packtpub.com` and apply today. We have worked with thousands of developers and tech professionals, just like you, to help them share their insight with the global tech community. You can make a general application, apply for a specific hot topic that we are recruiting an author for, or submit your own idea.

Table of Contents

Preface

Welcome to *Tkinter GUI Programming by Example*. We will be exploring how to use the Tkinter library, which is included alongside most Python installs. This framework is very simple to use, and has a powerful event-handling system and an open license, perfect for anyone who wishes to quickly write and share graphical applications.

Throughout this book, we will be creating three powerful desktop applications, learning about the variety of widgets available in Tkinter. After we have these applications polished, we will then learn how to share them with other people by packaging them up for sharing. When you have finished this book, you will have in-depth knowledge of Tkinter, its widgets, GUI-design principles, and packaging Python projects.

Who this book is for

Do you have a great Python script, which runs via the command line that you wish could have a nice user interface? Or, do you know of a problem which could be resolved with a program containing a graphical interface? If so, this book is for you. All you need is some basic Python knowledge—things such as function declarations, if statements, for loops, and writing to files via the with statement. Everything else, including the use of Python's class system, will be covered in as much detail as you should need to complete each chapter.

What this book covers

Chapter 1, *Meet Tkinter*, introduces us to the Tkinter library itself. We will look at ensuring that it is installed, how to use its widget system, and how to display widgets inside a window. Once the basics are down, we will have a play with some of the easier widgets, including using a Label widget to display text and a Button widget to provide interactivity.

Chapter 2, *Back to the Command Line – Basic Blackjack*, has us return to our roots as Python programmers and create a command-line only version of blackjack. This will get us up to speed with the common situation where we a command-line application, which we want to convert to a nicer interface. We will also discuss Python's class system and how to structure an application for conversion to a graphical interface.

Chapter 3, *Jack is Back in Style – the Blackjack GUI*, starts off the process of converting command-line blackjack to a graphical application. We will learn about the powerful Canvas widget and how we can use it to draw both shapes and images on the user's screen. This chapter will end with us having a working game of blackjack with a graphical interface.

Chapter 4, *The Finishing Touches – Sound and Animation*, teaches how to use the Canvas widget to create animations, which we will use to spruce up our game of blackjack. Of course, animations wouldn't be complete without accompanying sounds, so we will also have a look at how to play sound effects.

Chapter 5, *Creating a Highly Customizable Python Editor*, begins our second application, a text editor. We explore Tkinter's Text widget and its capabilities for handling events. We will also look at the themed widgets, which come with Tkinter in its ttk module, giving our applications a much more professional look.

Chapter 6, *Color Me Impressed! – Adding Syntax Highlighting*, covers how we can use Tkinter's tag system to affect different parts of certain widgets. We will be taking advantage of this system to add syntax highlighting for the Python language to our text editor. We will also explore the indexing system, which Tkinter uses to locate items inside some of its widgets.

Chapter 7, *Not Just for Restaurants – All about Menus*, teaches how we can add different types of menu to our applications—from the top menu bar that most applications have, to right-click context menus.

Chapter 8, *Talk Python to Me – a Chat Application*, begins our third and final application, an online instant messenger. We will learn how to plan the layout for a more complicated application, then piece together all of the different components needed for a chat program. We will also learn how to combine images and text by implementing smileys into the chat.

Chapter 9, *Connecting – Getting our Chat Application Online*, explains how we can use web technologies, including flask, requests, and sqlite3, to get desktop GUI applications communicating with the internet.

Chapter 10, *Making Friends – Finishing our Chat Application*, covers adding a friend's system and blocking system to improve socializing within our application. We will also learn how to manipulate images in Python using PIL by introducing user avatars. We will also learn why threads are great for computationally expensive or repeated tasks inside a GUI application.

Chapter 11, *Wrapping Up – Packaging our Applications to Share*, finishes off the book by briefly covering some widgets, which we did not get the opportunity to use in our three example application. Afterward, we will look at packaging a Python and Tkinter application up for distribution among users of the three biggest desktop operating systems, Windows, Linux, and macOS.

To get the most out of this book

This book assumes that you have:

- A basic understanding of the Python language and its syntax, including functions, if statements, while and for loops, and file handling
- A computer (desktop or laptop) running Windows, Linux, or macOS, which has Python version 3.6 (or higher) installed
- Pip and Virtualenv installed along with Python
- An internet connection to download any external dependencies, which will be needed for our projects

Download the example code files

You can download the example code files for this book from your account at www.packtpub.com. If you purchased this book elsewhere, you can visit www.packtpub.com/support and register to have the files emailed directly to you.

You can download the code files by following these steps:

1. Log in or register at www.packtpub.com.
2. Select the **SUPPORT** tab.
3. Click on **Code Downloads & Errata**.
4. Enter the name of the book in the **Search** box and follow the onscreen instructions.

Once the file is downloaded, please make sure that you unzip or extract the folder using the latest version of:

- WinRAR/7-Zip for Windows
- Zipeg/iZip/UnRarX for Mac
- 7-Zip/PeaZip for Linux

The code bundle for the book is also hosted on GitHub
at `https://github.com/PacktPublishing/Tkinter-GUI-Programming-by-Example`. In case
there's an update to the code, it will be updated on the existing GitHub repository.

We also have other code bundles from our rich catalog of books and videos available
at `https://github.com/PacktPublishing/`. Check them out!

Download the color images

We also provide a PDF file that has color images of the screenshots/diagrams used in this
book. You can download it here: `http://www.packtpub.com/sites/default/files/`
`downloads/TkinterGUIProgrammingbyExample_ColorImages.pdf`.

Conventions used

There are a number of text conventions used throughout this book.

`CodeInText`: Indicates code words in text, database table names, folder names, filenames,
file extensions, pathnames, dummy URLs, user input, and Twitter handles. Here is an
example: "To specify the position within the `grid`, the `row`, and `column` keywords are
used."

A block of code is set as follows:

```
self.label_text = tk.StringVar()
self.label_text.set("Choose One")
```

When we wish to draw your attention to a particular part of a code block, the relevant lines
or items are set in bold:

```
def say_hello(self):
    message = "Hello there " + self.name_entry.get()
    msgbox.showinfo("Hello", message)
```

Any command-line input or output is written as follows:

```
>>> import tkinter
>>> tkinter.TkVersion
```

Bold: Indicates a new term, an important word, or words that you see onscreen. For
example, words in menus or dialog boxes appear in the text like this. Here is an example:
"The last thing to do is to create the method that will be responsible for placing it into
our **Tools** menu."

Warnings or important notes appear like this.

 Tips and tricks appear like this.

Get in touch

Feedback from our readers is always welcome.

General feedback: Email feedback@packtpub.com and mention the book title in the subject of your message. If you have questions about any aspect of this book, please email us at questions@packtpub.com.

Errata: Although we have taken every care to ensure the accuracy of our content, mistakes do happen. If you have found a mistake in this book, we would be grateful if you would report this to us. Please visit www.packtpub.com/submit-errata, selecting your book, clicking on the Errata Submission Form link, and entering the details.

Piracy: If you come across any illegal copies of our works in any form on the Internet, we would be grateful if you would provide us with the location address or website name. Please contact us at copyright@packtpub.com with a link to the material.

If you are interested in becoming an author: If there is a topic that you have expertise in and you are interested in either writing or contributing to a book, please visit authors.packtpub.com.

Reviews

Please leave a review. Once you have read and used this book, why not leave a review on the site that you purchased it from? Potential readers can then see and use your unbiased opinion to make purchase decisions, we at Packt can understand what you think about our products, and our authors can see your feedback on their book. Thank you!

For more information about Packt, please visit packtpub.com.

1
Meet Tkinter

Hello, and welcome to *Tkinter GUI Programming by Example*. In this book, we will be building three real-world desktop applications using Python and Tkinter. You will gain the knowledge to fully utilize Tkinter's vast array of widgets to create and lay out any application you choose.

So why use Tkinter? Tkinter comes bundled with Python most of the time, meaning there's no arduous installation process. It's also licensed under a free software license, meaning, unlike some other GUI frameworks, there's no complicated licensing model to battle against when you want to release your software to the outside world.

Tkinter is also very quick and easy to learn. Code can be written both procedurally or using object-oriented practices (which is the preferred style for anything non-experimental), and runs perfectly on any operating system supporting Python development, including Windows, macOS, and Linux.

In this first chapter, we will cover the following topics:

- Ensuring Tkinter is installed and available
- Creating a main window in which to display your application
- Laying out widgets inside the window via geometry managers
- Creating widgets and displaying them inside your main window
- Displaying static information via a `label` widget
- Creating interactivity with the `Button` widget
- Tying widgets to Python functions
- Using Tkinter's special variables
- Displaying pop-up messages easily
- Getting information from the user

Installation

Most of the time, you will not need to install Tkinter as long as you have Python installed. To check, open an instance of the interactive interpreter and type `import tkinter` (Python 3) or `import Tkinter` (Python 2). If you don't see an error, then Tkinter is already installed and you are ready to go! Some flavors of Linux will not come with Tkinter by default, and if you receive an error message while performing the previous step, search your distribution's package manager. On Debian-based distributions such as Ubuntu, the package should be called `python3-tk`. On RPM-based distributions, including Fedora, you may instead find a package called `python3-tkinter`.

Examples in this book will be written using Python 3.6.1 and Tkinter 8.6. I recommend you also use these versions, or as close to them as possible, when following along. To check your Tkinter version, open an interactive Python prompt and type the following:

```
>>> import tkinter
>>> tkinter.TkVersion
```

Once you've got Tkinter installed and ready, we can move on to a brief overview of how we will be structuring a Tkinter application and then dive in and write our first program.

How will the code be structured?

Tkinter exposes many classes. These are known as widgets. A widget is typically any part of the application that needs to be drawn onto the screen, including the main window.

A Tkinter application always needs to have a main window. This is what will be drawn on the screen for the user to see. This is crucial for any GUI application, so much so that if you do not define one, Tkinter will try to create one for you (though you should never rely on this!). The widget that performs this job is called `Tk`.

The `Tk` widget exposes various window properties, such as the text within the top bar of the application, the size of the application, its position on screen, whether it can be resized, and even the icon which appears in the top right-hand corner (on Windows only).

Because of this feature exposure, it is very common for the main class of an application to inherit from the `Tk` widget, though any Tkinter widget can be subclassed to add program-specific functionality.

There is no set convention for what the subclass should be called. Some like to call it `Root`, some choose `App`, and others (such as myself) prefer to name it after the program itself. For example, a shopping list program would have a class called `ShoppingList` that inherits from `Tk`. Bear this in mind when looking through other sources of information on Tkinter.

Once you have a main window defined, you can begin adding other widgets into it. All other widgets must belong to a parent which has the ability to display them, such as a `Tk` or `Frame`. Each widget is only visible if its parent is. This allows us to group widgets into different screens and show or hide groups of them as need be.

Widgets are placed into their parents using special functions called **geometry managers**. There are three geometry managers available in Tkinter – `pack`, `grid`, and `place`. Let's take a look at each of them in detail.

Geometry managers

Geometry managers serve the purpose of deciding where in the parent widget to render its children. Each of the three geometry managers uses a different strategy and therefore takes different arguments. Let's go over each one in detail, looking at how it decides the positions of new widgets and what sort of arguments need to be provided.

pack

The `pack` geometry manager acts based on the concept of using up free space within the parent widget. When packing, you can specify at which end of the free space to put the widget, and how it will grow along with said free space (as the window itself grows and shrinks). The geometry manager than assigns widgets into said free space, leaving as little empty space as possible.

The `pack` geometry manager is primarily controlled by three keyword arguments:

- `side`: On which end of the available space do you want to place the widget? The options are defined as constants within Tkinter, as `LEFT`, `RIGHT`, `TOP`, and `BOTTOM`.
- `fill`: Do you want the widget to fill any available space around it? The options are also constants: `X` or `Y`. These are Cartesian, meaning `X` is horizontal and `Y` is vertical. If you want the widget to expand in both directions, use the `BOTH` constant.
- `expand`: Should the widget resize when the window does? This argument is a Boolean, so you can pass `True` or `1` to make the widget grow with the window.

These are not the only arguments that can be provided to `pack`; there are others which handle things such as spacing, but these are the main ones you will use. The `pack` geometry manager is somewhat difficult to explain, but tends to create very readable code thanks to its use of words to describe positions.

The order in which widgets are packed matters greatly. Suppose you have two buttons which you wish to stack vertically, with one underneath the other. The first button, which you call `pack(side=tk.BOTTOM)` on, will be at the very bottom of the main window. The next widget, which is packed with `side=tk.BOTTOM`, will then appear above it. Bear this in mind if your widgets appear to be out of order when using `pack` as your geometry manager.

grid

The `grid`—as the name suggests—treats the parent widget as a `grid` containing rows and columns of cells. If you are familiar with spreadsheet software, `grid` will work in the same way. The `grid` lines will not be visible, they are just conceptual.

To specify the position within the `grid`, the `row` and `column` keywords are used. These accept integer values and begin at `0`, not `1`. A widget placed with `grid(row=0, column=0)` will be to the left of a widget at `grid(row=0, column=1)`. Underneath these would sit a widget placed at `grid(row=1, column=0)`.

To make a widget span more than one cell, use `columnspan` for a horizontal size increase and `rowspan` for a vertical increase. So, to make our hypothetical bottom widget sit below both, the full argument set would be `grid(row=1, column=0, columnspan=2)`.

By default, a widget will sit in the center of its assigned cell(s). In order to make the widget touch the very edge of its cell, we can use the `sticky` argument. This argument takes any number of four constants: `N`, `S`, `E`, and `W`. These are abbreviations for North, South, East, and West. Passing in `W` or `E` will align the widget to the left or right, respectively. `S` and `N` will align to the bottom and top.

These constants can be combined as desired, so `NE` will align top right and `SW` will sit the widget bottom left.

If you wish for the widget to span the entire vertical space, use `NS`. Similarly, use `EW` to stretch to the full size in the horizontal direction.

If you instead want the widget to fill the whole cell edge to edge, `NSEW` will let you do this.

 The `pack` and `grid` are both intended to lay out the entire content of a parent widget and apply different logic to decide where each new widget added should go. For this reason, they cannot be combined inside the same parent. Once one widget is inserted using `pack` or `grid`, all other widgets must use the same geometry manager. You can, however, `pack` widgets into one `Frame`, `grid` widgets into another, then `pack`/`grid` both of those `Frame` widgets into the same parent.

place

Unlike `pack` and `grid`, which automatically calculate where each new widget is added, `place` can be used in order to specify an exact location for a particular widget. `place` takes either *x* and *y* coordinates (in pixels) to specify an exact spot, which will not change as the window is resized, or relative arguments to its parent, allowing the widget to move with the size of the window.

To place a widget at (5, 10) within the window, you would write `widget.place(x=5, y=10)`.

To keep a widget in the direct center, you would use `widget.place(relx=0.5, rely=0.5)`.

`place` also takes sizing options, so to keep a widget at 50 percent width and 25 percent height of the window, add `(relwidth=0.5, relheight=0.25)`.

place is rarely used in bigger applications due to its lack of flexibility. It can be tiresome keeping track of exact coordinates for a widget, and as things change with the application, widgets may resize, causing unintended overlapping.

For a smaller window with only one or two widgets – say a custom pop-up message – place could be a viable choice of geometry manager, since it allows for very easy centering of said widgets.

One thing to note is that place can be used alongside pack or grid within the same parent widget. This means that if you have just one widget which you need to put in a certain location, you can do so quickly without having to restructure your already packed or gridded widgets.

To pack or to grid?

Using pack versus grid in your application is mostly down to personal preference. There doesn't seem to be a particularly dominant reason to use one over the other.

The main advantage of pack is the code tends to be very readable. pack uses words such as *left* and *top* to make it clear where the programmer wants the widget to go.

When using pack, sections of the window are also split using frames to allow for much greater control. When variables are named sensibly, this allows anyone changing the code to know exactly which part of a window the widget will end up in (by its parent Frame) and prevents them from having unexpected consequences when changing widgets, such as resizing a widget in the top-left corner of an application, knocking a widget at the bottom out of alignment.

The grid can also take advantage of Frame widgets too, but this can sometimes cause alignment issues.

Finally, pack works out widget positions based mainly on the argument and the order in which they are added. This means that when a new widget is added among existing ones, it is usually quite easy to get it into the correct spot. Simply adjust the order in which your widget.pack() calls occur. When using grid, you may need to change quite a few row and column arguments in order to slot the widget where you need it and keep everything else in their correct positions.

The great advantage of `grid` is its code simplicity to layout complexity ratio. Without the need to split your application into frames, you can save many lines of code and lay out a complicated window design with essentially just one line of code per widget.

You also don't need to worry about the order in which you add your widgets to their parent as the numerical `grid` system will apply regardless.

In the end, both prove to be good tools for the job and there is no need to use one if you prefer the other.

My personal preference is to use `pack` for main windows which may change quite a bit during development, and sometimes `grid` for smaller windows or layouts which are written in one go. Any additional windows for an application which would require more than two `Frame` widget are often better off being managed by `grid` for simplicity's sake.

Examples in this book will cover both `grid` and `pack`, so you will be able to practice both and decide which you prefer.

Getting going

Now that we have the basic understanding of the concept of widgets and how to add them into a window, it's time to put this into practice and make ourselves an application!

As with almost all programming examples, we will start with a `Hello World` application. Don't feel cheated though, it will have interactive aspects too! Let's begin with the most important step for any GUI application—showing a window. Start by opening your choice of text editor or IDE and putting in the following code:

```python
import tkinter as tk

class Window(tk.Tk):
    def __init__(self):
        super().__init__()
        self.title("Hello Tkinter")

        label = tk.Label(self, text="Hello World!")
        label.pack(fill=tk.BOTH, expand=1, padx=100, pady=50)


if __name__ == "__main__":
    window = Window()
    window.mainloop()
```

Let's break this first step down. We begin by importing Tkinter and giving it the alias of `tk` for brevity. Every example in this book should include this line so that we have access to all of Tkinter's widgets, including the main window.

Speaking of widgets, we begin this example by subclassing Tkinter's main window widget—`Tk`. Doing so allows us to change various aspects of it, including the title which will display inside the window's top bar. We set the title to `Hello Tkinter` in this example.

Next, we want to display some text within our window. To do this, we use a `Label` widget. A `Label` widget is typically non-interactive and is used to display either text or an image.

When defining Tkinter widgets, the first argument is always the parent (sometimes called master) which will hold the widget. We use `self` to refer to our main window in this case. Afterward, we have a vast array of keyword arguments to use in order to change their properties. The text argument here will take a string which tells the label what to display. Our label will say **Hello World!**

Now that we have two widgets, we need to place the label inside of our main window (`Tk`) so that they both display. To do this with Tkinter, we utilize one of the geometry managers we covered earlier. For our first example, we will be using `pack`. Pack has been given the following arguments:

- `fill`: This tells the widget to take all the space in both directions

- `expand`: This tells the widget to expand when the window is resized

- `padx`: Padding (empty space) of 100 pixels in the x direction (left, right)

- `pady`: Padding of 50 pixels in the y direction (above, below)

With that, our `Hello World` is ready to run. In order to tell the main window to show itself, we call the `mainloop` method. This is all enclosed within the (hopefully familiar) if __name__ == "__main__" block. Utilizing this block allows widgets from one file to be imported into another file for reuse without creating multiple main windows.

Execute the code via your preferred method and you should see a little window appear. Congratulations! You have now written your first GUI application with Tkinter!:

Our Hello World application

Adding interactivity

Of course, without any interactivity, this is just a message box. Let's add something for the user to do with our application. Bring the source code back up and change the __init__ method to look like this:

```
class Window(tk.Tk):
  def __init__(self):
    super().__init__()
    self.title("Hello Tkinter")

    self.label = tk.Label(self, text="Choose One")
    self.label.pack(fill=tk.BOTH, expand=1, padx=100, pady=30)

    hello_button = tk.Button(self, text="Say Hello",
                              command=self.say_hello)
    hello_button.pack(side=tk.LEFT, padx=(20, 0), pady=(0, 20))

    goodbye_button = tk.Button(self, text="Say Goodbye",
                                command=self.say_goodbye)
    goodbye_button.pack(side=tk.RIGHT, padx=(0, 20), pady=(0, 20))
```

Our label has changed to say Choose one to indicate that the user can now interact with the application by selecting one of the two buttons to click. A button in Tkinter is created by adding an instance of the Button widget.

The Button widget is exactly what you would imagine; something the user can click on to execute a certain piece of code. The text displayed on a Button is set via the text attribute, much like with a Label, and the code to run when clicked is passed via the command argument.

Be sure to remember that the argument passed to command must be a function, and should not be called (by adding parentheses). This means your code will *not* behave as intended if you use command=func() instead of command=func.

Our two buttons are placed within our main window using pack. This time, we use the side keyword argument. This tells the geometry manager where to place the item inside the window. Our hello_button will go on the left, and our goodbye_button will go on the right.

We also use padx and pady to give some spacing around the buttons. When a single value is given to these arguments, that amount of space will go on both sides. When a tuple is passed instead, the format is (above, below) for pady and (left, right) for padx. You will see in our example that both buttons have 20 pixels of padding below them; our leftmost button has 20 pixels of padding to its left, and our rightmost has 20 pixels to its right. This serves to keep the buttons from touching the edge of the window.

We now need to define the functions which will run when each button is pressed. Our **Say Hello** button calls say_hello and our **Say Goodbye** button calls say_goodbye. These are both methods of our Window class and so are prefixed with self. Let's write the code for these two methods now:

```
def say_hello(self):
    self.label.configure(text="Hello World!")

def say_goodbye(self):
    self.label.configure(text="Goodbye! \n (Closing in 2 seconds)")
    self.after(2000, self.destroy)
```

In say_hello, we will update the text of our label widget to Hello World! as it was before. We can change attributes of Tkinter widgets using the configure method. This then takes a keyword argument and value, just like when we created them initially.

Our say_goodbye method will also update the label's text and then close the window after two seconds. We achieve this using the after method from our Tk widget (which we have subclassed into Window). This method will call a piece of code after a certain amount of time has elapsed (in milliseconds).

The destroy method can be called on any Tkinter widget, and will remove it from the application. Destroying the main window will cause your application to exit, so use it carefully.

Leave the `if __name__ == "__main__"` block as it was before and give this application a try. You should see now that both buttons will do something. It may not look like many lines of code, but we have now covered quite a lot of the things a GUI application will need to do. You may be getting the following output:

Our application now with two buttons

We have provided user interactivity with `Button` widgets and seen how to link a button press to a piece of code. We've also covered updating elements of the user interface by changing the text displayed in our `Label` widget. Performing actions outside of the main loop has also happened when we used the `after` method to close the window. This is an important aspect of GUI development, so we will revisit this later.

Using variables

Instead of using `configure` to repeatedly change the text within our label, wouldn't it be better if we could assign a variable to it and just change this variable? The good news is you can! The bad news? Regular Python variables aren't perfectly compatible with Tkinter widgets. Shall we take a look?

Our first try

Let's give it a try the regular way. Open up your previous code and change it to look like this:

```
class Window(tk.Tk):
    def __init__(self):
        super().__init__()
        self.title("Hello Tkinter")
        self.label_text = "Choose One"
```

```
        self.label = tk.Label(self, text=self.label_text)
        self.label.pack(fill=tk.BOTH, expand=1, padx=100, pady=30)

        hello_button = tk.Button(self, text="Say Hello",
                                    command=self.say_hello)
        hello_button.pack(side=tk.LEFT, padx=(20, 0), pady=(0, 20))

        goodbye_button = tk.Button(self, text="Say Goodbye",
                                    command=self.say_goodbye)
        goodbye_button.pack(side=tk.RIGHT, padx=(0, 20), pady=(0, 20))

        def say_hello(self):
            self.label_text = "Hello World"

        def say_goodbye(self):
            self.label_text="Goodbye! \n (Closing in 2 seconds)"
            self.after(2000, self.destroy)


if __name__ == "__main__":
    window = Window()
    window.mainloop()
```

Give this code a whirl and click on your **Say Hello** button. Nothing happens. Now try your **Say Goodbye** button. The label will not update, but the window will still close after 2 seconds. This goes to show that the code written is not invalid, but will not behave as we may expect it to.

Creating Tkinter-compatible variables

So, how would we go about using a variable to update this label? Tkinter comes with four built-in variable objects for us to handle different data types:

- `StringVar`: This holds characters like a Python string.
- `IntVar`: This holds an integer value.
- `DoubleVar`: This holds a double value (a number with a decimal place).
- `BooleanVar`: This holds a Boolean to act like a flag.

To create a variable, just instantiate it like any other class. These do not require any arguments. For example:

```
label_text = tk.StringVar()
```

Using and updating

Since these variables are objects, we cannot assign to them a statement like `label_text = "Hello World!"`. Instead, each variable exposes a `get` and `set` method. Let's have a play with these in the interactive shell:

```
>>> from tkinter import *
>>> win = Tk()
>>> sv = StringVar()
>>> sv
<tkinter.StringVar object at 0x05F82D50>
>>> sv.get()
''
>>> sv.set("Hello World!")
>>> sv.get()
'Hello World!'
>>> sv.set(sv.get() + " How's it going?")
>>> sv.get()
"Hello World! How's it going?"
```

These variables are passed to widgets inside their keyword arguments upon creation (or at a later stage, using `configure`). The keyword arguments expecting these special variables will usually end in `var`. In the case of a label, the argument is `textvar`.

Fixing our application

Let's get our `Hello World` application working as intended again using our new knowledge of Tkinter variables. After setting the title, change the `label_text` property as follows:

```
self.label_text = tk.StringVar()
self.label_text.set("Choose One")
```

Now, alter our other two methods like so:

```
def say_hello(self):
    self.label_text.set("Hello World")

def say_goodbye(self):
    self.label_text.set("Goodbye! \n (Closing in 2 seconds)")
    self.after(2000, self.destroy)
```

Once again, run the application and click both buttons. Everything should now be all working as before.

Great! We now know how to take advantage of Tkinter's special variables, and it's super easy.

Showing messages

Often, a GUI application will need to tell the user something. Using what we have learned at the moment, we could make several `Label` widgets which update depending on the results of some other functions. This would get tedious and take up a lot of space within the application's window.

A much better way to achieve this is to use a pop-up window. These can be created manually, but Tkinter also comes with a few pre-built pop-ups which are already laid out and ready to display any message the programmer passes to them.

Let's adjust our `Hello World` application to utilize these windows to display the chosen message to the user.

Import the `messagebox` module with the following statement:

```
import tkinter.messagebox as msgbox
```

Now update the non-init methods to utilize this module:

```
def say_hello(self):
    msgbox.showinfo("Hello", "Hello World!")

def say_goodbye(self):
    self.label_text.set("Window will close in 2 seconds")
    msgbox.showinfo("Goodbye!", "Goodbye, it's been fun!")
    self.after(2000, self.destroy)
```

Run this version of our application and try out both buttons.

Showing information with showinfo

You should be able to see what the two arguments to `showinfo` do.

The first argument is the window's title bar text. If you didn't notice, click the **Say Hello** button again – you should see the word **Hello** inside the title bar of the pop-up window.

Clicking the **Say Goodbye** button will yield a pop-up message with **Goodbye!** in the title bar.

The second argument is a string containing the information which will be written inside the box.

The showinfo box contains just one button—an **OK** button. Clicking this button dismisses the window:

A showinfo box

While a messagebox window is displayed, the main window is effectively paused. The **Say Goodbye** button demonstrates this well. The line which tells the main window to close after 2 seconds does not get executed until the messagebox is dismissed.

Try clicking the **Say Goodbye** button and waiting for more than 2 seconds. You will see that the main window stays open until 2 seconds after you click OK to close the messagebox window. This is important to remember.

If, for example, you are processing a large list of items and you wish to alert the user to their status, it's best to wait until all of the items are processed before using showinfo. If you put a showinfo box after each item, the user will have to continually close them in order to allow the main window to continue processing.

Showing warnings or errors

If the information to convey is more serious, you can let the user know with showwarning.

If something goes wrong, tell the user with showerror instead.

Both of these function the same as the showinfo box that we have practiced but display a different image inside the box.

Try changing the `showinfo` in `say_hello` to a `showwarning` and the `showinfo` in `say_goodbye` to a `showerror` to see what these boxes will look like.

Getting feedback from the user

Should you require something back from the user, Tkinter has four more message boxes for you:

- `askquestion`
- `askyesno`
- `askokcancel`
- `askretrycancel`

`askquestion` will allow any question to be passed in and provides **Yes** and **No** answers. These are returned to the program as the string literals `"yes"` and `"no"`.

`askyesno` does the same, but will return 1 on **Yes** and nothing on **No**.

`askokcancel` provides **OK** and **Cancel** buttons to the user. **OK** returns 1 and **Cancel** nothing.

`askretrycancel` provides **Retry** and **Cancel** buttons. **Retry** returns 1 and **Cancel** nothing.

Despite the seemingly large number of choices, these all do pretty much the same thing. There doesn't seem to be much of a use case for `askquestion` over `askyesno` since they provide the same button choices, but `askquestion` will produce cleaner code thanks to the return values.

Let's see `askyesno` in action within our `Hello World` application.

Change the `say_goodbye` method to the following:

```
def say_goodbye(self):
    if msgbox.askyesno("Close Window?", "Would you like to
                        close this window?"):
        self.label_text.set("Window will close in 2 seconds")
        self.after(2000, self.destroy)
    else:
        msgbox.showinfo("Not Closing", "Great! This window
                        will stay open.")
```

Run this application and try clicking the `Say Goodbye` button. You will now be asked whether you want to close the window. Give both **No** and **Yes** a try:

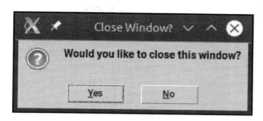

Our askyesno box

From the code for this function, you should see that the `askyesno` method can be treated like a Boolean statement. If you don't like doing this in one go, you could always use a variable such as the following:

```
close = msgbox.askyesno("Close Window?", "Would you like to close this
window?")
if close:
    self.close()
```

Getting text input

We now know how to get Boolean information from our user, but what if we want to get something more detailed, such as text?

Tkinter provides us with the perfect widget to do just this – `Entry`.

An `Entry` widget is a one-line text entry box which is put into a parent widget just like a `Label` or `Button`. The special Tkinter variables can be attached to an `Entry` to make getting the value out a breeze.

Why don't we add some personalization to our `Hello World` application? Grab your code and adjust it to the following:

```
class Window(tk.Tk):
    def __init__(self):
        super().__init__()
        self.title("Hello Tkinter")
        self.label_text = tk.StringVar()
        self.label_text.set("My Name Is: ")

        self.name_text = tk.StringVar()
```

```
self.label = tk.Label(self, textvar=self.label_text)
self.label.pack(fill=tk.BOTH, expand=1, padx=100, pady=10)

self.name_entry = tk.Entry(self, textvar=self.name_text)
self.name_entry.pack(fill=tk.BOTH, expand=1, padx=20, pady=20)

hello_button = tk.Button(self, text="Say Hello",
                         command=self.say_hello)
hello_button.pack(side=tk.LEFT, padx=(20, 0), pady=(0, 20))

goodbye_button = tk.Button(self, text="Say Goodbye",
                           command=self.say_goodbye)
goodbye_button.pack(side=tk.RIGHT, padx=(0, 20), pady=(0, 20))
```

If you run this version of the code, you will now see a text box in which to enter your name. As we enter our name in the Entry widget, its value is automatically assigned to the name_text StringVar thanks to the textvar keyword argument:

Our application now with an Entry widget

The buttons will still function the same, however, so let's do something about that:

```
def say_hello(self):
    message = "Hello there " + self.name_entry.get()
    msgbox.showinfo("Hello", message)

def say_goodbye(self):
    if msgbox.askyesno("Close Window?", "Would you like to
                        close this window?"):
        message = "Window will close in 2 seconds - goodybye " +
self.name_text.get()
        self.label_text.set(message)
        self.after(2000, self.destroy)
    else:
        msgbox.showinfo("Not Closing", "Great! This window
```

```
will stay open.")
```

These functions demonstrate both of the ways we can now grab the value back out of our Entry widget. We can either call the get method of the Entry itself, or grab the value out of our StringVar (also with the get method).

If the Entry box itself is the only part of your application which will need to use its value, I would recommend just grabbing it directly via .get() and foregoing the use of a StringVar. If, however, its value will be needed by other parts of your application, using a StringVar is probably the best way. This allows you to use the set method to adjust its value programmatically.

Summary

With this, our Hello World application has taught us all we should need to know with regard to basic GUI functionality. We have learned how to spawn a window containing various GUI elements by utilizing Tkinter's built-in widgets. We can place these widgets into the window using special functions called geometry managers, of which we have three to choose from.

The messagebox module allows us to easily convey information to the user without having to use any widgets within our main window, and can also be used to get feedback from a user and control how our window will behave.

We've added three simple, but effective widgets to our arsenal (not including the main window): the Label, for displaying static information; the Button, which allows a user to execute functions by clicking on it; and the Entry, which gathers textual information and allows for its use by our applications.

Next on our agenda is something a little different—a game of blackjack! By writing this game, we will also cover a very common starting point among programmers interested in GUI development: having a command-line application which could be improved by becoming a graphical one. In order to do this, we will briefly step back to the world of the CLI.

Back to the Command Line – Basic Blackjack

2

Blackjack is a casino game involving just a deck of cards. The aim of the game is to get as close as possible to a hand worth 21 points – but go over and you're out!

Number cards are worth their face value, picture cards are worth 10, and an ace is worth either 1 or 11 depending on your other cards. Players are initially dealt two cards and can either choose to hit (receive another card) or stick (submit their current hand).

Players face off against the dealer, who has one card face down and one face up. When all players have chosen to stick or are out (having a hand over 21), the winner is the one with a hand closest to 21.

Why am I telling you about blackjack? Because we're going to make a blackjack game using Tkinter! Not only will this chapter introduce you to powerful widgets, such as the `canvas` and `Frame` widgets, but it will also teach something that I come across a lot in the world of GUI programming—having a CLI program and the desire to make it a GUI, but not knowing how.

We will begin with a simple CLI version of blackjack that is playable, then build the interface around it, keeping the core functionality and logic the same.

Within this chapter, we will cover the following topics:

- What a class is and how to create one in Python
- How inheritance works
- How to apply polymorphism
- Using classes to model aspects of blackjack
- Creating and exiting a game loop

Before we begin coding our blackjack game, it's important we clear up how object-oriented programming works, since we will need to utilize classes even for the command-line version of our game.

Python's class system

A class can be thought of as a way of assigning a name to a set of specific functions and variables that are all associated with a common piece of an application.

The code for a class differs in two main ways from regular Python code.

Firstly, you will see the `class` keyword before the name of the class, followed by a colon and an indented scope. This is the syntax for telling Python that everything within this scope belongs to the class.

Secondly, all functions defined will have `self` as their first argument (unless they are static or class methods). This is automatically passed in via Python itself and so will cause calls to the function to appear to need one fewer argument than the definition.

The purpose of the `self` argument is to give each function (which, when in the scope of a class, is known as a method instead) access to the instance's other attributes and methods.

Certain types of variables called attributes are available when using classes. Attributes function as regular variables do, but their scope extends to the class instance itself. This means these variables can be shared among all functions defined within the class without the need to use the `global` keyword.

Attributes are differentiated from regular variables by the use of `self.` in front of them. For example, the line `age = 20` creates a variable called age, whereas `self.age = 20` creates an attribute against the class instance.

Once you have determined which attributes and methods to bundle together into a class, you can then create instances of it.

Instances

An instance is one particular implementation of a class. Each separate instance of the same class can be completely independent from the others, or they can share attributes if the need arises.

Python uses a method called __init__ in order to initialize each instance of a class. This method can be used to set initial variables which differ between instances.

The easiest way to wrap your head around using classes is to see an example:

```
class Dog:
    def __init__(self, name):
        self.name = name

    def speak(self):
        print("Woof! My name is", self.name)
```

This code gives us a class called Dog. The _init_ function of Dog takes two arguments: self and name.

The methods of a class require the first argument to be self in order to give them access to the instance's attributes. This argument is passed automatically, so you will not need to worry about it. You will also see that the self argument is required for the speak method too.

All arguments following self are passed to the methods when calling them as normal.

Now, any instance of a Dog has access to its attributes (name) and its methods (speak). Let's create some instances of Dog:

```
dog_one = Dog('Rover')
dog_two = Dog('Rex')

dog_one.speak()
dog_two.speak()
```

Run this code and you should see two lines printed:

```
Woof! My name is Rover
Woof! My name is Rex
```

Both Dog instances have access to the same speak method, but each one calls it differently based on its attributes. This is the core concept of a class instance in a nutshell. The print function itself has been reused but has produced a slightly different outcome depending on the instance's attributes.

The main reason we use classes so much in GUI development is the ability to inherit the abilities of a widget but to better customize them to our particular application. Inheritance in Python is very simple to do.

Inheritance

Inheritance is the idea that a class which is created off the back of another class can use features from said other class. This subclass can also change them, or build upon them as necessary.

Let's use inheritance to alter the behavior of some dogs. Add these new classes underneath your Dog class:

```
class Greyhound(Dog):
    def __init__(self, name):
        super().__init__(name)

    def speak(self):
        print("Zoom! My name is", self.name)

    def race(self, opponent):
        print(self.name, "is running faster than", opponent.name)

class JackRussell(Dog):
    def __init__(self, name, color):
        super().__init__(name)
        self.color = color

    def get_color(self):
        print(self.name, "is", self.color)
```

In order to inherit from an existing class, we place its name in brackets after the name of our new class. This ensures that Greyhound is a subclass of Dog.

When initializing our Greyhound instance, we can reuse the initializing code from our Dog class by accessing it via super(). Once again, the self argument is passed automatically, so we only need to pass the name over to the __init__ function of Dog. The name attribute of our Greyhound will be set using the code from Dog, so we do not need to do anything more in our init of Greyhound.

The Greyhound class also demonstrates the ability to overwrite methods in the original class by simply declaring another one with the same name. We redefine speak here so that our more specific speak method of our Greyhound will be called instead of the Dog one from any Greyhound instance.

We can add new methods to the Greyhound class as normal. Here, we have added a race method.

The `race` method demonstrates another important concept which occurs with using classes: polymorphism. The argument passed to this method can be anything, since Python is dynamically typed. This means that we can use any class instance which has an attribute called `name` as the opponent in our race method. Since our `Dog` class defines a `name` attribute, we can use any kind of `Dog` to race against our `Greyhound`.

The `JackRussell` class shows that additional, more specific attributes can be added onto classes which derive from another within the __init__ method. These attributes behave as normal.

Let's try out these new classes. Remove the code regarding `dog_one` and `dog_two` and add this in its place:

```
greyhound = Greyhound("Tessa")
jack_russell = JackRussell("Jack", "brown")
dog = Dog("Boris")

greyhound.speak()
jack_russell.speak()
dog.speak()

greyhound.race(jack_russell)
greyhound.race(dog)

jack_russell.get_color()
```

The preceding code first demonstrates that each `Dog` still has the ability to speak, and the `Greyhound` will speak differently to the others. Note that even though the `JackRussell` class does not have a `speak` method defined, it has acquired it from the base class – `Dog`.

We then show that either type of `Dog` will work for racing against the `Greyhound`, since both have a `name` attribute.

Finally, we demonstrate that the `JackRussell` has access to its unique `color` attribute as normal.

Try adding `dog.get_color()` after the `JackRussell` class call. You should get an `AttributeError`, since inheritance is only one way. `JackRussell` can call the `Dog` speak method, since the `JackRussell` inherits from it, but the `Dog` class does not receive anything back from the `JackRussell` class. This is important to remember when using polymorphism to accept multiple classes as method arguments. Always ensure that the method relies on attributes of the base class, not a specific attribute from a subclass.

Now that we have an understanding of how to write and use classes, we can begin writing our blackjack game.

Blackjack's classes

We will begin by defining the classes which will be used in order to separate out different aspects of the game of blackjack. We will model three of the components of the game:

- Card: A basic playing card. The card belongs to a suit and is worth a certain value.
- Deck: A collection of cards. The deck shrinks as cards are drawn and contains 52 unique cards.
- Hand: Each player's assigned cards. A hand is what defines each player's score and thus who wins.

Let's begin with the simplest concept—the Card.

The Card class

The Card class will be the first class we define, as both of our other classes will need to use it. Open up a new file and type the following code:

```
import random

class Card:
    def __init__(self, suit, value):
        self.suit = suit
        self.value = value

    def __repr__(self):
        return " of ".join((self.value, self.suit))
```

The only import we will need for our game is the random module. This will allow us to shuffle our virtual deck of cards at the beginning of every game.

Our first class will be one representing the playing cards. Each card will have a suit (hearts, diamonds, spades, and clubs) and a value (ace to king). We define the __repr__ function in order to change how the card is displayed when we call print on it. Our function will return the value and the suit, for example, King of Spades. This is all we need to do for a Card.

Next up, we need to create a `Deck` of these `Card` classes.

The Deck class

The `Deck` will need to contain 52 unique cards and must be able to shuffle itself. It will also need to be able to deal cards and decrease in size as cards are removed:

```
class Deck:
    def __init__(self):
        self.cards = [Card(s, v) for s in ["Spades", "Clubs", "Hearts",
                     "Diamonds"] for v in ["A", "2", "3", "4", "5", "6",
                     "7", "8", "9", "10", "J", "Q", "K"]]

    def shuffle(self):
        if len(self.cards) > 1:
            random.shuffle(self.cards)

    def deal(self):
        if len(self.cards) > 1:
            return self.cards.pop(0)
```

When creating an instance of the `Deck`, we simply need to have a collection of every possible card. We achieve this using a list comprehension which contains lists of every suit and value. We pass each combination over to the initialization for our `Card` class to create 52 unique `Card` instances.

Our `Deck` will need to be able to be shuffled, so that every game is different. We use the `shuffle` function in the `random` library to do this for us. To avoid any potential errors, we will only shuffle a deck which still has two or more cards in it, since shuffling one or zero cards is pointless.

After shuffling, we will need to deal cards too. We utilize the `pop` function of a list (which is the data structure holding our cards) to return the top card and remove it from the deck so that it cannot be dealt again.

The final utility concept to be created for our game to work is the concept of a `Hand`. All players have a hand of cards, and each hand is worth a numerical value based on the cards it contains.

The Hand class

A `Hand` class will need to contain cards just like the `Deck` class does. It will also be assigned a value by the rules of the game based on which cards it contains.

Since the dealer's hand should only display one card, we also keep track of whether the `Hand` belongs to the dealer to accommodate this rule:

```python
class Hand:
    def __init__(self, dealer=False):
        self.dealer = dealer
        self.cards = []
        self.value = 0

    def add_card(self, card):
        self.cards.append(card)
```

Much like the `Deck`, a `Hand` will hold its cards as a list of `Card` instances.

When adding a card to the hand, we simply add the `Card` instance to our `cards` list.

Calculating the value of a `Hand` is where the rules of the game come into play the most:

```python
def calculate_value(self):
    self.value = 0
    has_ace = False
    for card in self.cards:
        if card.value.isnumeric():
            self.value += int(card.value)
        else:
            if card.value == "A":
                has_ace = True
                self.value += 11
            else:
                self.value += 10

    if has_ace and self.value > 21:
        self.value -= 10

def get_value(self):
    self.calculate_value()
    return self.value
```

We first initialize the value of the hand to 0 and assume the player does not have an ace (since these are a special case). We then loop through the Card instances and try to add their value as a number to the player's total.

If the card's value is not numerical, we will then check to see whether the card is an ace. If it is, we begin by adding 11 to the hand's value and setting the has_ace flag to True. If this increase of 11 points brings the hand's value over 21, we make the ace worth 1 point instead, and so subtract 10 from the hand's value.

If the card is not numerical or an ace, we simply add 10 to the hand's value.

We need some way for the game to display each hand's cards, so we use a simple function to print each card in the hand, and the value of the player's hand too. The dealer's first card is face down, so we print hidden instead:

```python
def display(self):
    if self.dealer:
        print("hidden")
        print(self.cards[1])
    else:
        for card in self.cards:
            print(card)
    print("Value:", self.get_value())
```

Now that we have all of our underlying data structures written, it's time for the game loop. This will be contained in a Game class for simplicity's sake.

The Game class and main loop

We will define the game's main loop within the class __init__ method so that to begin playing, we simply need to create an instance of this class:

```python
class Game:
    def __init__(self):
        playing = True

        while playing:
            self.deck = Deck()
            self.deck.shuffle()

            self.player_hand = Hand()
            self.dealer_hand = Hand(dealer=True)
```

```
for i in range(2):
    self.player_hand.add_card(self.deck.deal())
    self.dealer_hand.add_card(self.deck.deal())

print("Your hand is:")
self.player_hand.display()
print()
print("Dealer's hand is:")
self.dealer_hand.display()
```

We start off our loop with a Boolean which will be used to track whether or not we are still playing the game.

If we are, we need a shuffled `Deck` and two `Hand` instances—one for the dealer and one for the player.

We use the `range` function to deal two cards each to the player and the dealer. Our `deal` method will return a `Card` instance, which is passed to the `add_card` method of our `Hand` instances.

We now want to display the hands to our player. We can use the `display` method on our `Hand` instances to print this to the screen.

This marks the end of the code which needs to run at the beginning of every new game. Now we enter a loop which will run until a winner is decided. We again control this with a Boolean:

```
game_over = False

while not game_over:
    player_has_blackjack, dealer_has_blackjack = self.check_for_blackjack()
```

We first need to check for blackjack. If either player has been dealt an ace and a picture card, their hand will total 21, so they automatically win. Let's jump to the function which does this:

```
def check_for_blackjack(self):
    player = False
    dealer = False
    if self.player_hand.get_value() == 21:
        player = True
    if self.dealer_hand.get_value() == 21:
        dealer = True

    return player, dealer
```

We need to keep track of which player may have blackjack, so we will keep a Boolean for the player and dealer.

Next, we need to check whether either's hand totals 21, which we will do using two `if` statements. If either has a hand value of 21, their Boolean is changed to `True`.

If either of the Booleans are `True`, then we have a winner, and will print the winner to the screen and `continue`, thus breaking us out of the game loop:

```
if player_has_blackjack or dealer_has_blackjack:
    game_over = True
    self.show_blackjack_results(player_has_blackjack, dealer_has_blackjack)
    continue
```

To print the winner to the screen, we have another function named `show_blackjack_results` which will handle displaying the correct winner:

```
def show_blackjack_results(self, player_has_blackjack,
                           dealer_has_blackjack):
    if player_has_blackjack and dealer_has_blackjack:
        print("Both players have blackjack! Draw!")

    elif player_has_blackjack:
        print("You have blackjack! You win!")

    elif dealer_has_blackjack:
        print("Dealer has blackjack! Dealer wins!")
```

If neither player had blackjack, the game loop will continue.

The player can now make a choice—whether or not to add more cards to their hand (hit) or submit their current hand (stick):

```
choice = input("Please choose [Hit / Stick] ").lower()
while choice not in ["h", "s", "hit", "stick"]:
    choice = input("Please enter 'hit' or 'stick' (or H/S) ").lower()
```

We use the `input` function to collect a choice from the user. This will always return us a string containing the text the user typed into the command line.

If you are following along with Python 2, make sure to use `raw_input` in place of `input`. In Python 2, `input` will try and evaluate what is typed in, which is not what we need here.

Since we have a string, we can cast the user's input to lowercase using the `lower` function to avoid having to check combinations of upper case and lower case when parsing their reply.

If their input is not recognized, we will simply keep asking for it again until it is:

```
if choice in ['hit', 'h']:
    self.player_hand.add_card(self.deck.deal())
    self.player_hand.display()
```

Should the player choose to hit, they will need to add an extra card to their hand. This is done in the same way as before—using `deal()` and `add_card()`.

Since their total has changed, we will now need to check whether they are over the allowed limit of 21. We'll jump to a function which does this now:

```
def player_is_over(self):
    return self.player_hand.get_value() > 21
```

This simple function merely checks whether the player's hand value is over 21 and returns the information as a Boolean. Nothing too complicated here. Back to our main loop:

```
if self.player_is_over():
    print("You have lost!")
    has_won = True
```

If the player's hand has a value over 21, they have lost, so the game loop needs to break and we set `has_won` to `True` (indicating that the dealer has won).

When the player decides to stick with their hand, it is time for their score to be compared with the dealer's:

```
else:
    print("Final Results")
    print("Your hand:", self.player_hand.get_value())
    print("Dealer's hand:", self.dealer_hand.get_value())

    if self.player_hand.get_value() > self.dealer_hand.get_value():
        print("You Win!")
    else:
        print("Dealer Wins!")
        has_won = True
```

We use the `else` statement here because we have already established that the user's answer was either `hit` or `stick`, and we have just checked `hit`. This means we will only get into this block when the user answers `stick`.

The value of both the player's and the dealer's hand are printed to the screen to give the final results. We then compare the values of each hand to see which is higher.

If the player's hand is a higher value than the dealer's, we print You Win!. If the scores are equal, then we have a tie, so we print Tie!. Otherwise, the dealer must have a higher hand than the player, so we show Dealer wins!:

```
again = input("Play Again? [Y/N] ")
while again.lower() not in ["y", "n"]:
    again = input("Please enter Y or N ")
    if again.lower() == "n":
        print("Thanks for playing!")
                playing = False
    else:
        has_won = False
```

Outside of our while loop, we check whether the user wishes to play again.

We once again use the combination of lower and a while loop to ensure our answer is a y or n.

If the player answers with n, we thank them for playing and set our playing Boolean to False, thus breaking us out of the main game loop and ending the program.

If not, they must have answered y, so we set has_won to False and let our main loop run again. This will take us right back to the top at self.deck = Deck() to set up a brand new game.

To run this code, we simply create an instance of the Game class:

```
if __name__ == "__main__":
    game = Game()
```

Now we have a game, give it a play. While playing, be sure you can follow exactly where you are in the game's main loop.

This version of blackjack is kept simple in order to give us a command-line application which we can now convert to a GUI-based game. The dealer will never hit and there is no concept of betting. Feel free to try and add these features yourself if you wish, or carry on with the next chapter, where we will begin to add graphics by going back over to the Tkinter library.

Command line versus GUI

Since we now have a working game, what is the motivation to continue with this project? Isn't the command-line interface good enough for a lot of games?

Let's briefly compare the suitability of command-line interfaces versus graphical interfaces for Python programs.

Interactivity

When creating a program which runs on the command line, there are essentially only two ways to get input from the user.

The first is by parsing command-line arguments. These are the extra information written on the same line when running an executable from the command line. For example: `python3 -i blackjack.py`. Here, we have passed in a flag of `-i` telling the interpreter to end in interactive mode, and the filename `blackjack.py`.

The second is the one which we have used throughout our blackjack game – `input`. The `input` function allows the user to type anything in to the command line and returns this as a string. As you may have noticed from our constant need to use the `lower` function and a `while` loop to validate the user's choices, this is far from ideal.

Compare this to the various ways with which we collected information from the user in `Chapter 1`, *Meet Tkinter*. We replicated the `input` function's capabilities with an `Entry` widget. Whilst we could use multiple `Entry` widgets and validation loops in a graphical interface, this would not solve the problem.

In order to collect a choice of two options from the user, such as in the case of choosing between hit and stick, we could simply use two buttons. This means the user cannot pick an option which was not given.

When choosing to play again, it would make more sense to use one of the message box windows to get the user's choice. The `askyesno` box seems like the perfect choice for this job. This again removes the need to validate whether the user's answer is one we expected.

Even if the command-line version of the game had a way of conveniently gathering user input, there's also the question of familiarity.

Familiarity

While developers may be very used to using the command line to interact with programs, the average user may not even know how to use it.

The majority of applications which people use come with some sort of graphical interface. It is only usually very niche and specific tools which will come with only a command-line interface.

If you want your applications to be accessible to as many people as possible, it is worth creating a graphical interface to make as many people as possible feel familiar when using them.

Ease of use

When a user needs help with a command-line-based application, they usually have two options for documentation: a website or the command-line manual, also called man pages.

Having to locate and read a web page in order to use an application could be considered a lot of hassle, which could deter new users of an application.

Similarly, the man pages within a terminal can be difficult to navigate. It is not intuitive how to search them for a specific keyword and the inability to scroll with a mouse can be offputting to some people.

Within most GUI applications, you will likely see a menu bar at the top. Inside this menu bar can often be found a **Help** option. This is a rather self-explanatory way for a user to locate instructions on how to use a particular application. The developer also has all of the tools to lay out this section of the application as they have for the main application itself, so they can enable things such as mouse scrolling and hyperlinks to make searching and navigating the help document very easy.

On the flip side of this, if an application has a huge number of different functions, translating this into a graphical interface can get very messy. There may simply be too many buttons and configuration choices to cram into a graphical window whilst retaining all possible features. Something like the Git version control system comes to mind here. Whilst graphical interfaces do exist, they can be much more complicated to use than simply memorizing the command-line options.

Size and portability

The main advantage a command-line application has over a graphical one is the file size. Without the need to include a graphical library and all of its code, a command-line application can be significantly smaller. This not only allows for quicker downloads, but the ability to package the application on smaller forms of physical media.

Since all OSes will have a command-line interface by default, the potential issue of incompatibilities between a user's system and the graphical library in use will also be eliminated. Your application will also be able to run on machines which do not include a means of drawing graphical windows, such as servers, ensuring it can be run by as many users as possible.

Overall, the choice of interface for an application is largely down to what the application itself does and its intended audience. If you are building a simple application which you wish as many people as possible to use, then a graphical interface seems to be the way to go.

If you are creating a specific and very complicated program which is tailored toward people who are familiar enough with computers to not be intimidated by the command line, then the time and disk space savings of a command-line interface could be of real benefit.

Summary

In this chapter, we have gone over how to create and use classes in Python. We have seen that they allow for code reuse by defining methods, but these methods can have different outcomes depending on which attributes the particular instance of a class holds.

We have briefly looked at the concept of polymorphism and how easy it is to do using Python's dynamic typing.

Our basic command-line version of the blackjack game has been written and is fully playable. We are now prepared to take this up to the next level in the following chapter by utilizing some new Tkinter widgets.

The choice of interface options has been discussed so that we now know why learning a graphical framework such as Tkinter is a good idea to allow for familiarity and ease of use for our applications. This serves as our motivation for the next step with our game, so that we may make it interesting and enjoyable for as many people as possible.

Jack is Back in Style – the Blackjack GUI

3

Now that we have a working game with a solid, reusable data structure in place, it's time to take it to the next level by adding graphics. Not only will the graphics make the game look so much nicer to play, but we can take advantage of the ease of taking user input via graphical means.

At the end of this chapter, we will have the same blackjack game as before but with a completely new look and feel.

In this chapter, we will cover the following:

- Converting a CLI application to use a GUI
- Collecting user input via `Button` widgets
- Creating images that can be used by Tkinter
- Displaying images with a `Canvas` widget
- Controlling the layout using the pack geometry manager
- Separating display logic from application logic

Moving from the command line to a graphical interface

It is very common to see people asking for advice on how to move a command-line-only application that they have already written to a graphical interface, for reasons discussed at the end of the previous chapter, such as ease of use and familiarity.

How easy this is to do is largely dependent on the choice of data structure used within the application. If the application's main logic is too intertwined with data collection and storage, then porting can become a nightmare. If you find yourself with a command-line application that you wish to convert, take the time to consider how separable these two pieces are.

If you are not using classes, could you split certain pieces out into small, reusable classes which could then be shared into a new file? Since classes are almost a necessity for building graphical applications, it's a good idea to ensure that your current application takes advantage of them before attempting to make it graphical.

If your application takes a lot of text input from the user via the `input` (or `raw_input`) function, think about what type of information you need from it. Since the `input` function will always return a string, consider which information you may be casting to an integer (via the `int` function), what is being treated as some sort of list (a big clue is if you are asking the user to comma-separate words), and what things require the user to enter a choice of predetermined responses.

Whilst numerical entries can be made using a text field (known as the `Entry` widget to Tkinter), there is also a numerical field known as the `Spinbox` widget which will ensure that the value entered is a number between a certain range.

Lists of multiple values can be collected in multiple ways depending on whether or not the options are set by the developer or the user. If the options are limited, then a `Listbox` widget will allow the user to select multiple options from a preset list, or the good old `Checkbox` widget could be used as well. If the user decides exactly what will be entered, then the GUI programmer can use dynamically created widgets to collect as many options as can fit on the screen.

When providing a single choice from a predetermined set of responses, Tkinter provides regular buttons, radio buttons, a drop-down menu, and a single-choice `Listbox`, depending on the designer's preference.

If your command-line application collects many different forms of input from the user, it is recommended that you take the time to decide what type of information each input statement is after and map out what widgets would do the job of collecting this information in the right way. Familiarize yourself with each widget that you intend to use and make sure it can do what you would need it to, for example, in terms of validation of data.

As well as this, make sure that your choice of widgets can be laid out in a way that will look appealing. If you have too many individual data-entry widgets, the user interface may look cluttered, so see what can be grouped in a logical way and perhaps look into using a `Menu` widget to hide anything non-essential away from your main window.

Applying this advice to our blackjack game, we know that we have chosen a reusable data structure in the form of our `Hand`, `Deck`, and `Card` classes. Whilst these depend on each other, and the `Hand` class knows a bit about the rules of the game of blackjack via its `get_value` method, the classes are not dependent on any form of data collection or display in order to function properly.

There are two main points at which user input is collected – when deciding whether to *hit* or *stick*, and when choosing whether to play another game or quit. Since both of these points in the game involve a specific choice of one of two predetermined answers, we can use two `Button` widgets to collect an answer from the user.

In terms of layout, we will need only three interactive widgets—a `Canvas` widget to display our game's graphics, and two button widgets to collect the hit or stick choices from our user. These buttons can change, based on which stage of the game we are at, since we don't need to display one set while the other set is active. This allows us to help keep the interface as uncluttered as possible and avoids confusing the users.

We have had a look at using a `Button` widget in `Chapter 1`, *Meet Tkinter*, but have not yet looked at the extremely powerful `Canvas` widget. Before we begin writing our code, let's look at an overview of this crucial part of our game.

The Canvas widget

The `Canvas` widget is Tkinter's primary widget for displaying graphics. With a vast range of built-in functions for creating graphics manually, it is the perfect choice for the display piece of a computer game.

Let's have a quick introduction to the `Canvas` widget's built-in drawing capabilities. Open up a new file and type in the following:

```
import tkinter as tk

window = tk.Tk()

canvas = tk.Canvas(window, bg="white", width=300, height=300)
canvas.pack()
```

```
canvas.create_oval((0, 0, 300, 300), fill="yellow")

canvas.create_arc((50, 100, 100, 150), extent=180, fill="black")
canvas.create_arc((200, 100, 250, 150), extent=180, fill="black")

canvas.create_line((50, 200, 110, 240), fill="red", width=5)
canvas.create_line((110, 240, 190, 240), fill="red", width=5)
canvas.create_line((190, 240, 250, 200), fill="red", width=5)

window.mainloop()
```

Run this code and you should see a nice smiley face appear on your computer screen:

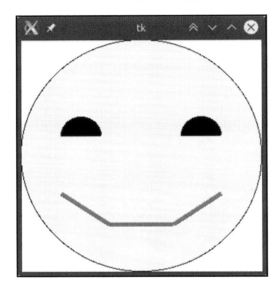

Let's go over exactly how we create this image:

1. We begin by importing `tkinter` and abbreviating it to `tk` as usual.
2. Next, we create a main window using the `Tk` widget.
3. Inside our main window, we place a 300 pixel by 300 pixel canvas. We color this white to make it more apparent.
4. We use the `pack` geometry manager to get this canvas into our main window.
5. Now that we have our canvas inside a window, we are ready to begin drawing.
6. In order to create the face's shape, we use a circle. The `Canvas` widget has a `create_oval` method which will create circles (provided we make the bounding box a square).

The `Canvas` widget handles coordinates with a Cartesian system, with the origin in the top-left of the window. The *Y* coordinate will go down the window as its value increases, which may take some getting used to if you are familiar with other software in which a positive *Y* value instead goes upwards. The *X* coordinate goes further right as it increases, as with most other systems.

The first argument of `create_oval` is a 4-tuple containing the coordinates of the bounding box in which the oval will be contained. In order, these are top left *X*, top left *Y*, bottom right *X*, bottom right *Y*.

7. For this demo, we will use the entire canvas to display our face, so we put the top left of the bounding box at the origin: `0, 0`. We then place the bottom right of the bounding box at the bottom-right corner of our canvas widget: `300, 300` (we know this because we specified the size of our canvas as 300 by 300).

8. We use the `fill` argument to specify that we want our face to be yellow. Luckily, Tkinter can recognize a large number of strings and interpret them as colors. This allows us to use the string literal `yellow` to color our face.

   This code creates a yellow circle which spans the entirety of our window, since the window only contains the canvas.

9. To draw the eyes, we need a semi-circle. The `Canvas` widget has a `create_arc` method which allows us to do this.

   The `create_arc` method relies on the same bounding box principle as `create_oval`. We again use a 4-tuple to specify the coordinates of the bounding box.

   The default size of an arc is 90 degrees, which will only make a quarter-circle. To instead achieve a semi-circle, we use the `extent` argument and set this to 180.

10. We again use the `fill` argument to color our eyes black.

11. Finally, to draw a smile, we will use three individual lines. The `Canvas` widget provides `draw_line` to let us do this.

    Another 4-tuple of coordinates specifies where the line begins and where it ends.

12. We color the line red using the `fill` argument, and make it much thicker than the default by specifying the width argument.

Now all of our drawing is done, we simply need to display our main window. We do this with the usual `mainloop` method.

While this image isn't going to win any design competitions, hopefully you now have an idea of the drawing capabilities of a Tkinter `Canvas`.

 Other drawing methods include `create_rectangle`, `create_polygon`, and `create_text`. We will certainly make use of `create_text` within our blackjack game in order to convey information to the user.

The rest of the graphics of our game will be displayed by converting existing image files into a format usable by Tkinter's canvas, so don't fret about having to draw each playing card using lines and rectangles!

When it comes to animations, the `Canvas` widget also has us covered there. Not only can we delete and then redraw elements, but the `Canvas` widget contains methods like `move` and `itemconfig` which will allow us to update positions and sizes of elements to create easy animation.

These methods can be bound to keyboard and mouse events (we will learn how to do this later), creating game-like interaction capabilities, too.

Speaking of which, let's get going with porting our command-line game over to a `Canvas` widget. You can either open a new file or try just modifying your code from `Chapter 2`, *Back to the Command Line – Basic Blackjack*. Let's get started.

Creating a graphical blackjack game

 In order to display images within our blackjack game, we need to obtain them first. If you are the arty kind, you can draw them yourself. I am not a great artist so I have chosen to acquire artwork online. The images used in the pictures in this book came from the Open Game Art website, and can be downloaded from `https://opengameart.org/content/playing-cards-0`.

As usual, we will begin our file with the necessary imports:

```
import os
import random
import tkinter as tk
```

This project will need three imports now:

- os: To access the assets folder
- random: To shuffle the Deck
- tkinter: To use graphical features

We begin with a variable that will be used by multiple classes, and so is defined outside of the scope of a class, the assets_folder. We use the os module to construct the full path to our images so that this will work on multiple machines:

```
assets_folder = os.path.abspath(os.path.join(os.path.dirname(__file__),
'..', 'assets/'))
```

In this case, the images are stored in a folder named assets, which is in the same directory as our code folder.

We use os.path.dirname to get the directory of the current file, then we use os.path.join to join up .., which goes back one directory, then assets, which is the name of the folder full of our images.

We wrap this all up in os.path.abspath, so that we have the absolute path to this folder, allowing us to use it anywhere.

To clarify the directory structure being used, it looks like this:

```
- D: Code/
    - D: assets/
        - F: image1.png
        - F: image2.png
        - F: ...
    - F: blackjack.py
```

D represents a directory and F represents a file. All of our images are placed into the assets folder.

Now that we have this variable available, we can begin defining the classes which will make up our game.

Card, Deck, and Hand

First, copy over the `Card` class from the code you wrote for Chapter 2, *Back to the Command Line - Basic Blackjack*. There are no changes to the existing methods in this class, but we need to add one more for our graphical implementation:

```
@classmethod
def get_back_file(cls):
    cls.back = tk.PhotoImage(file=assets_folder + "/back.png")

    return cls.back
```

This new method will use a decorator to make it into a class method. A class method functions much like a regular method (or function), except that it does not require an instance of the class to work.

For this reason, we name the first variable `cls` instead of `self`. Python will automatically pass a reference to the class itself to a class method, meaning just as is the case with a regular method, we will call it with one fewer argument than it is defined with.

Our `get_back_file` class method returns the image `back.png` stored in our `assets` folder. This allows the graphical piece of our application to acquire and draw this particular image onto the screen when the dealer has a card which is face down.

In order for an image to be usable by Tkinter, we need to create a `PhotoImage` instance. When we initialize a `PhotoImage`, we can use the `file` argument to supply the path to the image file, then Tkinter will handle the rest.

 Something important to note when using a `PhotoImage` in Tkinter is that the object will be garbage collected if no reference to it is kept. In order to avoid this, we assign the `PhotoImage` to the `back` attribute of our `Card` class. This allows us to keep a reference to it for as long as a `Card` instance sticks around.

Our `Deck` class does not need to change for now. If you are using a new file, simply copy and paste this code over from the previous chapter.

Our `Hand` class does not need anything new either, although there is no longer any need for the `display` method since we are not using `print` at all anymore, so either delete the method or don't copy it over.

Instead of a class holding our game loop, we will maintain a GameState class which handles the state of the current game. Our GameScreen class, which handles the graphical elements of the game, can use this class to access the state of the game at any time it needs to redraw graphics.

The GameState class

We will put the code which needs to run at the beginning of any game into the GameState __init__ method. This code will then run any time we make a new game:

```
class GameState:
    def __init__(self):
        self.deck = Deck()
        self.deck.shuffle()

        self.player_hand = Hand()
        self.dealer_hand = Hand(dealer=True)

        for i in range(2):
            self.player_hand.add_card(self.deck.deal())
            self.dealer_hand.add_card(self.deck.deal())

        self.has_winner = ''
```

Inside the __init__ method, we create and shuffle our Deck, assign a Hand to our player and dealer, and initialize the winner as nobody (using an empty string).

Our player_is_over method now sits in this class. Copy it over if you are using a new file.

We will slightly modify our old check_for_blackjack function, and rename it someone_has_blackjack to signify the difference:

```
def someone_has_blackjack(self):
    player = False
    dealer = False
    if self.player_hand.get_value() == 21:
        player = True
    if self.dealer_hand.get_value() == 21:
        dealer = True

    if player and dealer:
        return 'dp'
    elif player:
```

```
        return 'p'
    elif dealer:
        return 'd'

    return False
```

Since we no longer are using a terminal window to display results, there is no longer any need for the previous calls to the `print` function.

As graphical displaying of information to the user is now separate from the game logic, we need to indicate to the caller of this function which contestant (if any) is the one with blackjack. We use a simple string to indicate this information: d for the dealer, p for the player, and dp for both.

If nobody has blackjack, then we will just return `False`. This allows the results of this method to be treated as a Boolean and used in the condition of an `if` statement.

Now we will need a way for the player to add cards to their hand when they choose to hit.

When the player chooses to hit, we will call the `hit` method from this class. The body of this method is much like it was in the previous chapter:

```
def hit(self):
    self.player_hand.add_card(self.deck.deal())
    if self.someone_has_blackjack() == 'p':
        self.has_winner = 'p'
    if self.player_is_over():
        self.has_winner = 'd'

    return self.has_winner
```

We add a card to the user's hand with the familiar `add_card` method, called with the Deck class' deal method as an argument.

Since their hand's value has changed, we should check for blackjack. We use the `someone_has_blackjack` method and check if it returns the p string indicating that the player's hand is worth 21. If it is, we assign this p string to our `has_winner` attribute to indicate that the game has finished and the player has won.

We should also check if the player is now over 21. If so, we assign the d string to our `has_won` attribute to indicate that the dealer has won this round.

Between each hit, we need to send information about the table's state over to our graphical `GameScreen` class so that the board can be drawn and shown to the user.

We will represent the board state using a simple dictionary.

The GameScreen will need to know:

- The cards in the player's hand
- The cards in the dealer's hand
- If there is a winner or not
- If the winner has blackjack or not

We will need a method to obtain this dictionary, which we will call get_table_state:

```
def get_table_state(self):
    blackjack = False
    winner = self.has_winner
    if not winner:
        winner = self.someone_has_blackjack()
        if winner:
            blackjack = True
    table_state = {
        'player_cards': self.player_hand.cards,
        'dealer_cards': self.dealer_hand.cards,
        'has_winner': winner,
        'blackjack': blackjack,
    }

    return table_state
```

We will use a Boolean to store whether a user has blackjack.

The winner will be represented by the use of a string, d for the dealer, p for the player, and dp for a tie. This is all handled by the someone_has_blackjack method from before.

Before checking for blackjack, we will see if our has_winner attribute contains a winner string already. If so, the player has gone over 21 and so there's no need to check for blackjack.

 We do not need to check whether the player has over 21 in this method, as the initial deal cannot produce a hand of more than 21, and there is already a call to player_is_over in the hit method.

Once we have determined whether or not we have a winner, we can begin building our return dictionary, which will be used by the GameScreen class.

The player's and dealer's cards are accessed via their attributes in this class.

When the player chooses to stick with their hand, then the game enters the final state. This means there will be no more changes to the cards in the player's hand, and so we will need to compare their score with the dealer's and determine a final winner:

```python
def calculate_final_state(self):
    player_hand_value = self.player_hand.get_value()
    dealer_hand_value = self.dealer_hand.get_value()

    if player_hand_value == dealer_hand_value:
        winner = 'dp'
    elif player_hand_value > dealer_hand_value:
        winner = 'p'
    else:
        winner = 'd'

    table_state = {
        'player_cards': self.player_hand.cards,
        'dealer_cards': self.dealer_hand.cards,
        'has_winner': winner,
    }

    return table_state
```

In order to obtain the final state, we first obtain both the player's and the dealer's score from our attributes. We now need to compare them to see which is higher.

We do not need to check for a loss or blackjack here since this is checked after each time the player decides to hit.

If the player and the dealer have the same value in their hand, the winner is assigned as the string dp.

If the player has a higher score, the winner becomes p.

If the dealer has the larger hand, we use the string d.

We now pass this information over as a dictionary, very similar to the get_table_state method, so that it can be used by the GameScreen class in the same way.

The final piece of information the GameScreen will need from the GameState is the player's score. This will be displayed as text on our canvas. Since this is stored as an integer, we need to convert it to a string before it can be displayed:

```
def player_score_as_text(self):
    return "Score: " + str(self.player_hand.get_value())
```

We concatenate the word Score: to the player's hand value so that the GameScreen can just display all of the text returned by this method. This also tells the user what they are looking at, as a number by itself on the screen may not be all that self explanatory.

Now that we have completed the class which will hold all of the information about our game state and logic, we can move on to displaying our graphical elements.

The GameScreen class

Our GameScreen class will hold the window attributes for our game as well as all of the graphical widgets. It makes sense for us to make this the main window of our application too, so we will inherit from the Tk widget in order to do this. Let's have a look at how we are going to set up our application:

```
class GameScreen(tk.Tk):
    def __init__(self):
        super().__init__()
        self.title("Blackjack")
        self.geometry("800x640")
        self.resizable(False, False)
```

We begin by initializing the Tk superclass. This ensures all of our graphical elements behave as they should.

We set the title of our application to Blackjack. If you can think of a quirkier name for the application, then feel free to change this!

The geometry method of a Tk widget is used to set the size of the window which is spawned. It can also set the location on screen at which the window initially opens up if desired. We use the string 800 x 600 to set the width of our window to 800 pixels and the height to 600 pixels.

The resizable method allows us to control which directions, horizontally or vertically, the window is allowed to be stretched and shrunk.

The first argument to the resizable method controls the *X* direction, and the second the *Y* direction.

We will set both of these to `False`, preventing the user from resizing the window entirely. This is for the purpose of simplicity. If we allow the user to resize the window, we would have to constantly change the size of our canvas and alter and redraw the images. To prevent this hassle, we do not allow the user to adjust the window's size.

After we set the window size and disable resizing, we need to define a few constants which will be used to position graphical elements on the screen:

```
self.CARD_ORIGINAL_POSITION = 100
self.CARD_WIDTH_OFFSET = 100

self.PLAYER_CARD_HEIGHT = 300
self.DEALER_CARD_HEIGHT = 100

self.PLAYER_SCORE_TEXT_COORDS = (400, 450)
self.WINNER_TEXT_COORDS = (400, 250)
```

`CARD_ORIGINAL_POSITION` is the *X* coordinate at which we will place the first card dealt to the player and dealer. This is set to `100`, meaning the first card will appear 100 pixels to the right of the left edge of the window.

`CARD_WIDTH_OFFSET` is how much space will be between each playing card in the *X* direction. The center of each card will be 100 pixels to the right of the previous card.

`PLAYER_CARD_HEIGHT` sets the *Y* coordinate at which the player's cards will be displayed.

`DEALER_CARD_HEIGHT` is the *Y* coordinate at which the dealer's cards are drawn.

Since a higher *Y* value actually goes down the window as opposed to up, the player has a higher *Y* value for its card display. This means the player's cards will be shown at the bottom of the screen and the dealer's cards toward the top of the screen.

`PLAYER_SCORE_TEXT_COORDS` defines the coordinates at which the `Score: XX` text will be displayed inside the canvas.

`WINNER_TEXT_COORDS` defines where on the canvas to place the text, which indicates the winner of the game. Since our display area will be 800 pixels wide and 500 pixels tall, the value of `WINNER_TEXT_COORDS` places the text in the center of the screen.

With the constants taking care of positioning for images drawn on our canvas, we can now begin creating graphical elements which will be stored as attributes of our GameScreen class:

```
self.game_state = GameState()
```

We store an instance of the GameState class covered earlier. This will keep track of the game logic and allow us to draw the state of the game onto our canvas. In order to begin a new game, all we will need to do is replace our game_state instance with a fresh copy:

```
self.game_screen = tk.Canvas(self, bg="white", width=800, height=500)
```

The Canvas on which we will draw all of our graphics is created next. We set the width and height of our game_screen to fixed values of 800 pixels and 500 pixels respectively. This allows us to know the exact coordinates of where to place images (as defined earlier in our constants) and allows us to create a background image which will always be the exact size of our Canvas.

We also know that since our application is 800 pixels by 640, we have 140 pixels left to function as the bottom part of our application. This is where we will display our buttons for the user to interact with.

In order to claim this space and make it usable, we will use a Frame widget:

```
self.bottom_frame = tk.Frame(self, width=800, height=140, bg="red")
self.bottom_frame.pack_propagate(0)
```

Our Frame widget also has a fixed width and height, as well as a background color specified by the bg argument. Feel free to change this to suit your own preferences.

Frame widgets behave differently to Canvas widgets when they have their sizes specified. By default, a Frame widget will only be as big as it needs to be in order to hold all of its child widgets. If we want to force the size when placing our Frame widget into its parent using the pack geometry manager, we need to call pack_propagate(0) on it. This forces the Frame to be the size specified by the keyword arguments of width and height.

Now that we have a Frame to hold our Button widgets, let's add some Button widgets to our class:

```
self.hit_button = tk.Button(self.bottom_frame, text="Hit", width=25,
command=self.hit)
self.stick_button = tk.Button(self.bottom_frame, text="Stick", width=25,
command=self.stick)
```

```
self.play_again_button = tk.Button(self.bottom_frame, text="Play Again",
width=25, command=self.play_again)
self.quit_button = tk.Button(self.bottom_frame, text="Quit", width=25,
command=self.destroy)
```

We define four buttons, which can go into our `Frame`.

The `hit_button` and `stick_button` act as our main gameplay controls. These will call the `hit` and `stick` methods which will be defined on this class, so we pass `self.hit` and `self.stick` to their `command` argument.

For consistency, we want the buttons to all be the same size. We achieve this by passing in the `width` argument of `25`.

We also define two more buttons: `play_again_button` and `quit_button`. At the end of the game, these buttons will display, allowing the user to decide whether or not they wish to play another game. These will also call functions defined on this class, so we pass these to the `command` argument.

```
self.hit_button.pack(side=tk.LEFT, padx=(100, 200))
self.stick_button.pack(side=tk.LEFT)
```

We only pack our `hit_button` and `stick_button` in the __init__ method since we do not need to show the other buttons until a game is over.

We pack these over to the left so that they line up side by side. We also add some padding to the `hit_button`, which will be over on the left-hand side, to space it away from the left edge of the screen, and to put some spacing between itself and our `stick_button`.

We now need to place our `Frame` and `Canvas` into our window to complete the layout:

```
self.bottom_frame.pack(side=tk.BOTTOM, fill=tk.X)
self.game_screen.pack(side=tk.LEFT, anchor=tk.N)
```

We put our bottom frame at the bottom of the window by using `side=tk.BOTTOM` and stretch it horizontally by using `fill=tk.X`.

We pack our `game_screen` to the left and use `anchor=tk.N` to ensure that this begins in the very top-left corner of the window.

Now all we need to do is draw the graphical elements into our `Canvas`, and we will use a method named `display_table` to do so:

```
self.display_table()
```

With that, our __init__ is complete. Let's take a look at what `display_table` will do to give our `game_screen` some life:

```
def display_table(self, hide_dealer=True, table_state=None):
    if not table_state:
        table_state = self.game_state.get_table_state()

    player_card_images = [card.get_file() for card in
                            table_state['player_cards']]
    dealer_card_images = [card.get_file() for card in
                            table_state['dealer_cards']]
    if hide_dealer and not table_state['blackjack']:
        dealer_card_images[0] = Card.get_back_file()
```

We allow for two arguments for this method.

The first tells the `game_screen` whether or not to hide the dealer's first card. During the gameplay, the dealer's first card will need to be face down, but when the user chooses to stick with their hand, we will flip the dealer's card face up to reveal their score.

We may also need to call the method with a pre-calculated table state. This also happens when the user decides to stick with their hand.

By default, the dealer's first card will be hidden and we will not have a `table_state`.

If a table state was not provided, then we need to ensure we get it. We call the `get_table_state` method from our `game_state` instance to generate one.

Now that we definitely have our table state, we can display some card images. We grab both the player's and dealer's cards from the `table_state` dictionary and use them within a list comprehension, calling their `get_file` method to return the location of the relevant image file to our `assets` folder.

If we are hiding the dealer's first card then we do not want to display its image. We instead replace the first element in our `dealer_card_images` list with the back file, which we obtain using the `Card` class's `get_back_file` method. This means the first card will appear to be face down to the player.

Now that we have some image file locations, it's time to start drawing them onto the `game_screen`. We begin by drawing the tabletop, which will function as our background:

```
self.game_screen.delete("all")
self.tabletop_image = tk.PhotoImage(file=assets_folder + "/tabletop.png")

self.game_screen.create_image((400, 250), image=self.tabletop_image)
```

Between each draw of the screen, we will delete everything currently drawn onto our `Canvas`. This ensures that we are only drawing what we need, and anything old will not be left over. We do this using the `Canvas` widget's `delete` method and by passing the string `all` to instruct it to delete everything.

Now that we have a clean slate, we will begin by drawing the background. We create a `PhotoImage` instance containing the `tabletop.png` image from our `assets` folder and keep a reference to it as the `self.tabletop_image` attribute.

The `tabletop.png` file can be any image which is 800 pixels wide and 500 pixels tall. The one which is used in the images of this book was created by me, so is included in the code bundle which goes along with this book.

Our `PhotoImage` can now be drawn onto our `game_screen`. We do this using the `create_image` method in our `Canvas`.

The first argument to `create_image` is a 2-tuple of the coordinates for the center of the image. Since the image is the exact size of our `Canvas`, we want to put the center of the image at the center of our `Canvas`. We know they are both 800 by 500, so we pass `(400, 250)` as our coordinates.

The image to place onto the `Canvas` is passed to the `image` argument. We pass our `PhotoImage` instance as the value here.

With that, we now have our background on our `game_screen`. The next thing we need to draw is the cards:

```
for card_number, card_image in enumerate(player_card_images):
    self.game_screen.create_image(
        (self.CARD_ORIGINAL_POSITION + self.CARD_WIDTH_OFFSET *
card_number, self.PLAYER_CARD_HEIGHT),
        image=card_image
    )

for card_number, card_image in enumerate(dealer_card_images):
    self.game_screen.create_image(
        (self.CARD_ORIGINAL_POSITION + self.CARD_WIDTH_OFFSET *
card_number, self.DEALER_CARD_HEIGHT),
        image=card_image
    )
```

To correctly position our player's cards, we need to know which card we are drawing—their first, second, third, and so on. We use the `enumerate` function to loop over our list of `player_card_images` and also obtain the index each is at.

Calculating the coordinates at which to place each card is done using our classes constants.

Each card is initially placed at the *X* coordinate defined by our `CARD_ORIGINAL_POSITION` constant, then subsequent cards will be placed a distance of 100 pixels (as defined by `CARD_WIDTH_OFFSET`) to the right of this. We get these numbers by multiplying the list index of the card we are looking to place by the `CARD_WIDTH_OFFSET` constant and adding the result to the `CARD_ORIGINAL_POSITION` value.

The *Y* value of our card's coordinates is always going to be the same as the number we have stored in `PLAYER_CARD_HEIGHT`, since that defines how close to the bottom of the `game_screen` to draw our cards, and we always want them to line up horizontally.

We apply the same logic when placing the dealer's card images, except we use our `DEALER_CARD_HEIGHT` constant to set the *Y* coordinate.

Now that the player can see their cards, we should show their score as well so that they do not have to tally their total in their head:

```
self.game_screen.create_text(self.PLAYER_SCORE_TEXT_COORDS,
text=self.game_state.player_score_as_text(), font=(None, 20))
```

We use the `create_text` method from our `Canvas` widget to draw text onto our screen.

The first argument to this method is once again the coordinates as a 2-tuple. We have these defined as a constant, `PLAYER_SCORE_TEXT_COORDS`, so we use that as the first argument.

The `text` argument controls what the text drawn to the screen actually says. We have the score as a string available in our `game_state` instance, so we can call this method and use the result as the value passed.

In order to change the font size, we can use the `font` argument. The `font` argument takes a tuple.

The first value in the tuple will be a string containing the font name, for example, `Ariel`. Since we are providing `None` in this case, the system's default font will be used.

The second value defines the font's size. We pass in 20 to make the text bigger and thus more readable.

With that added, all of the graphics which should always be drawn are accounted for. However, if somebody wins, we should display a message portraying this:

```
if table_state['has_winner']:
    if table_state['has_winner'] == 'p':
        self.game_screen.create_text(self.WINNER_TEXT_COORDS,
                                text="YOU WIN!", font=(None, 50))
    elif table_state['has_winner'] == 'dp':
        self.game_screen.create_text(self.WINNER_TEXT_COORDS, text="TIE!",
                                font=(None, 50))
    else:
        self.game_screen.create_text(self.WINNER_TEXT_COORDS,
                                text="DEALER WINS!", font=(None, 50))

    self.show_play_again_options()
```

We first check whether or not the `table_state` contains a winner. If it does not, then we won't want to display any more text.

If we do have a winner, then we will once again use the `create_text` method to draw some text onto the screen, letting the player know that the current game is now over.

If our winner string is set to p, then the player has won and we will show `YOU WIN!`.

If our winner string is dp, then we have a tie and we will show `TIE!`.

Otherwise, the dealer must have won, so we show `DEALER WINS!`.

The location of this text is stored in our `WINNER_TEXT_COORDS` constant, and so this is the first argument passed to our call to `create_text`. These coordinates are again the middle point of the `Canvas` so that this text will be centered on the screen.

We again use the `font` argument to increase the size of our default font. This time, we want it even bigger, so we set it to 50.

As the game is now over, we no longer need to offer the `hit_button` or `stick_button`—we instead need to ask the player if they would like to play another game. We handle the replacing of these buttons with a method called `show_play_again_options`. Let's look at this now:

```
def show_play_again_options(self):
    self.hit_button.pack_forget()
    self.stick_button.pack_forget()

    self.play_again_button.pack(side=tk.LEFT, padx=(100, 200))
    self.quit_button.pack(side=tk.LEFT)
```

In order to unpack the `hit_button` and `stick_button`, we call the `pack_forget` method on them. This does not delete them but simply removes them from being displayed by the parent widget.

To show our `play_again_button` and `quit_button`, we pack them with the same parameters as attributed to our `hit_button` and `stick_button`. This ensures that they will be put in the exact same place as the previous buttons.

Since we are on the topic of our game's buttons, let's have a look at what each will do, starting with our `hit_button`:

```
def hit(self):
    self.game_state.hit()
    self.display_table()
```

This method simply calls the hit method over on our `game_state` instance which deals with the game logic side of the player receiving a card. Once that has happened, the state of the table will have changed, so we need to draw it again. We call `self.display_table` to do this.

If they instead click the `stick_button`, we will do the following:

```
def stick(self):
    table_state = self.game_state.calculate_final_state()
    self.display_table(False, table_state)
```

Since clicking the `stick_button` ends any further game logic, we need to obtain the final table state from our `game_state` instance. We can then pass this over to `display_table` in order to draw it on the screen. We also pass `False` to the `hide_dealer` argument in order to show the player what the dealer had in their hand.

Now that the game has ended, our other two buttons will be displayed. The `quit_button` calls the built-in `destroy` method of the `Tk` widget in order to close the window.

Our `play_again_button` will reset the `game_state` so that a new game can begin:

```
def play_again(self):
    self.show_gameplay_buttons()
    self.game_state = GameState()
    self.display_table()
```

When a new game begins, the user will need to see the hit and stick buttons again. We do this by using a method called `show_gameplay_buttons`, which will be covered next.

The `game_state` instance we store is replaced by a new one, meaning we have a new shuffled deck and two new hands, as well as no winner.

We then display this new `game_state` by calling `display_table`:

```
def show_gameplay_buttons(self):
    self.play_again_button.pack_forget()
    self.quit_button.pack_forget()

    self.hit_button.pack(side=tk.LEFT, padx=(100, 200))
    self.stick_button.pack(side=tk.LEFT)
```

The `show_gameplay_buttons` method just does what our `show_play_again_options` method did but in reverse. Instead of forgetting the `hit` and `stick` buttons, it forgets the `quit` and `play again` buttons and re-packs the `hit` and `stick` buttons in their place.

This is all that is needed in order to have our game function. Now we just need to piece it together.

Playing our game

To make and display a window for our game, we just need an instance of our `GameScreen`. Since this inherits from the `Tk` widget, we will also need to call its `mainloop` method to make it show.

We will do this within an `if __name__ == "__main__"` block to allow our classes from this file to be imported into another, in case someone wanted to write another card game using our `Card` and `Deck` classes, for example:

```
if __name__ == "__main__":
    gs = GameScreen()
    gs.mainloop()
```

Add the preceding code to the very bottom of your code file of this chapter and run the program. You should now have a fully working game of blackjack:

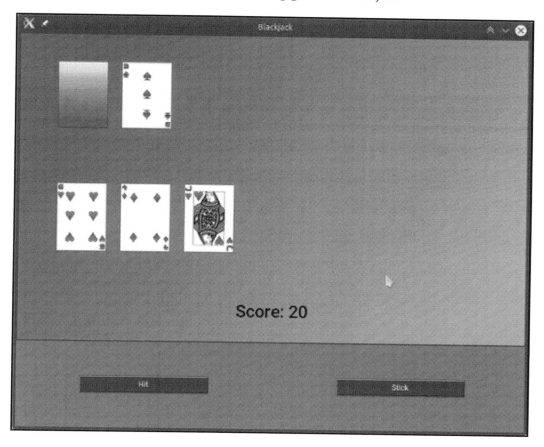

Our game of blackjack

Hopefully, you will agree that this is much more enjoyable than the command-line version. Feel free to have a play around with any of the constants, colors, or image files in order to make the game more personal to you.

Summary

With the completion of this chapter, we now have a fully graphical version of a game which was previously playable only over the command line. We have identified the key decisions to make before porting the interface of a command-line application over to a graphical one.

The benefits of making programs follow a reusable, class-based data structure have been made clear during the upgrading of our interface, allowing for a lot of code reuse between the previous chapter and this one.

We have learned about the drawing abilities of Tkinter's `Canvas` widget—we practiced drawing natively via lines and polygons, as well as inserting an image file at certain coordinates.

More detailed controls of the pack geometry manager have been shown, including the use of `pack_propagate(0)` to keep a `Frame` at its defined size and `pack_forget` to replace widgets with others.

While impressive, our blackjack game is not quite complete yet. We will be adding the ability to bet money and continue playing until we run out (or cash out early with a profit). Most games on sale also feature more flashy features, including animations and sound effects. Next on our agenda is to make our game feel more lifelike by adding these features.

The Finishing Touches – Sound and Animation

With our game now wearing its flashy graphical outfit, it's time to step it up one more notch on the scale of professionalism with some sound effects. These will help to engage the user by tapping into another of their senses.

To go along with the sound, we should also make some of the movement more realistic so that it better appears that our game is generating these noises.

Luckily, Tkinter's `Canvas` widget is well equipped to handle displaying animations and comes with some great built-in tools to make animating a breeze.

We can also take advantage of a popular Python game development library called `pygame` to make playing sounds incredibly simple.

By the end of this chapter, we will have covered the following:

- Making graphics move on a canvas
- Keeping control of the GUI while animations are playing
- Integrating the pygame library with Tkinter and playing sounds
- Expanding and re-structuring a larger application using Python's module system

With such a vast expansion of our application's features, it makes sense to try and abstract some of it into easily reusable chunks. We have already seen that defining classes can help to achieve this, but there is also one further step we can take – using Python's module system. Let's have a look into how this works before we begin refactoring our game.

Python's module system

Python's module system is something we have been using throughout the book. It is what lies behind the `import` statements.

All that we need to do in order to create a module is make a Python file. It really is that simple. Let's take a small example. Create a new folder to hold our example and add a short simple file:

```python
# mymod.py
myvariable = 15

def do_a_thing():
    print('mymod is doing something')

def do_another_thing():
    print('mymod is doing something else, and myvariable is', myvariable)
```

This may look the same as any normal Python file, but we can treat this as a reusable module if we want to. To demonstrate, open up a terminal window, change into the directory you have just created with this file in, and then run the Python REPL:

```
>>> import mymod
>>> mymod.do_a
mymod.do_a_thing( mymod.do_another_thing(
>>> mymod.do_a_thing()
mymod is doing something
>>> mymod.do_another_thing()
mymod is doing something else, and myvariable is 15
```

Since we are in the directory in which the `mymod.py` file is stored, we are able to import it in the same way as anything from the standard library. This is due to how importing works.

When you add `import mymod` to a Python file, you are telling it to look for a file or package with the name `mymod`. Python won't scan the whole computer though, only the places defined in your Python install's default `path`, as well as in a special `os` variable called `PYTHONPATH`. These variables simply tell the Python interpreter which folders to check for the imported files or packages.

To check out our `path` and `PYTHONPATH`, we can go back to our REPL and do this:

```
>>> import sys
>>> import os
>>> sys.path
['', '/usr/lib/python36.zip', '/usr/lib64/python3.6',
'/usr/lib64/python3.6/lib-dynload', '/usr/lib64/python3.6/site-packages',
'/usr/lib64/python3.6/_import_failed', '/usr/lib/python3.6/site-packages']
>>> os.environ['PYTHONPATH']
Traceback (most recent call last):
  File "<stdin>", line 1, in <module>
  File "/usr/lib64/python3.6/os.py", line 669, in __getitem__
    raise KeyError(key) from None
KeyError: 'PYTHONPATH'
```

From the previous code, we can note that my machine does not have a `PYTHONPATH` environment variable configured, so all modules will be located from the default path found in `sys.path`.

Speaking of which, the locations listed in `sys.path` are all displayed, the first of which is an empty string, signaling that the first place that will be searched is the current directory that the file is being executed from. This is why the interpreter was able to find my `mymod.py` file even though we had just created it in a normal folder.

Once a module has been imported, its classes, functions, and variables are all accessible to the importer (unless specifically protected). Depending on the type of import performed, they will be accessed differently.

To better demonstrate this point, we'll need to change `myvariable` to a list:

```
myvariable = ['important', 'list']
```

Now let's have a look at importing `mymod` the regular way:

```
>>> import mymod
>>> dir()
['__annotations__', '__builtins__', '__doc__', '__loader__', '__name__',
'__package__', '__spec__', 'mymod']
>>> dir(mymod)
['__builtins__', '__cached__', '__doc__', '__file__', '__loader__',
'__name__', '__package__', '__spec__', 'do_a_thing', 'do_another_thing',
'myvariable']
>>> mymod.myvariable
['important', 'list']
>>> mymod.do_another_thing()
mymod is doing something else, and myvariable is ['important', 'list']
```

```
>>> myvariable = ['silly', 'list']
>>> mymod.myvariable
['important', 'list']
>>> mymod.do_another_thing()
mymod is doing something else, and myvariable is ['important', 'list']
```

When importing with a plain `import mymod` statement, we are able to inspect the module via Python's `dir` function. This lists all of the available attributes, methods, and variables within the module.

We also use `dir` to inspect the global namespace to see that we do not have direct access to anything inside `mymod`. To use its features, we must prepend `mymod.` to them.

You will notice that the variable `myvariable` is accessed as `mymod.myvariable`, meaning we are free to define another `myvariable` without affecting the one used by our `mymod` module. Even when we redefine `myvariable` to `['silly', 'list']`, our `mymod` module will still have access to the original value of `['important', 'list']`.

Let's try the other import type using `from` and `*`:

```
>>> from mymod import *
>>> dir()
['__annotations__', '__builtins__', '__doc__', '__loader__', '__name__',
'__package__', '__spec__', 'do_a_thing', 'do_another_thing', 'myvariable']
>>> myvariable
['important', 'list']
>>> myvariable.append('junk')
>>> do_another_thing()
mymod is doing something else, and myvariable is ['important', 'list',
'junk']
>>> myvariable.remove('important')
>>> do_another_thing()
mymod is doing something else, and myvariable is ['list', 'junk']
```

When using a wildcard import, all features are added to the global namespace. Whereas before we had to use `mymod.` to access parts of it, they are now available without that prefix.

While this offers a bit of brevity, the trade-off is the ability to accidentally overwrite parts of a module without realizing it. In this example, we were able to access `myvariable` from the global namespace and change it. In doing this, we have also changed the result produced by the `do_another_thing` function. Needless to say, this could cause some unwanted effects and difficult-to-trace bugs.

While in the first example we still could have changed the value of `myvariable` and affected the result of `do_another_thing`, the need to place the modulus's name directly in front of it acts as a safeguard against accidental modification. This means the regular `import` statement is just as capable as the wildcard, but safer to do. This is why the plain import is considered preferable to a wildcard.

If we find ourselves with many different modules that belong to an overall group, we can make them easier to import by combining them into a package.

A package is defined by a folder containing a file named __init__.py. This __init__.py file is run when the package is imported and anything within its namespace becomes available to the importer.

To try creating a package, let's make a new folder called `counter` and place three files inside it:

```
# counter/countdown.py
def count_down(max):
    numbers = [i for i in range(max)]
    for num in numbers[::-1]:
        print(num, end=', ')
```

This module provides a function that will simply count down from the specified number.

If you are not familiar with the syntax, `[::-1]` is used to reverse an iterable:

```
# counter/countup.py
def count_up(max):
    for i in range(max):
        print(i, end=', ')
```

This module gives us a function that will count up from the given number.

The final file to make is __init__.py, which tells the Python interpreter that the folder containing this file is a package that is importable. In our case, this file can be completely blank, it just needs to exist.

Now we have created a package called `counter`. If we launch the REPL from the folder containing our `counter` folder (not the `counter` folder itself), we are able to make use of the `counter` package:

```
>>> from counter import countdown
>>> countdown.count_down(10)
9, 8, 7, 6, 5, 4, 3, 2, 1, 0,
```

```
>>> from counter.countup import count_up
>>> count_up(10)
0, 1, 2, 3, 4, 5, 6, 7, 8, 9,
>>> import counter
>>> counter.countdown.count_down(3)
2, 1, 0,
```

From the preceding example it is clear that we can use the functions provided by our modules in three ways.

Firstly, we can use a `from` statement to import just the module we require from the `countdown` package. This gives us access to the functions provided by that module, but this requires the module's name as a prefix much like with our first `mymod` example. We demonstrate this by executing the `count_down` function.

Secondly, the function can be brought into the global namespace by importing it directly from the package and the module. We access a module within a package by putting a dot between them, as we have with `counter.countup`. This allows us to use the `count_up` function without the need to prepend the `countup` module's name, but does not expose any underlying variables that may be used by the function. We again demonstrate this by executing the function.

Finally, we can import the `counter` package, as a whole. This provides the most protection against accidentally changing parts of a program used by modules, but requires the most amount of typing in order to access functions and variables exposed by the package's modules.

After importing the whole `counter` package we need to prepend the package name first, followed by the module name, and finally the function name. This is a lot more verbose, but ensures the programmer knows exactly which function is being run.

That's all there is to grouping modules into packages. We will be using packages to split up some aspects of our blackjack game so that we do not get distracted by one very large file as we add more and more depth to the game.

We will also then have created a package that allows us to quickly emulate another casino card game in the future without re-writing any of the underlying structural pieces.

Let's begin creating the packages needed for the new and improved blackjack game.

The blackjack packages

Begin the rejuvenation of the blackjack game by creating a new folder to hold our new game. For simplicity, I will call this folder `blackjack`.

Within this folder, create two others: `casino` and `casino_sounds`.

The `casino` folder will become a package holding various aspects of a typical casino. This includes our old `Hand`, `Deck`, and `Card` classes.

The casino package

Within your `casino` folder, create three files to house these. Name them `hand.py`, `deck.py`, and `card.py`.

In each one, paste in the code from the relevant class.

If you are using an IDE with syntax checking, you may notice a few errors. These are due to the now-missing imports.

In `deck.py`, ensure you have the following imports:

```
import random

from .card import Card
```

The `random` module is needed to shuffle our deck.

The `Deck` class also relies on having instances of our `Card` class, so we need to ensure we have access to it. We achieve this by using a relative import.

The relative import is indicated by a single or double dot in front of the module name. In this case, `.card` tells Python to import from a module named card, which is in the same directory as our `deck.py` file.

To fix our `card.py` file, ensure you have the following at the top of the file:

```
import os
from tkinter import PhotoImage

assets_folder = os.path.abspath(os.path.join(os.path.dirname(__file__),
'../..', 'assets/')
```

The os module will allow us to build the path to our assets_folder, which will live in this file for simplicity's sake.

The Player class will represent the user who is playing our game. We will use it to hold their hand of cards and control their money, as well as shorten certain function calls that are repeatedly used in the main flow of the game by utilizing Python's @property decorator:

```python
from .hand import Hand


class Player:
    def __init__(self):
        self.money = 50
        self.hand = Hand()

    def add_winnings(self, winnings):
        self.money += winnings

    def can_place_bet(self, amount):
        return self.money >= amount

    def place_bet(self, amount):
        self.money -= amount

    def receive_card(self, card):
        self.hand.add_card(card)

    def empty_hand(self):
        self.hand.cards = []
```

When initializing our Player, we need their hand and money. For simplicity we will start each player off with a fixed £50 of stake money. Their hand will be an instance of the Hand class, as expected.

If the player wins a round, they should receive the money that was bet. To achieve this, we use an add_winnings method, which increases their money attribute by the specified amount.

Before a player can place their share of the bet, we need to check whether they have sufficient funds. The can_place_bet method handles this by comparing the player's money total with the amount to bet against. We return whether or not the player has as much, or more, than the required bet.

In order to place a bet, we remove the needed amount from the player's total money.

The Hand instance assigned to the player will be managed via the Player instance. In order to add a card to the player's hand, we now need simply to call the Player class' receive_card method with the relevant Card instance.

To clear the Player class' hand between rounds, we have an empty_hand method.

Now we will use some class properties to streamline accessing the player's statistics from within the game logic:

```
@property
def score(self):
    return self.hand.get_value()

@property
def is_over(self):
    return self.hand.get_value() > 21

@property
def has_blackjack(self):
    return self.hand.get_value() == 21

@property
def cards(self):
    return self.hand.cards
```

Instead of calling get_value on the Hand instance every time, we can now get the player's score by accessing player.score.

We can remove the player_is_over method from our game logic by accessing player.is_over.

Similarly, the someone_has_blackjack method can be shortened by accessing the player.has_blackjack property from our Player instance.

Finally, the player's cards are accessed by player.cards.

With these changes, we no longer need to directly access any Hand instances from the game logic—all classes that need to affect a hand will now just deal with the player instances. This ensures that our game logic is as loosely coupled with our implementations of the casino elements as possible.

For the sake of naming clarity, we also define a `Dealer` class in this module. The `Dealer` will be a subclass of `Player` with no additional logic. This allows us to create an instance of a `Dealer` within our game logic, and if we decide that we want to add any dealer-specific functionality at a later date, we are already set up to do so:

```
class Dealer(Player):
    pass
```

With these two classes, our casino modules are complete.

Now we need to make sure that we can import them easily when we need to use them in our main `blackjack.py` file. To do this, we simply need to create a file called `__init__.py` in our casino folder. Inside this file, type the following:

```
from .card import Card, assets_folder
from .deck import Deck
from .hand import Hand
from .player import Player, Dealer
```

These `import` statements don't appear to do anything in this file, but they will allow us to access each of these classes from the `casino` package's namespace. This means we do not need to know about the internal file structure used by our `casino` package in order to use its classes.

In practical terms, this means we only need to type `from casino import Deck` instead of `from casino.deck import Deck`.

Just like that, our `casino` package is finished! We now have a simple, reusable collection of classes that emulate various aspects of a real-life casino.

There is just one more package that we will need to make: the `casino_sounds`. This will be a simple package containing a class that makes playing audio clips easy.

The casino_sounds package

We will use the popular game development library called `pygame` in order to play our audio. `Pygame` is primarily a game-development library for Python, providing its own set of game-related features, one of which is a very simple API for playing audio files. This is how we will handle adding sound to our game.

You may not already have this library installed. This presents us with a good opportunity to look at using virtual environments in order to manage our Python libraries.

Setting up a virtual environment

A virtual environment is simply a set of folders created in a project's directory that contain all of the necessary binaries and libraries needed to run that project.

To create a virtual environment for our blackjack game to use, open up a terminal window and move into the outer `blackjack` directory. Now type the following:

```
$ python3 -m venv env
$ source env/bin/activate
```

This first command will create a folder called `env` in your `blackjack` folder. This folder contains everything that will be needed to run our blackjack application.

The next command tells our terminal to use the content of our virtual environment instead of the system-wide versions of Python and its packages.

To confirm this, open up the REPL now and check out the system path:

```
>>> import sys
>>> sys.path
['', '/usr/lib/python36.zip', '/usr/lib64/python3.6',
'/usr/lib64/python3.6/lib-dynload',
'/home/David/Dropbox/packtbook/Code/blackjack/env/lib64/python3.6/site-
packages',
'/home/David/Dropbox/packtbook/Code/blackjack/env/lib/python3.6/site-
packages']
```

Take note of the last two items in my path. Both now contain my virtual environment's `env` folder, showing that the Python interpreter is checking inside it for packages.

Now that we have created a separate environment for our blackjack game to run from, we can install the `pygame` library. We could do this in one of two ways.

If we have no intentions of moving or sharing our blackjack game, simply running `pip install pygame` will bring in the library ready for use.

However, if we wish to make our game as portable as possible, or if we had a much larger amount of external dependencies, we could create a `requirements.txt` file. This file would contain a newline-separated list of packages that our application requires to run and ensures that anyone else obtaining the code is able to easily locate and install them all.

As our application only requires the `pygame` library, this `requirements.txt` file would just contain the word `pygame`. We would then install the `pygame` library with the command `pip install -r requirements.txt`.

Go ahead and install `pygame` by either of the two methods mentioned earlier.

With the dependencies handled, we can now create our `casino_sounds` package.

Creating the package

Create another `__init__.py` file, this time in your `casino_sounds` folder. Add the following code:

```
import os

import pygame
from casino import assets_folder

class SoundBoard:
    def __init__(self):
        pygame.init()
        self.sound_folder = os.path.join(assets_folder, 'sounds')
        self.place_sound = self.load_sound('cardPlace1.wav')
        self.shuffle_sound = self.load_sound('cardShuffle.wav')
        self.chip_sound = self.load_sound('chipsStack6.wav')
```

Our `SoundBoard` class will make use of the inbuilt `os` module for some file path validation, as well as make use of our newly-installed `pygame`. We also import the `assets_folder` from our `casino` package to allow us to store sound files inside it.

We begin our `SoundBoard` class's `__init__` method by initializing `pygame`. Without this, our sound will not work.

The next thing we need is access to the folder that holds our audio files. I have placed these in the `assets` folder, under a new folder named `sounds`. We access this path by combining the string `"sounds"` with the `assets_folder` variable that we imported from our `casino` module. We use `os.path.join` to achieve platform-independent file paths.

Each sound we wish to play will become its own attribute of our `SoundBoard` class. We assign each attribute by passing the name of the audio file to a method called `load_sound`. Let's check this out:

```
def load_sound(self, sound):
    file_location = os.path.join(self.sound_folder, sound)
    if os.path.isfile(file_location):
        return pygame.mixer.Sound(file_location)
    else:
        raise Exception('file ' + file_location + ' could not be found')
```

We combine the passed-in audio filename with the `sounds` folder, which we have saved as our `sound_folder` attribute. This creates the full path to the supplied audio file.

 The audio files I have used in this chapter were obtained from the Open Game Art website, and are located at `https://opengameart.org/content/54-casino-sound-effects-cards-dice-chips`. Due to flexible licensing, they are also included in the `assets` folder for this chapter in the GitHub repository, which accompanies this book.

Before trying to load this with `pygame`, we need to check that it is indeed an existing file path. We achieve this using `os.path.isfile`. This will check that there is a file at the supplied path. If there is not, we will raise an `Exception`, letting the user know that they require this file in order to run the game.

If the `isfile` check passes, we can use `pygame.mixer.Sound` to create a playable `Sound` object, passing it along the full path to our specified audio file. This `Sound` object is what will be assigned to each class attribute.

Now that this is done, all we need to do to play one of these sounds is call `.play()` on our `SoundBoard` instance's relevant attribute.

That's all there is to adding sound effects to our blackjack game. We now have a reusable class that will play any sound effect we decide to put into our `assets` folder and assign as an attribute.

With the `casino_sounds` package finished, we have all of the necessary tools to begin refactoring our game.

The blackjack.py file

Before we begin adjusting our game's main engine, take a moment to clarify that the directory structure for your project matches the following exactly:

```
- D: assets/
  - D: sounds/
    - F: cardPlace.wav
    - F: cardShuffle.wav
    - F: chipsStack6.wav
  - F: tabletop.png
  - F: back.png
  - F: Clubs2.png
  - F: Clubs3.png
```

```
    - F: ...
  - D: blackjack/
    - D: casino/
      - F: __init__.py
      - F: card.py
      - F: hand.py
      - F: deck.py
      - F: player.py
    - D: casino_sounds/
      - F: __init__.py
    - F: blackjack.py
```

Change things around to match this if necessary, then open up blackjack.py for editing. If you still have this file left over from the previous chapter, it will probably be easier to begin a new one and copy over some parts from it where possible, instead of trying to re-work the old file.

Begin in your new blackjack.py file with the following imports:

```
import tkinter as tk

from functools import partial

from casino import Card, Deck, Player, Dealer, assets_folder
from casino_sounds import SoundBoard
```

As well as the usual tkinter import, we will also make use of the functools module from the Python standard library. We only need the partial function, so we do not need to import the entirety of functools. The use of this will become clear later on.

We will also grab what we need from our casino and casino_sounds packages.

Our GameScreen logic from before will now be handled by a class called GameWindow. We will instead use the name GameScreen for our Canvas widget, which will need to be subclassed now in order to handle a lot more logic.

Initializing the GameWindow class

Let's look at the new GameWindow class and how it manages our application's main window and widgets. A lot of this code will feel familiar from our previous GameScreen class:

```
class GameWindow(tk.Tk):
    def __init__(self):
        super().__init__()
```

```
self.title("Blackjack")
self.geometry("800x640")
self.resizable(False, False)

self.bottom_frame = tk.Frame(self, width=800, height=140, bg="red")
self.bottom_frame.pack_propagate(0)

self.hit_button = tk.Button(self.bottom_frame, text="Hit",
                    width=25, command=self.hit)
self.stick_button = tk.Button(self.bottom_frame, text="Stick",
                    width=25, command=self.stick)

self.next_round_button = tk.Button(self.bottom_frame,
        text="Next Round", width=25, command=self.next_round)
self.quit_button = tk.Button(self.bottom_frame, text="Quit",
                    width=25, command=self.destroy)

self.new_game_button = tk.Button(self.bottom_frame,
        text="New Game", width=25, command=self.new_game)

self.bottom_frame.pack(side=tk.BOTTOM, fill=tk.X)
```

You should see that the majority of the initialization code has remained from our earlier GameScreen class.

One new button is now added, the new_game_button, which will allow the user to start a new game when they have run out of money.

Our game_screen attribute is no longer a stock Canvas widget, but a new subclass, which we will call GameScreen. This will allow us to handle animations separately and separate the game logic from the game's main window.

Instead of displaying the table at the end of this function, we now pass over to the game_screen instance to display the opening animation:

```
self.game_screen = GameScreen(self, bg="white", width=800, height=500)
self.game_screen.pack(side=tk.LEFT, anchor=tk.N)
self.game_screen.setup_opening_animation()
```

Since the rest of the methods in this class revolve around packing and unpacking certain buttons, let's jump to the new GameScreen class to see where our GameWindow class is leading us.

The GameScreen class

Our `GameScreen` will be a subclass from Tkinter's powerful `Canvas` widget and contain all of the logic to do with our window's graphics and animations:

```
class GameScreen(tk.Canvas):
    def __init__(self, master, **kwargs):
        super().__init__(master, **kwargs)

        self.DECK_COORDINATES = (700, 100)

        self.CARD_ORIGINAL_POSITION = 100
        self.CARD_WIDTH_OFFSET = 100

        self.PLAYER_CARD_HEIGHT = 300
        self.DEALER_CARD_HEIGHT = 100

        self.PLAYER_SCORE_TEXT_COORDS = (340, 450)
        self.PLAYER_MONEY_COORDS = (490, 450)
        self.POT_MONEY_COORDS = (500, 100)
        self.WINNER_TEXT_COORDS = (400, 250)
```

We begin by initializing the super class, `Canvas`, with the arguments passed over by our `GameWindow`. We use the `**kwargs` argument to pass all of our options over to the `Canvas'` `__init__` method.

The first argument to our `GameScreen` is called `master`, and this will refer to our `GameWindow` instance. This allows our `GameScreen` to alter the GUI elements of the game by calling methods defined within our `GameWindow` class, referring to it by `self.master`.

Our constants will now sit in this class, with a few new ones added.

`self.DECK_COORDINATES` holds the position at which we will draw a card back image representing the deck of cards being dealt from. When a card is dealt to a player it will appear to slide from the deck of cards over to the calculated position on the table.

`self.PLAYER_MONEY_COORDS` holds the coordinates for text displaying the player's current amount of money.

`self.POT_MONEY_COORDS` holds the coordinates for text displaying the amount of money in the pot. The pot holds the total amount of money that will be given to the winner of the round.

With the constants taken care of, we can now define some regular attributes:

```
self.game_state = GameState()
self.sound_board = SoundBoard()

self.tabletop_image = tk.PhotoImage(file=assets_folder + "/tabletop.png")
self.card_back_image = Card.get_back_file()

self.player_score_text = None
self.player_money_text = None
self.pot_money_text = None
self.winner_text = None

self.cards_to_deal_pointer = 0
self.frame = 0
```

We grab instances of our `SoundBoard` and `GameState` classes so that we can access their methods within all methods in this class.

The images that we will need to draw every game are stored as attributes for our `GameScreen` class. This includes the tabletop background and the card back.

Each piece of text that needs to be drawn to the `GameScreen` has an attribute reserved for it, which is initially set to `None`.

The `cards_to_deal_pointer` and `frame` attributes will be used for displaying animations, and are covered in the relevant method explanation.

Now that we know what happens when creating a `GameScreen`, let's look at how it displays the opening animation of our game:

```
def setup_opening_animation(self):
    self.sound_board.shuffle_sound.play()
    self.create_image((400, 250), image=self.tabletop_image)

    self.card_back_1 = self.create_image(self.DECK_COORDINATES,
                                        image=self.card_back_image)
    self.card_back_2 = self.create_image((self.DECK_COORDINATES[0] + 20,
                self.DECK_COORDINATES[1]), image=self.card_back_image)

    self.back_1_movement = ([10] * 6 + [-10] * 6) * 7
    self.back_2_movement = ([-10] * 6 + [10] * 6) * 7

    self.play_card_animation()
```

This animation will simply show the deck of cards being shuffled.

We start by playing the sound for our deck shuffling so that the user knows what is being shown. We do this by calling the `play` method of the `shuffle_sound` attribute on our `sound_board` instance. This instructs `pygame` to play the audio file `cardShuffle1.wav`.

We now need to draw the tabletop, which serves as the background image for our `GameScreen`.

In order to give the illusion of a shuffling deck of cards, we will use two card back images moving back and forth horizontally.

To set this up, we need to draw two card back images on our canvas. These will be referred to as `card_back_1` and `card_back_2`.

We will draw one of them at the location of our `DECK_COORDINATES` and one 20 pixels over to the right.

The next thing to do is to make a list of steps to move each card back by. This may look a little strange if you are not familiar with list multiplication. The first step is to multiply a list of one value (such as `[10]`) by 6 to make a list of 6 x 10s (`[10, 10, 10, 10, 10, 10]`). Next, we reverse these steps by multiplying a list of—10s by 6 to make another list of 6 items. We add these together to create one list of 12 items. We multiply the resulting list by 7 in order to create a single list of 84 items.

To see the result of this, you can enter (`[10] * 6 + [-10] * 6) * 7` in the Python REPL.

We reverse the signs of the initial lists for the second card back so that both card backs will move in opposite directions each time. We store both of these lists as `back_1_movement` and `back_2_movement`.

Now that we have prepared the variables needed for our opening animation, it's time to make it play. We now call `play_card_animation` to get things moving:

```
def play_card_animation(self):
    if self.frame < len(self.back_1_movement):
        self.move(self.card_back_1, self.back_1_movement[self.frame], 0)
        self.move(self.card_back_2, self.back_2_movement[self.frame], 0)
        self.update()
        self.frame += 1
        self.after(33, self.play_card_animation)
    else:
        self.delete(self.card_back_2)
```

```
self.frame = 0
self.display_table()
```

We use the `frame` attribute to keep a reference of how far along each list we currently are.

While our `frame` number is less than the total number of steps in one of our `back_movement` variables, we call the `move` method to move each card back image by the number contained in that step (10 or -10).

To show these changes, we use the `update` method to refresh our `GameScreen` and re-draw the images in their new positions.

We increase the `frame` value so that we will call the next step of our animation the next time our loop runs, and finish off by scheduling this function once again after 33 milliseconds. The 33 milliseconds is chosen in order to approximate 30 frames per second as our animation speed.

Once we have exhausted all 84 of our frames, we remove one of the card back images, leaving one remaining to represent our shuffled deck.

We reset our current `frame` to 0, allowing us to play another animation if need be.

Now that all of our frames have played, our animation will have finished showing, and we can draw the initial table state as we did in the previous chapter. Unlike before, the initial table will also feature animations—cards will move across the table as if being dealt from the deck:

```
def display_table(self, hide_dealer=True, table_state=None):
    if not table_state:
        table_state = self.game_state.get_table_state()

    player_card_images = [card.get_file() for card in
                          table_state['player_cards']]
    dealer_card_images = [card.get_file() for card in
                          table_state['dealer_cards']]
    if hide_dealer and not table_state['blackjack']:
        dealer_card_images[0] = Card.get_back_file()
```

 The `get_table_state` method can be copied over from the previous chapter and added to the new `GameState` class. The only change to be made is replacing `self.player_hand.cards` with `self.player.cards` to make use of our new properties.

The beginning of this method looks the same as before. We once again grab the initial state of the table from our `GameState` instance, extract the player's and dealer's cards, and grab the card images from our `Card` class:

```
self.cards_to_deal_images = []
self.cards_to_deal_positions = []

for card_number, card_image in enumerate(player_card_images):
    image_pos = self.get_player_card_pos(card_number)
    self.cards_to_deal_images.append(card_image)
    self.cards_to_deal_positions.append(image_pos)

for card_number, card_image in enumerate(dealer_card_images):
    image_pos = (self.CARD_ORIGINAL_POSITION + self.CARD_WIDTH_OFFSET *
card_number, self.DEALER_CARD_HEIGHT)
    self.cards_to_deal_images.append(card_image)
    self.cards_to_deal_positions.append(image_pos)

self.play_deal_animation()

while self.playing_animation:
    self.master.update()
```

In order to set up for an animation, we need to pass two lists of information back over to our animating method – the card image files and the position at which to place them. We will use two list attributes in order to store them.

We again loop over the cards held by the player and calculate the position at which to place it within the canvas. This has been abstracted out to a new method, `get_player_card_pos`, but the code is the same as it was in the previous chapter:

```
def get_player_card_pos(self, card_number):
    return (self.CARD_ORIGINAL_POSITION + self.CARD_WIDTH_OFFSET *
card_number, self.PLAYER_CARD_HEIGHT)
```

We append each position and card image to our `cards_to_deal` attributes before doing the same process with the dealer's cards.

Now that we have the required information, we can play the deal animations by calling `play_deal_animation`.

Once the animation has begun playing, we want to wait for it to finish playing before continuing in this method, so we use an attribute called `playing_animation` to communicate this. We wait on this using a `while` loop, which simply tells the window to update its content, thus playing each frame of the animation. This has the added bonus of blocking in this method until the `play_deal_animation` method sets `playing_animation` to `False`.

Let's have a look at how the `play_deal_animation` will handle all of this:

```
def play_deal_animation(self):
    self.playing_animation = True
    self.animation_frames = 15

    self.card_back_2 = self.create_image(self.DECK_COORDINATES,
                                        image=self.card_back_image)

    target_coords = self.cards_to_deal_positions
                        [self.cards_to_deal_pointer]

    x_diff = self.DECK_COORDINATES[0] - target_coords[0]
    y_diff = self.DECK_COORDINATES[1] - target_coords[1]

    x_step = (x_diff / self.animation_frames) * -1
    y_step = (y_diff / self.animation_frames) * -1

    self.move_func = partial(self.move_card, item=self.card_back_2,
                            x_dist=x_step, y_dist=y_step)
    self.move_func.__name__ = 'move_card'

    self.move_card(self.card_back_2, x_step, y_step)
```

We begin by setting `playing_animation` to `True` and blocking the previous function.

Another attribute called `animation_frames` is used to control how long each card deal animation will play for. A value of 15 at roughly 30 frames per second means each deal animation will take around half a second.

To simulate a card being dealt from the deck, we will begin by drawing another card back image on top of the one that represents the deck. We use the `DECK_COORDINATES` constant to ensure that they are perfectly aligned.

We now need to calculate each of the 15 positions that the card will need to be drawn in to place it in the target position obtained from the `cards_to_deal_positions`.

The relevant target position is extracted from `cards_to_deal_positions` using our `cards_to_deal_pointer`, which was initialized to 0 in our __init__ method.

With this, we now need to find the total distance between the target position and the coordinates of our deck. We store these as `x_diff` and `y_diff`.

To calculate each step, we divide these total differences by the number of animation frames. This gives us how much we need to move in each direction per frame.

Since our deck is placed top-right of the dealing positions and our cards need to move to the bottom-left, we need to reverse the sign of each of our steps. We achieve this by multiplying the steps by -1. These steps are stored as `x_step` and `y_step`.

As we did when playing our shuffle animation, we need a function that we can repeatedly call using Tkinter's `after` method. The `partial` function from the `functools` library will allow us to do that.

A partial function is a function that has some (or all) of its arguments frozen at certain values. You can think of it as cloning another function but setting the default values of all of its arguments.

The first argument to the partial function is the function that needs its arguments fixed. We pass this through the `move_card` method, which will be detailed next. We then pass the `item` argument as our `card_back_2` image, the `x_step` as our calculated `x_step`, and the `y_step` as our calculated `y_step`.

In order to avoid an error, we set the __name__ attribute of this partial function to `"move_card"`. This allows our partial function to be compatible with Tkinter's `after` method.

Now we can call the first round of this method to begin the chain:

```python
def move_card(self, item, x_dist, y_dist):
    self.move(item, x_dist, y_dist)
    self.update()
    self.frame += 1
    if self.frame < self.animation_frames:
        self.after(33, self.move_func)
    else:
        self.frame = 0
        self.delete(self.card_back_2)
        self.show_card()
        self.sound_board.place_sound.play()
```

As with the previous animation function, we move our image the required distances with the `move` method, update the canvas to show the image in its new position, and then update our `frame` attribute to advance the animation counter.

If we still have frames left to display, then we reschedule our `move_func` partial for 33 milliseconds later using the `after` method.

Once we have exhausted all of our frames, we reset the frame counter back to 0 again. Next, the card back image needs to be removed and the face-up card image needs to be drawn in its place. We do this using the `show_card` method, which will be shown next. A sound is also played to represent the card hitting the table.

Showing the face up card simply involves creating the card image in the target position and updating our canvas to display it:

```
def show_card(self):
    self.create_image(
        self.cards_to_deal_positions[self.cards_to_deal_pointer],
        image=self.cards_to_deal_images[self.cards_to_deal_pointer]
    )
    self.update()
```

Back inside our `else` statement in `move_card`, we need to check if there are any more cards to play the dealing animation for:

```
if self.cards_to_deal_pointer < (len(self.cards_to_deal_images) - 1):
    self.cards_to_deal_pointer += 1
    self.play_deal_animation()
else:
    self.cards_to_deal_pointer = 0
    self.cards_to_deal_images = []
    self.cards_to_deal_positions = []
    self.playing_animation = False
```

If we have more cards to display, we update the pointer to refer to the next item in our `cards_to_deal` lists and call `play_deal_animation` once again.

When we have played our animation for each necessary card, our pointer is reset back to 0, our `cards_to_deal` lists are emptied out, and we set `playing_animation` to `False`, unblocking the `display_table` method.

Speaking of which, let's carry on with the rest of `display_table`. This code will sit underneath our `while` loop:

```
self.sound_board.chip_sound.play()
self.update_text()

if table_state['blackjack']:
    self.master.show_next_round_options()
    self.show_winner_text(table_state['has_winner'])
else:
    self.master.show_gameplay_buttons()
```

Since all of the cards have been dealt, it's time for the money to be bet. To indicate this, we play the sound of a casino chip being placed down.

We then call the `update_text` method to display various pieces of information on the screen.

The method is finished off by checking the game state for a winner. If someone was dealt blackjack from the beginning, we need to indicate the winner and tell the `GameWindow` to show the appropriate buttons at the bottom of the window. Otherwise, we get our `GameWindow` to display the hit and stick buttons with `show_gameplay_buttons`.

The `update_text` method is responsible for all `create_text` calls on our canvas:

```
def update_text(self):
    self.delete(self.player_money_text, self.player_score_text,
self.pot_money_text)

    self.player_score_text =
self.create_text(self.PLAYER_SCORE_TEXT_COORDS,
text=self.game_state.player_score_as_text(), font=(None, 20))
    self.player_money_text = self.create_text(self.PLAYER_MONEY_COORDS,
text=self.game_state.player_money_as_text(), font=(None, 20))
    self.pot_money_text = self.create_text(self.POT_MONEY_COORDS,
text=self.game_state.pot_money_as_text(), font=(None, 20))
```

When updating the text displayed, we first delete all of our text from the canvas. This ensures that there is no old text hanging around.

The three text items we create will display the player's score (as in the previous chapter), the player's money, and the money in the pot (which will be won at the end of the round).

All three of our text items are drawn at locations specified in our class' constants. Each item also has a method within the GameState to return their values as a string:

```
def player_score_as_text(self):
    return "Score: " + str(self.player.score)

def player_money_as_text(self):
    return "Money: £" + str(self.player.money)

def pot_money_as_text(self):
    return "Pot: £" + str(self.pot)
```

The only remaining text items that are not displayed by this method are the winner text, which gets its own method as it is not drawn at the beginning of each round, and the out-of-money text, which only displays at the end of a game. These also live in the GameState class:

```
def show_winner_text(self, winner):
    if winner == 'p':
        self.winner_text = self.create_text(self.WINNER_TEXT_COORDS,
                            text="YOU WIN!", font=(None, 50))
    elif winner == 'dp':
        self.winner_text = self.create_text(self.WINNER_TEXT_COORDS,
                            text="TIE!", font=(None, 50))
    else:
        self.winner_text = self.create_text(self.WINNER_TEXT_COORDS,
                            text="DEALER WINS!", font=(None, 50))

def show_out_of_money_text(self):
    self.winner_text = self.create_text(self.WINNER_TEXT_COORDS,
                        text="Out Of Money - Game Over", font=(None, 50))
```

These should seem familiar from the previous chapter – the relevant text is drawn at the center of our canvas.

With the animations displayed and the GameWindow showing our hit and stick buttons, it's time for the game logic to begin. Let's create our GameState class to handle the rules and variables we need to begin playing.

The GameState class

As in the previous chapter, the `GameState` class is responsible for all of the game logic, including handling the deck, determining each player's score, and who has won.

This time around, it will also determine how much money is needed to play each round:

```
class GameState:
    def __init__(self):
        self.BASE_BET = 5
        self.minimum_bet = self.BASE_BET
        self.current_round = 1
        self.pot = 0

        self.deck = Deck()
        self.deck.shuffle()

        self.player = Player()
        self.dealer = Dealer()

        self.begin_round()
```

This class contains one constant, `BASE_BET`, which defines both the original bet and how much the bet will increase per round. We have set this to 5, meaning the `minimum_bet` will be 5, 10, 15, and so on.

As we increase the bet based on the current round, we need to keep track of it. We use a `current_round` attribute to accomplish this.

The money in the pot will also be stored as an attribute of our `GameState`.

As with every iteration of our game, we begin by creating a deck and shuffling it. Instead of creating `Hand` instances to represent our player and dealer, we can now just create `Player` and `Dealer` instances.

With the variables initialized, it's time to begin the first round:

```
def begin_round(self):
    self.has_winner = ''

    for i in range(2):
        self.player.receive_card(self.deck.deal())
        self.dealer.receive_card(self.deck.deal())

    self.player.place_bet(self.minimum_bet)
    self.add_bet(self.minimum_bet * 2)
```

At the beginning of each round, we need to ensure that we do not still have a winner set, so we update our `has_winner` attribute to an empty string.

We then deal both players two cards as usual, this time using the `Player` class' new `receive_card` method.

The player then needs to place their bet, removing the minimum bet from their total money. The pot will increase by twice the minimum bet, so we use the `add_bet` method to add this amount to the game's `pot`:

```
def add_bet(self, amount):
    self.pot += amount
```

Now that our `GameState` has begun the round, we wait for the player to choose an action by clicking the hit or stick button.

Choosing to hit

When the player decides to click the hit button, the `GameWindow`'s hit method is called. This simply passes over to the `GameScreen` class to handle playing the deal animation:

```
def hit(self):
    self.game_screen.hit()
```

The `hit` method on our `GameScreen` needs to set up for the deal animation in much the same way as it did when displaying the initial table:

```
def hit(self):
    self.master.remove_all_buttons()
    new_card = self.game_state.draw()
    card_number = len(self.game_state.player.hand.cards)
    image_pos = self.get_player_card_pos(card_number)

    self.cards_to_deal_images.append(new_card.get_file())
    self.cards_to_deal_positions.append(image_pos)

    self.play_deal_animation()

    while self.playing_animation:
        self.master.update()
```

Before playing our animation, we need to remove the hit and stick buttons from our `GameWindow`. This prevents double-taps of the hit button from causing animation problems.

We draw a card from the deck, check the number of cards the player will now have, calculate its position on the table, and set up the deal animations using our `cards_to_deal` lists. The deal animation is played and we again wait for it to complete with another `while` loop:

```
self.game_state.hit(new_card)
self.update_text()
self.check_for_winner()
```

Once the animation has finished, we add the card to the `GameState`, update the text on screen, and check for a winner.

Adding the card on the game state simply passes the card instance over to our player:

```
def hit(self, card):
    self.player.receive_card(card)
```

To check for a winner, we pass back to the `GameState` object's `check_for_winner` method. If it finds a winner, we need to show the dealer's face-down card and the winner text in the middle of the screen. Then we can pass back to the `GameWindow`object's `on_winner` method to display the relevant GUI options:

```
def check_for_winner(self):
    winner = self.game_state.check_for_winner()

    if winner:
        self.show_dealers_cards(self.game_state.get_table_state())
        self.show_winner_text(winner)
        self.master.on_winner()
    else:
        self.master.show_gameplay_buttons()
```

The `GameState`object's `check_for_winner` method is much like it was previously, except we can use the player's properties to shorten it slightly:

```
def check_for_winner(self):
    if self.player.has_blackjack:
        self.has_winner = 'p'
    elif self.player.is_over:
        self.has_winner = 'd'

    return self.has_winner
```

If we did not find a winner, the `GameWindow` will just show our gameplay buttons. These are the usual hit and stick buttons:

```
def show_gameplay_buttons(self):
    self.next_round_button.pack_forget()
    self.quit_button.pack_forget()

    self.hit_button.pack(side=tk.LEFT, padx=(100, 200))
    self.stick_button.pack(side=tk.LEFT)
```

If, however, we did indeed create a winner from the last draw, we need to reveal the dealer's face-down card. We do this by using the `Card` class' `get_file` method to find the image of its front, then drawing it over the top of the card back image:

```
def show_dealers_cards(self, table_state):
    dealer_first_card = table_state['dealer_cards'][0].get_file()
    self.create_image((self.CARD_ORIGINAL_POSITION,
self.DEALER_CARD_HEIGHT), image=dealer_first_card)
```

The rest of the logic is handed over to the GUI elements under the `GameWindow` class:

```
def on_winner(self):
    self.show_next_round_options()

def show_next_round_options(self):
    self.hit_button.pack_forget()
    self.stick_button.pack_forget()

    self.next_round_button.pack(side=tk.LEFT, padx=(100, 200))
    self.quit_button.pack(side=tk.LEFT)
```

When a winner is found, the `hit` and `stick` buttons are removed from the bottom of the window and they are replaced with **next round** and **quit** buttons.

The **quit** button is the same as before, calling the `Tk` widget's `destroy` method:

```
def next_round(self):
    self.remove_all_buttons()
    self.game_screen.next_round()
```

Our `next_round` method removes all buttons from the GUI once again and passes over to the `GameScreen`, telling it to begin the next round:

```
def next_round(self):
    self.delete(self.winner_text)
    self.winner_text = None
    self.game_state.assign_winnings()
```

```
if self.game_state.player_can_place_bet():
    self.game_state.next_round()
    self.display_table()
else:
    self.show_out_of_money_text()
    self.master.on_game_over()
```

With the new round beginning, we no longer need to display who has won, so we delete the winner text with the `Canvas' delete` method. We also remove the attribute's value by setting it back to `None`.

The `GameState` now needs to give all of the money from the pot to the winner. This is handled by the `assign_winnings` method:

```
def assign_winnings(self):
    winner = self.has_winner
    if winner == 'p':
        self.player.add_winnings(self.pot)
        self.pot = 0
    elif winner == 'd':
        self.pot = 0
```

Should the player win the round, their money will increase by the amount in the pot. If the dealer won, there is no need to assign them the money since they cannot go bust, so the pot is just emptied. If the result was a tie, the pot will remain full, and the whole amount is left to play for in the next round (on top of that round's bet).

The `GameState` is then free to move on to the next round:

```
def next_round(self):
    self.current_round += 1
    self.minimum_bet = self.BASE_BET * self.current_round

    self.player.empty_hand()
    self.dealer.empty_hand()

    self.begin_round()
```

The `current_round` attribute is incremented and the new minimum bet is calculated from it. Both players then empty their hands to receive new cards, and the new round begins.

Choosing to stick

As you may remember from the previous chapters, when the player chooses to stick, the round is automatically over, and the winner needs to be determined by comparing the player's hand to the dealer's.

The method called by our stick button is that of the GameWindow itself. This method only passes on the stick choice to the GameScreen:

```
def stick(self):
    self.game_screen.stick()
```

The GameScreen grabs the final state from our GameState, then performs the same steps as it did when we found a winner during our hit logic:

```
def stick(self):
    table_state = self.game_state.calculate_final_state()

    self.show_dealers_cards(table_state)
    self.show_winner_text(table_state['has_winner'])
    self.master.on_winner()
```

The final state is calculated in the same way as in previous chapters. The code is shortened slightly by our new player properties:

```
def calculate_final_state(self):
    player_hand_value = self.player.score
    dealer_hand_value = self.dealer.score

    if player_hand_value == dealer_hand_value:
        winner = 'dp'
    elif player_hand_value > dealer_hand_value:
        winner = 'p'
    else:
        winner = 'd'

    self.has_winner = winner

    table_state = {
        'player_cards': self.player.cards,
        'dealer_cards': self.dealer.cards,
        'has_winner': winner,
    }

    return table_state
```

This dictionary is returned to the GameScreen so that it can flip the dealer's card and display the winner as text. The GameScreen will then pass back to the GameWindow to display the relevant buttons back to the user.

Running out of money

As the rounds go on, the amount of money needed to satisfy the minimum bet will grow. This means that if the player loses enough rounds, they will be unable to continue playing.

When this happens, the GameScreen will call the on_game_over method within our GameWindow so that it can adjust the GUI elements accordingly:

```
def on_game_over(self):
    self.hit_button.pack_forget()
    self.stick_button.pack_forget()
    self.new_game_button.pack(side=tk.LEFT, padx=(100, 200))
    self.quit_button.pack(side=tk.LEFT)
```

The hit and stick buttons are replaced with a **new game** button as well as our familiar **quit** button. The **new game** button will call a method named new_game on our GameWindow:

```
def new_game(self):
    self.remove_all_buttons()
    self.game_screen.refresh()
    self.game_screen.setup_opening_animation()
```

Upon starting a new game, the GameWindow will remove its buttons to prevent a double-click, then pass back over to the GameScreen to refresh its GameState instance and play the opening shuffle animation:

```
def refresh(self):
    self.game_state = GameState()
```

All that's needed from the GameScreen to restart itself is a new instance of the GameState, which will be set back at around 1.

With that, the game logic is all finished. You should now have three fairly big classes containing all of the window widgets, canvas animations, and game logic. All that's left to do is make it run.

Finishing off

To make our game runnable, we just need an instance of the `GameWindow` class. This class will handle the creation and initializing of the other two classes, making running the game effortless:

```
if __name__ == "__main__":
    gw = GameWindow()
    gw.mainloop()
```

As usual, we contain the creation of our window within an `if __name__ == "__main__"` block, create our instance, and call its `mainloop` method.

Make sure you have sourced your virtual environment, then give this code a run with `python3 blackjack.py`. You should be greeted by a window that looks much like the one from *Chapter 3*, *Jack is Back in Style - the Blackjack GUI*, but with a fancy shuffling animation playing. You should then see and hear each individual card being dealt to you, rather than have them appear all at once.

Give the game a play for a few rounds to get a feel for how each new round will begin, and see the minimum bet increase until you can no longer afford to play.

Congratulations, you have now finished a fully-working game featuring both sounds and animations!:

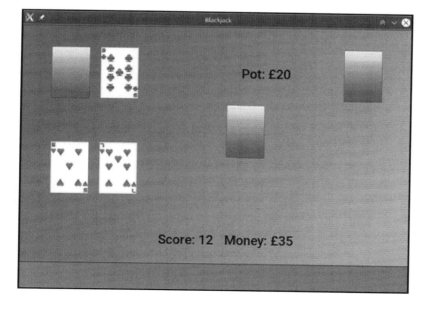

This is where we will leave our blackjack game. We have now created a fully playable game with both sound effects and animation. We also have a few reusable pieces of a casino card game that you may use to create other card games, such as poker, if you wish to continue along this path.

Summary

With the end of this chapter, and the end of our blackjack project as a whole, we now know how to add animations to a Tkinter project by making use of the powerful `Canvas` widget and its methods, such as `create_image`, `create_text`, `move`, and `update`. We know how to control their frame rate with the use of Tkinter's `after` method and how to block other functions until the animation is finished with a `while` loop.

Adding sound into a project has been made very easy by the use of the `pygame` library. Although the package we made for this chapter used casino-specific sounds, we have learned enough about reusability in order to create a sound collection package for any type of game and application, all we need is the audio files.

By looking into Python's packaging system, we have learned how to import and use other pieces of code within an application – both code written by us and external libraries. The advantages and dangers of specific `import` styles have been demonstrated so that we know how to balance conciseness of code with safety from accidentally editing things we should not.

Python's virtual environments have been explored and practiced so that we can consider portability of our applications as a whole, ensuring anybody who has the code will also have a list of its dependencies and the correct Python interpreter to go along with it.

In the next chapter, we will begin a new project—a text editor that handles syntax highlighting. With this project, we will be learning all about Tkinter's powerful `Text` widget, as well as general concepts of event handling and tagging.

5
Creating a Highly Customizable Python Editor

The next project we will be undertaking is a smart text editor for writing Python code. This text editor will have all of the features you would normally expect a text editor to have, including line numbers, a top menu bar, a right-click menu, various customizable key-bindings, a find/replace window, configurable syntax highlighting, and more!

Our first iteration will set up the foundations for our editor. We will start with the basic layout, some of the least complicated and familiar widgets, some key-bindings, and the creation of our find window.

In this chapter, we will cover:

- Using themed `ttk` widgets instead of regular `tk` ones
- Styling `tk` and `ttk` widgets
- Handling a large amount of text with the `Text` widget
- Scrolling with the `Scrollbar` widget
- Tkinter's event system
- Creating a second top-level window

With the increase in complexity of this new project, we should also ensure it looks as professional as possible. In order to improve the look and feel of our text editor, we will move on from Tkinter's stock widgets to those provided by a submodule named `ttk`. These will give our editor a much more native feel to the user. So, what is the `ttk` submodule?

The ttk submodule

The `ttk` submodule contains themed widgets that match those native to the system they are being run on. You may have noticed that the `Button` widgets used by our blackjack game looked a little out of place compared to buttons on a native application for your operating system. This is because Tkinter's regular widgets have a consistent look across all platforms and were likely designed before the operating system you are using was created.

To demonstrate what a difference `ttk` themed widgets make, open up a Python file and add the following code:

```python
import tkinter as tk
import tkinter.ttk as ttk

win = tk.Tk()

button_tk = tk.Button(win, text="tk")
button_ttk = ttk.Button(win, text="ttk")

button_tk.pack(padx=10, pady=10)
button_ttk.pack(padx=10, pady=10)

win.mainloop()
```

Run this code and carefully study each button. The `ttk` button should appear below the `tk` button, and should look similar to the buttons you are used to seeing on desktop applications for your operating system:

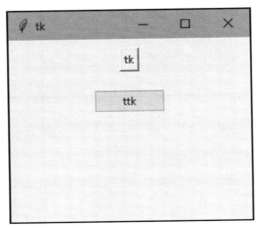

Given the native look, there is little reason to use regular tk widgets when there is a themed alternative provided in ttk.

The small advantage of a tk widget over a ttk equivalent is the ease of styling. If you plan on custom-styling a widget, then it is usually easier to stick with the tk version, since it will likely not look native after heavy custom styling is applied anyway.

Styling a tk widget

In order to style a tk widget, we simply use keyword arguments upon its creation, or the configure method if we wish to alter it afterwards.

Let's open up another Python file and have a go at styling some tk widgets:

```
import itertools
import tkinter as tk

style_1 = {'fg': 'red', 'bg': 'black', 'activebackground': 'gold',
'activeforeground': 'dim gray'}
style_2 = {'fg': 'yellow', 'bg': 'grey', 'activebackground': 'chocolate',
'activeforeground': 'blue4'}
style_cycle = itertools.cycle([style_1, style_2])

def switch_style():
    style = next(style_cycle)
    button.configure(**style)

win = tk.Tk()

button = tk.Button(win, text="style switch", command=switch_style)
button.pack(padx=50, pady=50)

win.mainloop()
```

In this file, we begin by creating two dictionaries full of keyword-argument to value mappings. The dictionary keys (fg, bg, and so on) are arguments which can be passed when initializing a widget, or to the configure method, to change its styling. The values of the dictionary are color names which will be assigned to these attributes.

The attributes we will be changing are:

- `fg`: The button's foreground (text) color
- `bg`: The button's background color
- `activebackground`: The button's background color when pressed
- `activeforeground`: The button's foreground (text) color when pressed

These two dictionaries are put into a list and passed to the `cycle` function from the `itertools` module. This function simply takes an iterable and returns each value when `next` is called on it. Once it reaches the end of the iterable, it then continues from the beginning, thus creating a cycle.

A function is then created named `switch_style`. This function will call `next` on our cycle and pass the arguments from the dictionary to the button's `configure` method. This will call the method and update the styling of our button.

The last four lines should look familiar. A main window is created with the `Tk` widget, a `Button` widget is created and bound to our `switch_style` function, the button is packed, and the window is displayed with `mainloop`.

Run this code and give the button a few clicks. Hold the mouse down on it and note the color change when the button is active which is shown in the following screenshot:

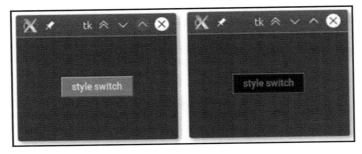

This is styling `tk` widgets in a nutshell. While I haven't covered every possible aspect of a widget that can be styled, the method of doing so will be the same.

A list of aspects and values can be found online. One possible source is http://effbot.org/tkinterbook/tkinter-widget-styling.htm.

Styling a `ttk` widget is quite different. These require a special `Style` object to be created for each widget type. Let's have a go at styling some `ttk` widgets.

Styling a ttk widget

In order to emulate the previous example with a `ttk` button, open up a new file and add the following code:

```
import itertools
import tkinter as tk
import tkinter.ttk as ttk

win = tk.Tk()
style = ttk.Style()

style_1 = {'foreground': 'red', 'background': 'black'}
style_2 = {'foreground': 'yellow', 'background': 'grey'}

mapping_1 = {'background': [('pressed', 'gold'), ('active', 'magenta')]}
mapping_2 = {'background': [('pressed', 'chocolate'), ('active', 'blue4')]}

style_cycle = itertools.cycle([style_1, style_2])
mapping_cycle = itertools.cycle([mapping_1, mapping_2])
```

To set up our style switching button, we use the following steps:

1. Though the imports are the same as before, we will also add `ttk` this time, so we start by adding this.
2. We create a main window, followed by the `ttk Style` object. This is the object that will be configured in order to affect multiple widgets in the application.
3. Another two style dictionaries are created, this time without `activebackground` or `activeforeground`, which are configured differently in `ttk`.
4. Two mapping dictionaries are created which will handle changing colors when the buttons are hovered over and pressed. These are in the form of a list of 2-tuples. The first value in the tuple is the state and the second is the color (as a string in this case).
5. Create two cycles to hold our styles and mappings.

Now that we have these variables set up, we can continue with the logic:

```
def switch_style():
    style_choice = next(style_cycle)
    mapping_choice = next(mapping_cycle)
    style.configure('TButton', **style_choice)
    style.map('TButton', **mapping_choice)

button = ttk.Button(win, text="style switch", command=switch_style,
style="TButton")
button.pack(padx=50, pady=50)

win.mainloop()
```

Our `switch_style` function now looks a bit different.

6. We get the next style and mapping dictionary from our cycles.
7. The `configure` method is called as before, but this time on the `Style` object rather than the button itself.
8. The string `TButton` is passed as the first argument to `configure`. This is a special string within `ttk` which will tell the `Style` object to apply the given styling to all `Button` widgets. The keyword arguments passed here come from our `style_choice` dictionary, as before.
9. In order to add the highlighting logic, we need to use the `map` function. This will map the attributes in the keys of our mapping dictionaries (just `background` in this case) to different style options, depending on their states.
10. The button is created. Upon creation, it is mapped to the `TButton` style. This assignment is actually pointless because the `TButton` styles will apply to all `Button` widgets by default, but it can be helpful to pass it as the argument to `style` just for clarification.
11. We finish the file by packing the button and displaying the window.

Give this file a try. Click the button a few times, again making sure to hold down the button to see how the coloring changes based on its state:

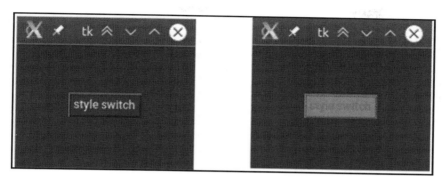

Now that we have a grasp of how to change some styling with both tk and ttk widgets, it is clear that styling a tk widget is much simpler, so it may be tempting to stick with tk widgets.

However, aside from the native look, there is another huge benefit to ttk widget styling—inheritance. One more example will allow us to explore how this concept works.

Ttk style inheritance

You know the drill by now—open up a blank file and fill in the following code:

```
import tkinter as tk
import tkinter.ttk as ttk

win = tk.Tk()

regular_button = ttk.Button(win, text="regular button")
small_button = ttk.Button(win, text="small button", style="small.TButton")
big_button = ttk.Button(win, text="big button", style="big.TButton")
big_dangerous_button = ttk.Button(win, text="big dangerous",
style="danger.big.TButton")
small_dangerous_button = ttk.Button(win, text="small dangerous",
style="danger.small.TButton")
```

After the imports and main window, we create five buttons. Each button will have different styling added to it:

- The first has no style argument, so will only have the global styling applied to it.
- The second has `small.TButton` styling applied.
- The third has `big.TButton` styling applied.
- The fourth has `danger.big.TButton` styling applied.
- The fifth has `danger.small.TButton` styling applied.

These style arguments are just strings. They won't do anything until we get a `Style` object to `configure` them:

```
style = ttk.Style()

style.configure('TButton', foreground="blue4")
style.configure('small.TButton', font=(None, 7))
style.configure('big.TButton', font=(None, 20))
style.configure('danger.small.TButton', foreground="red")
style.configure('danger.big.TButton', foreground="dark red")
```

We call configure with each of our `style` choices as the first argument:

- The global `TButton` sets the foreground (text) color to `blue4`.
- The `small.TButton` reduces the font size down to `7`.
- The `big.TButton` increases the font size to `20`.
- The `danger.small.TButton` sets the foreground color to `red`.
- The `danger.big.TButton` sets the foreground to `dark red`.

Now that we have the styles all set up, all we have left to do is pack the buttons and display the window:

```
regular_button.pack(padx=50, pady=50)
small_button.pack(padx=50, pady=50)
big_button.pack(padx=50, pady=50)
big_dangerous_button.pack(padx=50, pady=50)
small_dangerous_button.pack(padx=50, pady=50)

win.mainloop()
```

Run this code and look at the styling of each button. Hopefully, the way inheritance works is clear just from this example.

When defining a style name, the string which is used determines the logic used when styling the widget. Inheritance is applied via the use of the dots within the string.

Think of the rightmost word as the `base` of the inheritance chain. This will almost always be named after one of the `ttk` special strings, as they define exactly which widget the styling is applied to.

A list of all of these can be found online; for example, at `http://infohost.nmt.edu/tcc/help/pubs/tkinter/web/ttk-style-layer.html`.

Once you have found the appropriate base, you can edit all widgets of that type by configuring the base. This is what we did with this line of code:

```
style.configure('TButton', foreground="blue4")
```

Using this line, we changed all buttons to have blue text, unless overwritten by a new style.

In order to create a style which is only applied to certain widgets, add a new style name, followed by a dot, before the name of the base style. We did this as follows:

```
style.configure('small.TButton', font=(None, 7))
style.configure('big.TButton', font=(None, 20))
```

Any buttons using one of these two styles will have the relevant font size modifications from their leftmost style name. As well as this, they will inherit the blue text modification from the `TButton` base style. This is why all of the first three buttons have blue text.

This chain of inheritance can continue as far as necessary. In our example, we extended both big and small buttons one further time:

```
style.configure('danger.small.TButton', foreground="red")
style.configure('danger.big.TButton', foreground="dark red")
```

Each of these two buttons inherits both the font size and blue text from its middle and right style names, but the base name of `TButton`, which sets the text to blue, has been overwritten by the leftmost style name's shade of red:

This inheritance allows us to achieve effortless consistency across widgets of the same type within an application. We can configure a base style for each widget and update certain features of any widget which may need a slight difference in style without having to re-declare the base styling.

It also shortens our initializations significantly if we want to apply multiple default styles upon creation.

Now that we have an understanding of the differences between `tk` and `ttk` widgets, let's begin using some by building the first version of our text editor application.

Beginning our text editor

Before writing any code, be sure to make a new folder to hold the files for this chapter. Inside this folder, create a file called `textarea.py`. This file will hold the main part of our text editor—a subclass of the `Text` widget.

The `Text` widget is such as a `textarea` tag within HTML. It holds multiple lines of text and many formatting options. In the next chapter, we will see just how powerful this widget can be with the use of concepts like tags and indexing, which alter the text's appearance and give us control over certain regions of the text, allowing us to search all over the document within.

For now, we will just need a simple instance of the widget with a couple of configuration options set:

```
import tkinter as tk


class TextArea(tk.Text):
    def __init__(self, master, **kwargs):
        super().__init__(**kwargs)

        self.master = master

        self.config(wrap=tk.WORD)
```

Although initially short, this is all we need at the moment for our `Text` widget subclass.

After initializing the `Text` widget superclass, we assign the `master` widget as an attribute which will allow us to send information back to the main application window in the future.

We use the `config` method to tell our widget to wrap text on a whole word where possible. This will be configurable in a later iteration.

The next file to create in this folder will hold our main window, so I have called it `texteditor.py`:

```python
import tkinter as tk
import tkinter.ttk as ttk

from textarea import TextArea


class MainWindow(tk.Tk):
    def __init__(self):
        super().__init__()

        self.text_area = TextArea(self, bg="white", fg="black", undo=True)

        self.scrollbar = ttk.Scrollbar(orient="vertical",
                            command=self.scroll_text)
        self.text_area.configure(yscrollcommand=self.scrollbar.set)

        self.scrollbar.pack(side=tk.LEFT, fill=tk.Y)
        self.text_area.pack(side=tk.LEFT, fill=tk.BOTH, expand=1)
```

As usual, our main window will inherit from the `Tk` widget. We make an instance of our `TextArea` class, passing a default background and foreground color. The `undo` keyword argument is used to tell the widget that we want to keep a history of the user's actions to allow the familiar `undo` and `redo` commands to function.

After our `TextArea`, we create a `Scrollbar` widget. This will allow the user to quickly scroll around the `TextArea` widget by dragging the bar with their mouse.

We want this `Scrollbar` to be down the left-hand side of our window and handle scrolling up and down. We achieve this by passing the string `"vertical"` to the `orient` keyword. Much like a `Button`, the `Scrollbar` widget can take a command argument to call a piece of code when it is interacted with.

To tell the `TextArea` widget to receive scrolling information from our `Scrollbar`, we configure it with the `yscrollcommand` attribute assigned to the `Scrollbar` set property.

Both widgets are packed into the main window. We pack the `Scrollbar` in first to ensure it goes on the very left and tell it to fill the entire `Y` (vertical) space above and below it. We then pack the `TextArea` widget next to our `Scrollbar`, instructing it to take up all remaining space with the `fill` and `expand` arguments.

If you were to run this code as is (after making an instance of the `MainWindow` and calling `mainloop` on it), you would see that scrolling the text area will move the `Scrollbar` along with it, but you cannot click and drag the `Scrollbar` yet. In order to make that work, we need to assign its `command` function, which in our case is the `scroll_text` method:

```
def scroll_text(self, *args):
    self.text_area.yview_moveto(args[1])
```

The arguments supplied to this method will be the string `moveto` and an integer containing the position at which to move. We are catching these with a starred `args` parameter, for a reason which will become clear later on.

For now, all we need to do is call the `text_area yview_moveto` method with the supplied position and our `text_area` will be scrollable via the `Scrollbar`.

Finish up with the usual creation of an instance of the main window to allow the application to run:

```
if __name__ == '__main__':
    mw = MainWindow()
    mw.mainloop()
```

We can now run this file and have a look at our text editor. Try typing a lot of text and scrolling the widget with your mouse. Now try grabbing and pulling the `Scrollbar` as well.

Once you've explored scrolling, try some common keyboard shortcuts which you would expect to work. You should find that some of them will work fine, but others either do nothing or will do something different.

For example, *Ctrl + A* usually selects all text within a document, but this won't happen by default. *Ctrl + O* is usually to open a new file, but this will insert a blank line instead.

If we want to change these bindings, we will need to begin using Tkinter's event system to bind custom events to key combinations. Before diving in, let's take a brief look at how this event system is going to work.

Tkinter's event system

Each time the user interacts with a program in some way—usually via the use of a mouse and keyboard—an event is sent to the application. It is these events that cause things to happen, such as the letters appearing on my screen as I press keys on the keyboard while writing this book.

Tkinter's widgets have a default behavior for certain keys, and the operating system you are using will have default behaviors too. For example, *Alt + F4* will close the active window on a lot of operating systems, unless specifically unbound from this action.

When writing an application using Tkinter, there is a very simple and succinct API which allows the programmer to listen for keyboard presses or mouse movement and execute code in response.

Binding an event

The basic format of an event binding is as follows:

```
widget.bind('<Event-String>', function_name)
```

Each widget has the ability to listen to the system for one of many event types. Each event type has a particular string defined within Tkinter to allow it to be mapped over to the Python interface. When the event passed via this string occurs, the function passed as the second parameter is executed. Note that the function is passed and not executed, just like the `command` argument of a `Button` widget.

 When an application is written in an object-oriented manner, the function passed to the `bind` method is typically a regular class method. If the code is instead written procedurally, you will often see `lambda` functions used in order to access previously defined widgets. If you are not familiar with the way a `lambda` works, it is a good idea to familiarize yourself with that before continuing.

To try out some event bindings, get yourself another blank Python file and add the following code to it:

```
import tkinter as tk

win = tk.Tk()
can = tk.Canvas(win, width=300, height=300)
strvar = tk.StringVar()
```

```
lab = tk.Label(win, textvar=strvar)
strvar.set("Press a key")
```

Begin the file by creating a main window, `Canvas`, `StringVar`, and `Label`. The `StringVar` is set to a default value to make the `Label` show something when the window is first initialized.

Now we need a few functions to be called when our events are triggered, which are as follows:

```
def on_click(event=None):
    can.create_oval((event.x - 5, event.y - 5, event.x + 5, event.y + 5),
                    fill="red")


def on_key_down(event=None):
    strvar.set(event.keysym)


def on_ctrl_d(event=None):
    top = tk.Toplevel(win)
    top.geometry("200x200")
    sv = tk.StringVar()
    sv.set("Hover the mouse over me")
    label = tk.Label(top, textvar=sv)
    label.pack(expand=1, fill=tk.BOTH)
```

We have three functions which will be used to demonstrate three different events:

- `on_click`: When the left mouse button is clicked, we will draw a small red dot in our `Canvas`.
- `on_key_down`: When a key on the keyboard is pressed, we will display it using our `Label`.
- `on_ctrl_d`: When the control key is held and the *d* key is pressed, we will display a second window. There will be more to this function added shortly.

Each function takes a single argument—event. This is a special object that Tkinter will pass to a function which has been bound via the `bind` method. This object contains information regarding the event which took place, and has different properties based on the type of event which was captured.

When this object is spawned from a mouse event, for instance, it will contain the coordinates of where on the widget the user has clicked. These are stored in its x and y properties. We use these x and y properties in order to create the bounding box for our dot with our `on_click` function. This is how we know the dot will appear underneath where the user has clicked.

During a keyboard event, the `event` object will hold information about what key has been pressed. There are multiple properties holding various different bits of data, but the human-readable representation of the key will be stored in its `keysym` property. We set the value of the `StringVar` referenced by our `Label` to this string, allowing us to show the user what key has been pressed.

Now that we have the functions to be bound, all that's left is to do the binding. Add this to the following functions:

```
can.bind('<Button-1>', on_click)
win.bind('<KeyPress>', on_key_down)
win.bind('<Control-d>', on_ctrl_d)

can.pack()
lab.pack(side=tk.BOTTOM)

win.mainloop()
```

To bind to the left-click of the mouse, the special string is `<Button-1>`. Since the `Canvas` is what will draw our dots, we call the `bind` method on its instance.

On each keyboard's key press, both the `<KeyPress>` and `<KeyRelease>` events will trigger. The first occurs when the key is pushed in and the latter when the key is released.

In order to bind to a modifier key (such as control) and a regular key, we use the modifier key first, joined to the regular key with a hyphen. To bind to *Ctrl* and *D*, the string will be `<Control-d>`. Similarly, holding the shift key and pressing the *s* key would be `<Shift-s>`.

Our widgets are packed and our window is displayed.

Save and run this code, then try clicking over the canvas. You should be spawning small red dots each time you click.

Then try pressing keys on the keyboard and observe the text appearing at the bottom of the window. You can use this feature any time you are unsure of what the special name is for a key you are trying to bind an event to.

If you hold *Ctrl* and press the letter *D*, you should see a second window appear. Although it tells you to hover the mouse over it, nothing happens when you do. Let's fix this. Add the following to the `on_ctrl_d` function:

```
label.bind("<Enter>", lambda e, sv=sv: sv.set("Hello mouse!"))
label.bind("<Leave>", lambda e, sv=sv: sv.set("Goodbye mouse!"))
```

At first glance, you may assume the `<Enter>` event is the `Enter` key, but it is actually used to detect the mouse cursor entering the boundaries of a widget.

Conversely, the `<Leave>` binding detects the mouse leaving the bounds of a widget.

Using these two events, we can detect when the mouse is hovering over the `Label` and change its text. A `lambda` function is used to change the text of our `StringVar` variable depending on the position of the mouse.

Run this updated version of the code, press *Ctrl* + *D*, then move the mouse cursor in and out of the newly spawned window. You should see the text change as you do so.

Now we know how to add behavior to certain events. We also saw in our text editor application that some widgets will come with default events already programmed. These are changeable, too, but require an extra step.

Overwriting default events

What happens if we bind a key which already has default behavior on the target widget? Let's take a look at one example. You should remember from our text editor example that the combination of *Ctrl* + *O* inserted blank lines. We should overwrite that:

```
import tkinter as tk

win = tk.Tk()

text = tk.Text(win, fg="black", bg="white")

text.bind('<Control-o>', lambda e, t=text: t.insert(1.0, 'aaa'))

text.pack()
win.mainloop()
```

Run this example, type three lines of dummy text, then place your cursor in the middle somewhere. When you press *Ctrl + O*, you would expect the letters `aaa` to be inserted at the beginning of the editor. Well, they are, but the default behavior of adding blank lines also happens. If we are going to bind this shortcut to open a file, we don't want blank lines being added into the current file first!

When an event occurs in Tkinter, it will propagate from the instance level down to the class level. This means that any bindings which occur on the `Text` widget class itself, not specifically our instance, will also happen. This is why we get the additional blank line—the behavior has been bound to the `Text` widget at a class level.

To prevent this propagation, we need to return the string `break` during the instance level bindings.

Update the previous code snippet to do this:

```
def on_control_o(event=None):
    t.insert(1.0, 'aaa')

    return "break"

t.bind('<Control-o>', on_control_o)
```

When running this version of the code, pressing *Ctrl + o* will only add the `aaa` characters and no longer create the blank lines. This is because returning the special `break` string has prevented Tkinter from passing the keyboard event down to the class level.

With that cleared up, the last thing to look at regarding events is generating them.

Generating events

When generating a custom event, we first need to name it in a way Tkinter will recognize. We can name an event anything we want (assuming it is not already reserved), as long as we enclose it between two less-than and greater-than signs, for example `<<custom_event>>`.

We can emit this event whenever we like by using the `event_generate` method of a Tkinter widget. The first argument to this widget will be our custom name, and the remaining keyword arguments will define some properties which will be sent to the handler via the usual `event` object.

To receive and handle this event, the `bind` method is used just like before.

Let's have a go at an example program which uses custom events:

```
import random
import tkinter as tk

win = tk.Tk()
sv = tk.StringVar()
sv.set('You are walking around with an open wallet...')
lab = tk.Label(win, textvar=sv)
```

Our program will feature a main window, a `StringVar`, and a `Label`. It tells the story of the user walking with an open wallet. They will both drop and find money. Since this is only a demo program, there's no need to try and keep track of total money. The amounts dropped and picked up are merely for demonstration.

We now need a couple of functions which will act as event handlers to display each gain or loss of money:

```
def user_found_money(event):
    amount = event.x
    sv.set('You found £' + str(amount))


def user_lost_money(event):
    amount = event.x
    sv.set('You dropped £' + str(amount))
```

Each function updates the value of our `StringVar` to show how much money was picked up or dropped. This will be sent to the event handler by the `event x` attribute (since we cannot define arbitrary attributes):

```
lab.pack(padx=50, pady=50)

win.bind("<<Find>>", user_found_money)
win.bind("<<Lose>>", user_lost_money)
```

Our `Label` is packed and we bind the window to two custom events. These are named `<<Find>>` and `<<Lose>>` to fit in with Tkinter's demand for event name formatting. Each time one of these events is emitted, we will call the appropriate function to update the `StringVar` and show the user how much money was found or lost:

```
def emit_custom_event():
    choices = ['find', 'lose']
    choice = random.choice(choices)

    if choice == 'find':
```

```
            win.event_generate("<<Find>>", x=random.randint(0, 50))
        else:
            win.event_generate("<<Lose>>", x=random.randint(0, 50))

        win.after(2000, emit_custom_event)

    win.after(2000, emit_custom_event)

    win.mainloop()
```

A function to emit these events is defined as emit_custom_event. We use the random module to choose between a find or a lose string, then generate the relevant event using event_generate. We pass the necessary custom event name as the first argument and a random number to be stored in the x attribute of the event object which will be given to the handling functions.

Tkinter's after method is used to call the emit_custom_event function after 2 seconds, and the function will call itself every 2 seconds after that. This means the user will find or drop a random amount of money every 2 seconds while the application is open.

We finish up by calling mainloop to ensure our window displays when the program is run.

Run this program and watch as you find and lose money, all handled by our custom event objects.

With that, we now know how to create and listen for events within Tkinter. We can use this knowledge to build additional features into our basic text editor.

Events in our text editor

First things first: we should ensure that we have some expected key-bindings happening within our Text widget. We'll collate these in a method called bind_events and call this method from within our __init__:

```
def __init__(self):
    ...
    self.bind_events()

def bind_events(self):
    self.bind('<Control-a>', self.select_all)
    self.bind('<Control-c>', self.copy)
    self.bind('<Control-v>', self.paste)
    self.bind('<Control-x>', self.cut)
```

```
self.bind('<Control-y>', self.redo)
self.bind('<Control-z>', self.undo)
```

This function now ensures that six commonly used keyboard shortcuts will perform their expected behaviors.

Since these behaviors are already handled by the `Text` widget (except for `select_all`), we only need to emit the relevant events in order to get them to function. The `select_all` method is the only one we need to perform the logic for:

```
def cut(self, event=None):
    self.event_generate("<<Cut>>")

def copy(self, event=None):
    self.event_generate("<<Copy>>")

def paste(self, event=None):
    self.event_generate("<<Paste>>")

def undo(self, event=None):
    self.event_generate("<<Undo>>")

    return "break"

def redo(self, event=None):
    self.event_generate("<<Redo>>")

    return "break"
```

Our five built-in behaviors simply emit an event of the same name which will be handled by the `Text` widget at a class level. We return the `break` string in two of them in order to prevent the default behavior of their key combinations.

Now that we have defined these methods, we can be certain that key-bindings such as *Ctrl + c* will definitely copy text, and *Ctrl + v* will paste text. We do not need to return `break` for three of the events as there is no further default behavior, but if you wanted to do so for extra certainty, then it would not hurt:

```
def select_all(self, event=None):
    self.tag_add("sel", 1.0, tk.END)

    return "break"
```

In order to implement the `select_all` method, we add a tag of `sel` to the entire document. Don't worry about understanding how this works yet; we will go over tags and indexing in great detail in the next chapter.

That's all of the events for the `TextArea` widget. We can now make some more improvements to the `MainWindow` class.

A common feature of text editors is the ability to display line numbers. With the first iteration of our editor, we can implement a rough version of this feature (to be improved in Chapter 6, *Color Me Impressed! – Adding Syntax Highlighting*).

Go ahead and add the following to the __init__ method of the `MainWindow` class:

```
self.line_numbers = tk.Text(self, bg="grey", fg="white")
first_100_numbers = [str(n+1) for n in range(100)]

self.line_numbers.insert(1.0, "\n".join(first_100_numbers))
self.line_numbers.configure(state="disabled", width=3)
```

In order to represent the line numbers, we will be using another `Text` widget. The colors will be different from the `TextArea` widget to help differentiate between the two.

We use the `range` function to generate the first 100 numbers and insert them into our `Text` widget, separated by new line characters.

The `configure` method is then used to disable the widget, preventing the user from entering different text inside it, and also to set the `width` to three characters, which is as wide as it needs to be at the moment.

The line numbers will live on the left-hand side of the application now, so we will move the `Scrollbar` over to the right to make the interface a bit nicer:

```
self.scrollbar.pack(side=tk.RIGHT, fill=tk.Y)
self.line_numbers.pack(side=tk.LEFT, fill=tk.Y)
self.text_area.pack(side=tk.LEFT, fill=tk.BOTH, expand=1)
```

Give this code a whirl and check out the new layout.

If you enter many lines of text, you will still use the mouse and `Scrollbar` to scroll the `TextArea` widget, but you will notice that our line numbers don't move along with it. To fix this, we will revisit our `scroll_text` method:

```
def scroll_text(self, *args):
    self.line_numbers.yview_moveto(args[1])
    self.text_area.yview_moveto(args[1])
```

Running the code now, you will see that the `Scrollbar` will move the line numbers and `TextArea` together, but the mouse wheel still operates on each independently. To alter this behavior, we will need to use some event bindings.

We'll go ahead and use another `bind_events` method to collate all of these:

```
def bind_events(self):
    self.text_area.bind("<MouseWheel>", self.scroll_text)
    self.text_area.bind("<Button-4>", self.scroll_text)
    self.text_area.bind("<Button-5>", self.scroll_text)
```

Different operating systems will report different events, so we bind each possible one to our `scroll_text` method. This ensures all platforms will behave correctly.

We will now need to update the `scroll_text` method to handle the `event` argument which is passed by Tkinter's event system:

```
def scroll_text(self, *args):
    if len(args) > 1:
        self.text_area.yview_moveto(args[1])
        self.line_numbers.yview_moveto(args[1])
    else:
        event = args[0]
        if event.delta:
            move = -1 * (event.delta / 120)
        else:
            if event.num == 5:
                move = 1
            else:
                move = -1

        self.text_area.yview_scroll(int(move), "units")
        self.line_numbers.yview_scroll(int(move), "units")
```

Since the event system will pass a single `event` object as the only argument, we will only have one argument caught by our `args*` parameter. We can use this to detect whether or not we have entered this method by dragging the `Scrollbar` or moving the mouse wheel.

Our previous code is now in an `if else` block, with all new logic inside the `else`.

We grab the event object from the `args` list and check its properties. Again, different operating systems will populate different attributes in our `event` object.

If the `delta` attribute has been populated, we will need to scale it down to fit with Tkinter's scale. We do this by dividing it by `120`. We also need to reverse the direction, so we multiply it by `-1`. The result is stored in a variable named `move` which will be used to adjust how far, and in which direction, the widgets are scrolled.

If we do not have a `delta` attribute, then we should have a `num` attribute instead. Much like the mouse button codes, a `num` of 4 is a scroll up and a `num` of 5 is a scroll down. We decide the appropriate unit of movement with an `if` statement and again store it in our `move` variable.

Now that we have the unit of movement, we apply it to the widgets using the `yview_scroll` method. We cast this to an integer to ensure that the division from the `delta` attribute has not resulted in a float, and use the special `units` string to tell Tkinter that we are scrolling by one unit each time. The other option is `pages`, which would result in a much larger scroll.

With this method finished, our line numbers and `TextArea` will scroll together via both means. Despite this, the line numbers can still be scrolled by themselves, which we do not want to happen. We need to remove the default binding from the mouse wheel on this widget. We can use the `break` string to achieve this.

Add these three lines into the `bind_events` function:

```
self.line_numbers.bind("<MouseWheel>", lambda e: "break")
self.line_numbers.bind("<Button-4>", lambda e: "break")
self.line_numbers.bind("<Button-5>", lambda e: "break")
```

Using a `lambda` function to return the string `break` will prevent the class-level scrolling bindings from occurring on the `Text` widget we are using as line numbers.

Run this version of the text editor and try playing around with the scrolling properties. You should see that the line numbers and `TextArea` now scroll together, and you cannot scroll the line numbers independently by scrolling within their widget.

Due to the hardcoded amount of line numbers at the side, you will be able to scroll them down further than the `TextArea` widget, but this last small detail will be fixed in the next chapter when we begin dynamically populating the line numbers, so there is no need to worry about that yet.

The last thing to cover in this chapter will be creating a second top-level window. Luckily for us, Tkinter has a widget which will allow us to do just that. This widget will be great for our find/replace box.

A second top-level window

The new window that will spawn for our find/replace box shall be stored in a new file. Create a new script called `findwindow.py` and begin by entering the following:

```
import tkinter as tk
import tkinter.ttk as ttk


class FindWindow(tk.Toplevel):
    def __init__(self, master, **kwargs):
        super().__init__(**kwargs   )

        self.geometry('350x100')
        self.title('Find and Replace')

        self.text_to_find = tk.StringVar()
        self.text_to_replace_with = tk.StringVar()

        top_frame = tk.Frame(self)
        middle_frame = tk.Frame(self)
        bottom_frame = tk.Frame(self)
```

We will only need our usual Tkinter and `ttk` imports for this class.

We subclass Tkinter's `Toplevel` widget, which is a window that can act as a pop-up window to be displayed on top of a main window. It can be configured much like a regular `Tk` widget, but requires a `master` which needs to be an instance of the `Tk` widget as it cannot act as the main window of an application. A widget such as this is a great fit for our find/replace window, since it is much easier to spawn a new, smaller window above the main one than to try and place the relevant widgets somewhere around our `TextArea`.

After initializing the `Toplevel` widget class, we set this window's size to 350 pixels wide and 100 pixels tall using the `geometry` method. Then its title is changed to "`Find and Replace`" so that the user knows what it does.

We need two `StringVars` which will hold the text to be found and the text to replace that with.

To lay out our application, we will be using three `Frame` widgets. These will be stacked top, middle, and bottom, and span the entire horizontal space.

With the layout taken care of, we can begin adding functional widgets:

```
find_entry_label = tk.Label(top_frame, text="Find: ")
self.find_entry = ttk.Entry(top_frame, textvar=self.text_to_find)

replace_entry_label = tk.Label(middle_frame, text="Replace: ")
self.replace_entry = ttk.Entry(middle_frame,
textvar=self.text_to_replace_with)

self.find_button = ttk.Button(bottom_frame, text="Find",
command=self.on_find)
self.replace = ttk.Button(bottom_frame, text="Replace",
command=self.on_replace)
self.cancel_button = ttk.Button(bottom_frame, text="Cancel",
command=self.destroy)
```

The find window will need two places for the user to enter text, and these will need to be labeled so that they know which is which. We achieve this with two `Entry` widgets and two accompanying `Label` widgets. The `Label` widgets will have set text since they will not need to update, whereas the `Entry` widgets are bound to our `StringVar` so that we can easily get their values and adjust them if need be.

Along the bottom `Frame`, we will have three `Button` widgets. These buttons will be responsible for finding text in the `TextArea` widget which matches that in our `text_to_find` variable, replacing text in the `TextArea` widget with the text held in our `text_to_replace_with` variable, and canceling any further operations and closing the window.

The first two buttons are bound to methods within our `FindWindow` class, and the cancel button is bound to the top-level widget's `destroy` method, which we have looked at before.

The two methods will not do anything while our `FindWindow` is treated as its own class, but later on, when we link it to the rest of our application, it will be able to call methods from our other classes.

For now, enter the following code as these two methods:

```
def on_find(self):
    self.master.find(self.text_to_find.get())

def on_replace(self):
    self.master.replace(self.text_to_find.get(),
self.text_to_replace_with.get())
```

In order to preview our `FindWindow` before the next chapter, we will include a `Tk` widget as its `master`. Simply create an instance and call its `mainloop` as you usually would:

```
if __name__ == '__main__':
    mw = tk.Tk()
    fw = FindWindow(mw)
    mw.mainloop()
```

Run this code and you should have two windows pop up. One will be an empty main window, and the other our new `FindWindow`:

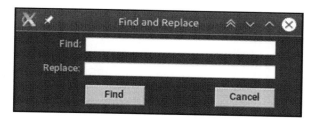

This is where we shall leave the first iteration of our text editor. We have a solid base on which we can add some sophisticated new features in the next chapter.

Summary

With the end of this chapter, the `ttk` set of widgets has now been added to our arsenal of tools, and we know why they would be used (to capture a more native feel) and how to style them using a `Style` object. Learning about style inheritance will enable us to better plan how we go about styling `ttk` widgets in a larger application.

We have also had a look at the styling options of the built-in widgets should we prefer to stick with those for their ease of use.

We have had a brief look at how Tkinter handles a large body of formatted text with the `Text` widget. We've previewed a couple of configurations and are ready to take a deeper dive into this widget in the next chapter, learning how to style and search this widget.

The built-in event system in Tkinter has been explored, allowing us to listen for keyboard and mouse input and execute Python code in response. We also understand that widgets may have their own default responses to some input, but we can overwrite them using the `break` string.

Our text editor application has its roots set with three classes handling the main window and widgets, the `Text` widget subclass, and a separate find/replace window, which we will be able to spawn atop our main window when we have combined them.

Next in line for our editor will be syntax highlighting. We will learn how to search around our `Text` widget quickly, finding keywords in the Python language and changing their color. We can then combine this ability to search with our find/replace window to make this function as it should.

6
Color Me Impressed! – Adding Syntax Highlighting

Now that we have a basic application laid out, it's time to dig deep into the `Text` widget and learn all about how to control its content while navigating around it. We will apply these concepts by adding syntax highlighting to our existing `TextArea` class. Along the way, we will also touch upon the concepts of tagging areas and parsing `config` files.

In this chapter, we will cover:

- Tkinter's indexing system for `Text` widgets
- Using the tag system to alter the display of text
- Locating specific content with the `search` function of a `Text` widget
- Parsing `config` files

Let's begin by looking at how we can use the indexing system to pinpoint locations within a `Text` widget.

Tkinter's indexing system

Indexing is handled in a somewhat coordinate-based way. An index is represented by two numbers separated by a single full stop. For example: `4.5`.

The first number (before the `.`) in this index can be thought of as the line number. This begins at `1`.

The second number (after the `.`) is how many characters into the line we are. This begins at `0`.

The first character within a `Text` widget will therefore be located at `1.0`. This means line 1, 0 characters in.

To ensure we fully understand this concept, let's create a demo application which will show us where the cursor is located at all times.

Getting the cursor's position

Open up a new Python file and enter the following code:

```python
import tkinter as tk

win = tk.Tk()
current_index = tk.StringVar()
text = tk.Text(win, bg="white", fg="black")
lab = tk.Label(win, textvar=current_index)
```

Begin with the normal importing and creation of a main window.

The things we will need for this application are a `StringVar` to hold the current cursor location, a `Text` widget to navigate around, and a `Label` to display our `StringVar`.

Now we need a function to hook to the `<KeyRelease>` event which will update our `StringVar` with the current cursor coordinates:

```python
def update_index(event=None):
    cursor_position = text.index(tk.INSERT)
    cursor_position_pieces = str(cursor_position).split('.')

    cursor_line = cursor_position_pieces[0]
    cursor_char = cursor_position_pieces[1]

    current_index.set('line: ' + cursor_line + ' char: ' + cursor_char +
                      ' index: ' + str(cursor_position))
```

In order to get the cursor's current position, we use the `index` method of the `Text` widget. This method will return the index of certain items which can reside within it. Since we want the location of the cursor, we use the built-in constant `INSERT` which refers to it.

This returns the index in the previously mentioned format of line number, full stop, and character number.

To separate these two pieces of information, we cast this to a string and use the `split` method to separate the two numbers from the full stop.

Each number is then stored in its own variable.

To make this information visible to the user, we create a string that contains the line number, character number, and complete index. This is then assigned to our `StringVar` with its `set` method.

Now we need to put these widgets into our main window, bind the `<KeyRelease>` event, and run the application:

```
text.pack(side=tk.TOP, fill=tk.BOTH, expand=1)
lab.pack(side=tk.BOTTOM, fill=tk.X, expand=1)

text.bind('<KeyRelease>', update_index)

win.mainloop()
```

Launch this application and type away in the `Text` widget (or copy and paste a bit of text) and move the cursor around. You should be shown the position at the bottom, and what it means:

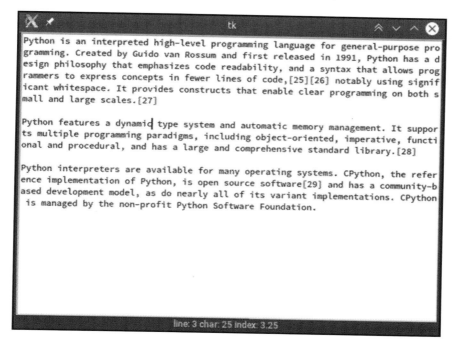

This covers the basics of cursor positioning. Most of the indexing you will need to do can be done like this, but there are certain tasks that will be tedious to calculate, for example, finding the last character of a line, or moving three characters forward. Luckily, Tkinter has a way of making this easy to do.

Named indexes

Much like the INSERT name we saw previously, Tkinter has many others we can use as shortcuts to finding locations within our Text widget. These include:

- CURRENT: The character closest to the mouse cursor. This updates when the mouse is moved and no buttons are pressed.
- END: The final character of the document. This is very useful for clearing the entire widget, as we know the start is always 1.0.
- SEL_FIRST: The first character which is selected.
- SEL_LAST: The last character which is selected.

These named indexes are not the only conveniences offered; there are also special strings that can be used to calculate indexes, but that do not reside in the built-in constants.

Special strings

There are some words that can be used in place of one of the numbers within a Tkinter index, which will remove the need to calculate them.

Line endings

To refer to the end of a line, for example, line five, we can use the word end instead of calculating and specifying a character number. With this example, we can use the 5.end index.

Horizontal movement

If we want to specify an index which is a certain number of characters forward from an existing index, we can append +nc, where n will be the amount of characters. Likewise, – nc will move backward n characters.

Suppose we want the range of the word `Python`, which we know begins at index `1.4`. We could cast this to a float, add `0.6` to it (since we know it is six characters long), and then cast back to a string. However, this becomes tedious and is unnecessary. Instead, we can refer to the ending index of this word with `1.4+6c`.

Vertical movement

To go up and down lines, you could again cast the index to a float and add `n.0` to it, but there is once again a much neater shortcut. This time, it is `+nl` or `-nl`, depending on the direction.

For example, if we had a shortcut to move the cursor three lines down, we could get its position with `pos = text.index(tk.INSERT)` and then set it to three lines lower with `pos = pos + "+3l"`.

Line beginning and end

The `linestart` and `lineend` strings will refer to the start and end of an index, respectively. These are most useful when you do not explicitly know the index you are working with.

For example, if you wish to add a feature that highlights the entire line at which the cursor is residing, you could get the necessary indexes with the following:

```
start = str(text.index(tk.INSERT)) + " linestart"
end = str(text.index(tk.INSERT)) + " lineend"
text.tag_add("sel", start, end)
```

This again removes the need for splitting off the line number and adding a `.0` and `.end` to it.

Word beginning and end

The last special strings to mention are `wordstart` and `wordend`. If you have an index which is in the middle of a word, you can use these two strings to refer to the beginning and end of it.

For example, if you knew that the y of `Python` was at `3.2`, then `3.2 wordstart` and `3.2 wordend` would refer to the beginning and end of this word.

Let's build upon our demo application by creating some keyboard shortcuts which will utilize a few of these tools.

Expanding our demo

Open back up the demo file we created earlier, which shows off the current cursor location. Underneath your `update_index` function, we will add four more bindings which will be used to practice the utilization of these special strings:

```
def down_three_lines(event=None):
    current_cursor_index = str(text.index(tk.INSERT))
    new_position = current_cursor_index + "+3l"
    text.mark_set(tk.INSERT, new_position)

    return "break"


def back_four_chars(event=None):
    current_cursor_index = str(text.index(tk.INSERT))
    new_position = current_cursor_index + "-4c"
    text.mark_set(tk.INSERT, new_position)

    return "break"
```

These two functions demonstrate the use of the +nl and −nc strings.

We get the cursor's current position in the same way as before, then add either `"+3l"` or `"-4c"` to create the new index at which we will move it to.

In order to move the cursor, we need to use the `mark_set` method, passing it the name of the mark (which is the `INDEX` constant again) and the new index which we have created.

Since these functions will be bound to keyboard shortcuts, we will return the `break` string to prevent any default behaviors:

```
def highlight_line(event=None):
    start = str(text.index(tk.INSERT)) + " linestart"
    end = str(text.index(tk.INSERT)) + " lineend"
    text.tag_add("sel", start, end)

    return "break"


def highlight_word(event=None):
    word_pos = str(text.index(tk.INSERT))
```

```
start = word_pos + " wordstart"
end = word_pos + " wordend"
text.tag_add("sel", start, end)

return "break"
```

To demonstrate the line and word navigations, we create two more functions which will be used to select different regions of the `Text` widget.

Demonstrating the line management, we will use a function which highlights the current line. This was mentioned before and is now demonstrated within our application.

We add the special tag `sel`, which is used to indicate selection, to the start and end of the cursor's current line, which we refer to by adding the `linestart` and `lineend` strings to its current index.

We then define a function that will highlight the word the cursor currently sits inside. We do this by again getting the cursor's current index, then appending `wordstart` and `wordend` to get our two indexes.

Once again, the `sel` tag is added between these indexes in order to create the selection.

Now we just need to bind these functions to keys as before:

```
text.bind('<Control-h>', highlight_line)
text.bind('<Control-w>', highlight_word)
text.bind('<Control-d>', down_three_lines)
text.bind('<Control-b>', back_four_chars)
```

Give this new version of the demo application a try. Again, type or copy over a few lines of text and press each keyboard shortcut to get a feel for how everything is working.

Hopefully, now you have a good grasp of how Tkinter's `Text` widget handles indexing and positioning. This will come in very handy when we search through our text to find Python keywords that require highlighting.

Speaking of which, it is now time to move on to tags. Tags are how the `Text` widget can style individual elements differently, and will be used to add the syntax highlighting.

We have already been adding one tag to our applications—`sel`—since this is a special tag which refers to the boundaries within the widget which are selected.

Using our knowledge of indexing, let's begin experimenting with adding tags to areas within a `Text` widget.

Using tags

In essence, a tag is simply a way of adding a name to certain parts of a widget. These names are then used as identifiers, and can be used either to separate certain parts, or group them, depending on your implementation of the principle.

To tag an area of text, you need:

- The starting index
- The ending index
- A tag name

The starting and ending indexes are as discussed in the previous section—they can be numbers joined by a full stop, or they can use any of the special strings as shortcuts, too.

The tag name is simply a user-defined string; the only rule is that it cannot contain spaces. It is therefore up to the developer to give their tags a meaningful name. The exception to this is the `sel` tag, which is reserved for selecting text, so should not be overwritten.

Once you have assigned tags to the necessary parts of the content, nothing new will happen by default—the tags themselves must be configured first (with the exception of `sel` once again).

Configuring a tag allows us to change certain styling properties of any areas which have that tag applied. Some of the options available are:

- `background`: The background (highlight) color of that area
- `foreground`: The foreground (text) color of that area
- `font`: The font and font size applied to that area
- `justify`: Whether the text is aligned to the left, right, or center
- `offset`: Vertically raise or lower the tagged text based on the argument provided (positive integer to raise, negative to lower)
- `underline`: Add a line underneath the tagged area

These configuration options are passed as keyword arguments to the `tag_configure` method of a `Text` widget.

Let's once again adjust our demo application to practice the use of tags.

Open up the demo file and add the following functions underneath the others:

```
def tag_alternating(event=None):
    for i in range(0, 27, 2):
        index = '1.' + str(i)
        end = index + '+1c'
        text.tag_add('even', index, end)

    text.tag_configure('even', foreground='orange')

    return "break"
```

Our first function will tag each alternating character with a tag named even.

We use the `range` function to generate all of the even numbers between 0 and 27, passing a 2 to the `step` argument so that we count up by two each time. We then add this number to a 1 and a full stop in order to create the full index.

To ensure we only tag one character, our ending index is created by adding the special string +1c to the end of the beginning index.

Now that we have the starting and ending index, we assign the tag to that area with the `tag_add` method, passing all three of the required arguments to it.

Once we have tagged all relevant areas, we need to make the tag we have defined actually do something. We achieve this by using the `tag_configure` method to set the `foreground` argument to orange for everything that has been tagged with our even tag. This means that each even character on the first line (for the first 26 characters) will become orange after this function has been run.

We end up returning the break string to prevent any default behavior from our chosen keyboard shortcut.

This example uses hard-coded indexes, which works for a small example such as this, but is not desirable for a proper application. There is a method called `tag_ranges` which will get the start and end indexes of all regions with a specific tag. Since the selection is defined with a tag, we can use this method to get the selected area.

Let's add two more methods which utilize this method to have a look at a couple more of the possible styling changes that can be applied by tags:

```
def raise_selected(event=None):
    text.tag_configure('raise', offset=5)
    selection = text.tag_ranges("sel")
    text.tag_add('raise', selection[0], selection[1])

    return "break"


def underline_selected(event=None):
    text.tag_configure('underline', underline=1)
    selection = text.tag_ranges("sel")
    text.tag_add('underline', selection[0], selection[1])

    return "break"
```

These functions begin again by configuring a tag name to have a particular styling change.

The `raise_selected` function assigns a positive integer to the `offset` option, which will raise the tagged area higher than the rest of the text on that line. Our `underline_selected` method sets the `underline` option to 1, which will underline the tagged text.

We use the `tag_ranges` method to get the start and end index of text which has the `sel` tag, meaning the selected text. A tag is then added to text between these ranges in order to change their properties, and the usual `break` string is returned.

To play with these functions, all we need to do is bind them to a keyboard shortcut:

```
text.bind('<Control-t>', tag_alternating)
text.bind('<Control-r>', raise_selected)
text.bind('<Control-u>', underline_selected)
```

Run this version of the demo application, add some dummy text, and press *Ctrl + t*. You should see each letter at an even index has now become orange.

Now select a small part of the text and press *Ctrl* and *r*. You should see the text rise above the rest of the text on that same line. Then give *Ctrl + u* a try; even on the same text range, it will add the underlining on top of all previous style changes. This is because the same range of text can have multiple tags affecting its styling:

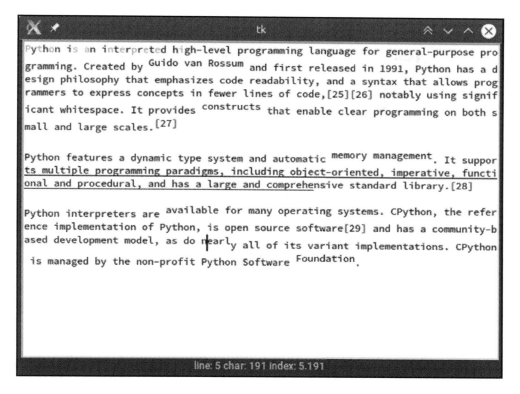

When multiple tags conflict, the tag that was configured last will have priority, regardless of what order they were added to the range in.

Now that we know how to apply a tag to an index range which will change its color, all we need to learn is how to discover the index ranges so that we can begin coloring certain words in our text editor. There's a very convenient method of Text widgets which will allow us to do just that.

Searching text

When we need to find a specific piece of text within a Text widget, there is a method called search which will allow us to do this easily.

The `search` method can take quite a lot of arguments:

- `pattern`: The pattern to match. This can be either an exact match or a regular expression.
- `index`: Where to begin the search from.
- `stopindex`: Where to stop ending a search. If this is not specified, the search will loop.
- `forwards`: Whether to search from the top to the bottom (this is the default).
- `backwards`: Whether to search from bottom to top.
- `exact`: Exact match instead of a regular expression (this is the default).
- `regexp`: Indicates that the pattern supplied is a regular expression.
- `nocase`: Whether to ignore case.
- `count`: A variable which will be updated with the length of the match.

The only mandatory arguments are the search pattern and the starting index.

The `Search` method will return the index of the beginning of the match and, if supplied, a variable for the `count` argument; the length of the match will be stored inside it.

For example, if your `Text` widget had one line containing `I like Python Programming` and you passed the string `Python` to the `pattern` argument, the return value of the function would be `1.8`, since the word Python begins at the eighth character of the line. Our `count` variable, if supplied, would contain the number `6`.

We can use these two pieces of information to construct the starting and ending index which we will need to tag this match. The easiest way to do this is using the special string of `+nc` along with the `count` variable—append this to the index which is returned by the method.

In our example, the tagging indexes would be `1.8` for the start and `1.8+6c` for the end.

Since this method returns after the first match is found, we will often need to run this in some sort of loop in order to find all pattern matches.

Let's get our heads around this by adding some code to our demo application which will detect and tag the word `python` throughout the `Text` widget.

Add this function alongside the others:

```
def tag_python(event=None):
    text.tag_configure('python', foreground="green")
    start = 1.0
    idx = text.search('python', start, stopindex=tk.END)
    while idx:
        tag_begin = idx
        tag_end = f"{idx}+6c"
        text.tag_add('python', tag_begin, tag_end)

        start = tag_end
        idx = text.search('python', start, stopindex=tk.END)

    return "break"
```

We will be using a tag called `python` to turn instances of the word `green`. We begin by configuring that tag and setting a starting variable to `1.0` (the beginning of the `Text` widget).

We then use the `search` method to find the word `python`. We use the `start` variable as the beginning index and the `END` constant to specify that we will finish at the end of the area.

The result of this method is stored in a variable called `idx`. This will contain the first occurrence of the word. Now, in order to find any further matches, we need to begin a loop. We use a `while` loop, which will exit once we no longer have a match index. This also ensures that the code inside will only run if we have at least one match.

Inside this loop, we create the tag range as mentioned before and add the Python tag to this range. We then update the `start` index to the calculated `end` index to ensure we begin searching from right after the match, and call the `search` method again.

This loop will continue to run until we reach the end of the text input area.

Bind this to a keyboard shortcut and run the application:

```
text.bind('<Control-p>', tag_python)
```

Write some text in the application which contains the word Python a few times. Pressing this keyboard combination will color all of them green.

This is the technique we will be using in order to implement syntax highlighting in our text editor. Instead of binding this to a keyboard combination, we will need our highlighting method to run as the user types, so we will be binding it to either `<KeyPress>` or `<KeyRelease>`.

Now that we have all of the tools and knowledge we need, we can finally begin with the syntax highlighting in our main text editor application.

Adding syntax highlighting to our text editor

Let's recap a bit and plan our next action before diving back into our text editor application.

We know that in order to add syntax highlighting, we will need to change the color of certain words which are considered keywords within the Python programming language. In order to change their colors, we must apply a tag to the range at which they appear within the `Text` widget.

Tkinter's indexing system is now familiar to us. We know that the general syntax is line number, full stop, and character number, and some special strings also exists which reduce the need to use mathematical calculations upon those numbers. This means we know exactly how to format the ranges to add our tags to.

In order to locate each range, the `search` method can be used to locate matches of provided words giving us the beginning index of a range, and we can use a special string +nc to make finding the end even easier.

In order to find every instance of a keyword match, we have a simple loop structure which we can transfer to our main application and use to find every occurrence of a given word.

In order for a tag to do anything, it must be configured to change the styling properties of all words sharing that tag. We have practiced this a couple of times and know that the `foreground` argument can be used to change text color.

To avoid putting too much logic in our `TextArea` class, this logic can all be encapsulated into a new class, which we will call `Highlighter`, to keep our `TextArea` as neat as possible.

The Highlighter class

Open up your text editor project from the last chapter and create a new file in its root folder called `highlighter.py`. We can now write our `Highlighter` class in here:

```
import tkinter as tk


class Highlighter:
    def __init__(self, text_widget):
        self.text_widget = text_widget
        self.numbers_color = "blue"
        self.keywords_color = "orange"
        self.keywords = ["True", "False", "def", "for", "while", "import",
                         "if", "elif", "else"]
        self.disallowed_previous_chars = ["_", "-", "."]

        self.tag_configure("keyword", foreground=self.keywords_color)
        self.tag_configure("number", foreground=self.numbers_color)

        self.text_widget.bind('<KeyRelease>', self.on_key_release)
```

Our `Highlighter` class will need to keep a reference to the `Text` widget which it is highlighting, so we require this as a parameter within our `__init__` method.

To start with, we will use a couple of attributes to hold the color of our numbers and keywords (we will make a more elegant solution shortly). Numbers will be blue and keywords will be orange. We also need a way of determining what a keyword is, so we hold a list of them too.

Both of the tags we will be using are configured to change the text color of any ranges which have the tags applied, and we bind a method to the `<KeyRelease>` event:

```
def on_key_release(self, event=None):
    self.highlight()
```

The `on_key_release` method will just call a `highlight` method, which is responsible for changing the color of our numbers and keywords:

```
def highlight(self, event=None):
    length = tk.IntVar()
    for keyword in self.keywords:
        start = 1.0
        keyword = keyword + "[^A-Za-z_-]"
        idx = self.text_widget.search(keyword, start, stopindex=tk.END,
                                      count=length, regexp=1)
```

We begin the `highlight` method with an `IntVar` which will hold the length of any match. We now need to iterate through all of our keywords and search for them inside the `Text` widget.

Since we want to start at the beginning of the text, we set the start variable to `1.0`.

As we want only whole-word matches, we are going to need to use the power of regex. The string `[^A-Za-z_-]` is added onto the end of each keyword. This small piece of regex is saying that we only want to match the word if it does not have any alphabet characters, an underscore, or a dash after it. For example, if we are searching to highlight the word `for`, we do not want to highlight the first three letters of `fortress`. This regex will prevent a match on the word `fortress` as it has an alphabet character (a `"t"`) after the word `for`.

 Our syntax highlighting will rely on regular expressions a lot. All programming languages have slight differences in capabilities when it comes to interpreting them. Tcl, the language behind Tkinter, differs from Python itself. To learn about Tcl's implementation of regular expressions, visit the Tcl documentation at `http://wiki.tcl.tk`.

We now search for the modified keyword with the `Text` widget's `search` method, passing in the argument `regexp=1` to tell it that our pattern text should be interpreted as a regular expression:

```
while idx:
    char_match_found = int(str(idx).split('.')[1])
    line_match_found = int(str(idx).split('.')[0])
    if char_match_found > 0:
        previous_char_index = str(line_match_found) + '.' +
                            str(char_match_found - 1)
        previous_char = self.text_widget.get(previous_char_index,
                            previous_char_index + "+1c")
```

As we have seen before, a `while` loop is utilized to ensure we will find every match within the `Text` widget.

To continue safeguarding against non-whole-word matches, we will need to check the character before the beginning of our match index. We cannot use the same regex expression as before since this would prevent matches which occur at the very beginning of a line (as is common with `import` statements).

In order to do this, we first split the index of the match on the full stop, separating the line number from the character number. We then check whether the character number is greater than 0, since this implies that the match was not the first word on this line. If it is indeed greater, then we will need to check if the preceding character is one of our disallowed ones:

```
if previous_char.isalnum() or previous_char in
self.disallowed_previous_chars:
    end = f"{idx}+{length.get() - 1}c"
    start = end
    idx = self.text_widget.search(keyword, start, stopindex=tk.END,
                        regexp=1)
```

If the character before our match is a letter, number, underscore, hyphen, or full stop, then we do not want to highlight the match. We do, however, need to continue the search from the end of our detected word.

To find the ending index of our match, we will use the +nc string. We add on the length of the match, which is stored in our length variable, but take one away to account for the character which will have been captured by our [^A-Za-z_-] regex.

We then set the start of our search to this ending index and fire off the search method once again to continue the loop:

```
else:
    end = f"{idx}+{length.get() - 1}c"
    self.text_widget.tag_add(category, idx, end)

    start = end
    idx = self.text_widget.search(keyword, start, stopindex=tk.END,
                        regexp=1)
```

If the previous character was not a disallowed one, then we can add the tag. We get the ending index in the same way as in the preceding code and use the tag_add method to add the necessary tag to the discovered range.

We then set the start to the calculated end and resume the search:

```
else:
    end = f"{idx}+{length.get() - 1}c"
    self.text_widget.tag_add(category, idx, end)

    start = end
    idx = self.text_widget.search(keyword, start, stopindex=tk.END,
                        regexp=1)
```

If the match was found at character 0, then we do not need to check the previous character since there isn't one. We can go ahead and add the tag and continue the search in the same way.

Once all of our keywords are tagged, we need to do the same with numbers. As we cannot store a list of all numbers we will need to use another regular expression. We can then run this through much the same loop as before:

```
start = 1.0
idx = self.text_widget.search(r"(\d)+[.]?(\d)*", start, stopindex=tk.END,
regexp=1, count=length)
while idx:
    end = f"{idx}+{length.get()}c"
    self.text_widget.tag_add("number", idx, end)

    start = end
    idx = self.text_widget.search(r"(\d)+[.]?(\d)*", start,
                        stopindex=tk.END, regexp=1, count=length)
```

The regular expression used here can be broken down as follows:

- `(\d)+`: Match one or more numbers
- `[.]?`: Match zero or one decimal point
- `(\d)*`: Match zero or more numbers following the decimal point

This regex will allow us to tag and color both integers and floating point numbers.

We have now tagged all of the keywords in our `keywords` attribute, as well as all numbers. Another thing which most editors will highlight is strings. These can be detected by searching for characters between either two speech mark characters (") or two apostrophe characters ('). Again, we would need to use a regular expression to match these.

To avoid repeatedly copying the number-highlighting code and making our highlight method huge, let's split it off into a new method. We can call this method `highlight_regex` and write it to perform our usual tagging loop on any regular expression.

Cut the last block of code from the `highlight` function and replace it with this:

```
self.highlight_regex(r"(\d)+[.]?(\d)*", "number")
```

Now, let's create a function called `highlight_regex` and paste the number-highlighting code inside it. Replace the number-detecting regex with an argument called `regex`, and the `number` tag with an argument called `tag`, so that it looks like this:

```
def highlight_regex(self, regex, tag):
    length = tk.IntVar()
    start = 1.0
    idx = self.text_widget.search(regex, start, stopindex=tk.END, regexp=1,
                                  count=length)
    while idx:
        end = f"{idx}+{length.get()}c"
        self.text_widget.tag_add(tag, idx, end)

        start = end
        idx = self.text_widget.search(regex, start, stopindex=tk.END,
                                      regexp=1, count=length)
```

Now that we have this function, we can add two more lines to the end of our `highlight` method:

```
self.highlight_regex(r"[\'][^\']*[\']", "string")
self.highlight_regex(r"[\"][^\']*[\"]", "string")
```

These regexes can be broken down as follows:

- `[\"]`: Match the string opening character (")
- `[^\"]*`: Match any number of characters which are not the string-closing character
- `[\"]`: Match the string-closing character

This will now add the `string` tag to any matches found in the `Text` widget.

Since we do not have a configured `string` tag, this will currently not do anything.

Hard-coding colors and keywords can get very tedious and clog up the code dramatically. As well as this, all of our keywords will be the same color, which is less than ideal. Instead of continuing our keyword configuring in this way, let's pass the configuration on to something which is better suited for it and utilize that.

The particular technology I have decided to use for this project is YAML. YAML is a configuration file syntax which has a Python library available to parse it.

Create a folder inside your root named `languages` and place a file called `python.yaml` inside. The following will go into that file:

```
categories:
  keywords:
    color: orange
    matches: [for, def, while, from, import, as, with, self]

  variables:
    color: red4
    matches: ['True', 'False', None]

  conditionals:
    color: green
    matches: [try, except, if, else, elif]

  functions:
    color: blue4
    matches: [int, str, dict, list, set, float]

numbers:
  color: purple

strings:
  color: '#e1218b'
```

The syntax of YAML should be straightforward. Keys are marked by an ending colon, subkeys are indicated by indentation, and values follow keys on the same line.

A comment in YAML is indicated by a hash (#) character, just like in Python. If we want to use this character when defining a color, we need to enclose it in quotation marks to indicate that it is a string instead.

 YAML's syntax is somewhat similar to Python's, so it should be fairly easy to pick up.

In order to read YAML files, we will need an external package. We can once again use a virtual environment to manage these. Enter the following three commands in your terminal, ensuring that you are in the root folder at which you are writing your text editor:

```
python3 -m venv env
source env/bin/activate
pip install pyyaml
```

This will install the `yaml` package into your Python environment, which you can now import at the top of the `highlighter.py` file, like so:

```
import yaml
```

We are now ready to write ourselves a method which will read and parse a given `.yaml` or `.yml` file and convert it into a Python dictionary:

```
def parse_syntax_file(self):
    with open(self.syntax_file, 'r') as stream:
        try:
            config = yaml.load(stream)
        except yaml.YAMLError as error:
            print(error)
            return
```

If you have ever worked with opening files in Python before, this should seem very familiar to you.

We use the `with` keyword in order to open the file which we will have set in our `syntax_file` attribute. We open it in read mode because we don't need to make any changes to it.

Within a `try: except` block, we attempt to load the content of the file into our `yaml` module using its `load` method. The module will return a `YAMLError` exception if the file's syntax is incorrect, so we catch that with our `except` statement, `print` the error to the console, and `return`, preventing any highlighting from taking place.

Assuming our YAML file loads without any problems, we can begin reading from the `config` variable as if it were just a Python dictionary.

If you want to see what the `config` variable looks like, add a `print(config)` call after the `with` statement:

```
        self.categories = config['categories']
        self.numbers_color = config['numbers']['color']
        self.strings_color = config['strings']['color']

        self.configure_tags()
```

Within our categories, we have stored different types of keywords, which we can assign different colors. We extract each category from our `config` dictionary and keep a record of it in our `categories` attribute. These contain the keyword patterns and colors, so there is no need to keep a separate reference to those anymore.

Our number and string colors are also found in the dictionary and stored in attributes, since this is the only information we need about these.

Now that we have extracted the information we need, it's time to configure our tags so they they have the ability to change the color of any matches.

In order to configure our tags properly, we must get the category name and color out of our `categories` attribute and pass them to the `tag_configure` method of our `Text` widget.

Our `categories` attribute is a dictionary of `dictionaries`; one entry will look as follows:

```
{
  'keywords': {
    'color': 'orange',
    'matches': ['for', 'def', 'while', 'from', 'import', 'as',
                'with', 'self']
  }
}
```

To get the relevant information out of this data structure, we will need to iterate over the keys of our `categories` dictionary and use each key to access its inner `color` data. We then have the key as our tag name, and the color as its foreground color:

```
def configure_tags(self):
    for category in self.categories.keys():
        color = self.categories[category]['color']
        self.text_widget.tag_configure(category, foreground=color)

    self.text_widget.tag_configure("number", foreground=self.numbers_color)
    self.text_widget.tag_configure("string", foreground=self.strings_color)
```

Using the `keys` method of our dictionary, we are able to iterate over each category and pass it back into the `self.categories` dictionary, along with the string `color`, to access each category's assigned color.

These two pieces of information are then passed to the `tag_configure` method to set up a matching tag.

We finish up the method by configuring tags for our numbers, and strings too. These are passed to the `numbers_color` and `strings_color`, which we extracted earlier.

In order to make this code run, we need to kick-off the chain of methods in our __init__ method. We will also need to receive a path to the YAML file to parse, which we will take as an argument.

Our __init__ method should now look like this:

```
def __init__(self, text_widget, syntax_file):
    self.text_widget = text_widget
    self.syntax_file = syntax_file
    self.categories = None
    self.numbers_color = "blue"
    self.strings_color = "red"
    self.disallowed_previous_chars = ["_", "-", "."]

    self.parse_syntax_file()

    self.text_widget.bind('<KeyRelease>', self.on_key_release
```

Now that our __init__ file has been taken care of, we still need to adjust our highlight method to allow it to create multiple tags, as it currently still only uses the keyword tag.

Luckily, only the beginning loop of this method will need altering:

```
def highlight(self, event=None):
    length = tk.IntVar()
    for category in self.categories:
        matches = self.categories[category]['matches']
        for keyword in matches:
            start = 1.0
            ...
```

Everything after the ellipses (. . .) here can be left the same as before; it is mainly the outer loop which needs to change. We now iterate over each category in our categories attribute and grab its matches by passing it back in, along with the matches string.

All calls to tag_add should be using our category variable instead of the hard-coded keyword tag. Replace all calls to tag_add with this:

```
self.text_widget.tag_add(category, idx, end)
```

We finish up this class running this code as an independent module:

```
if __name__ == '__main__':
    w = tk.Tk()
    h = Highlighter(tk.Text(w), 'languages/python.yaml')
    w.mainloop()
```

We can now launch this file with `python3 highlighter.py` and test it out. Try typing the words in your YAML file and watching them all change to their assigned color. Also try out numbers and strings. Perhaps copy the content of this file back into the window to see real Python code get highlighted:

```
def update_index(event=None):
    cursor_position = text.index(tk.INSERT)
    cursor_position_pieces = str(cursor_position).split('.')

    cursor_line = cursor_position_pieces[0]
    cursor_char = cursor_position_pieces[1]

    current_index.set('line: ' + cursor_line + ' char: ' + cursor_char + '
index: ' + str(cursor_position))

def highlight_line(event=None):
    start = str(text.index(tk.INSERT)) + " linestart"
    end = str(text.index(tk.INSERT)) + " lineend"
    text.tag_add("sel", start, end)

    return "break"

def highlight_word(event=None):
    word_pos = str(text.index(tk.INSERT))
    start = word_pos + " wordstart"
    end = word_pos + " wordend"
    text.tag_add("sel", start, end)
```

Once we are satisfied that everything is working as intended, it's time to integrate this class back into our main `TextEditor` application.

Using our Highlighter class

Before we can make use of our new `Highlighter` class, we need to import it:

```
from highlighter import Highlighter
```

We now simply need an instance of it, which we will pass to our `TextArea` instance and the path to a YAML file. Since we only have one YAML file currently, we will just hard-code the path to it. In the next chapter, we will add the ability to load different YAML files:

```
self.highlighter = Highlighter(self.text_area, 'languages/python.yaml')
```

That's all we need to do to get syntax highlighting into our `TextArea`, since the `Highlighter` class will bind to events in our `TextArea` and cause it to update itself.

With syntax highlighting complete, the next item on our agenda is to fix the line numbers. We will again split this into a new class to keep things organized.

Create a file in the same directory called `linenumbers.py`, ready for this class.

The LineNumbers class

Our `LineNumbers` class will remain as a disabled `Text` widget but will no longer just hold 100 numbers all of the time. Instead, it will respond to the size of the `TextArea` (or any `Text` widget) it is linked to and update its own content accordingly:

```python
import tkinter as tk


class LineNumbers(tk.Text):
    def __init__(self, master, text_widget, **kwargs):
        super().__init__(master, **kwargs)

        self.text_widget = text_widget
        self.text_widget.bind('<KeyPress>', self.on_key_press)

        self.insert(1.0, '1')
        self.configure(state='disabled')
```

Since the `LineNumbers` widget is just a `Text` widget, it will need a reference to a master object as well as the `Text` widget it will be paired to. We then capture any keyword arguments and pass them to the superclass's __init__ method.

The `Text` widget it is paired to is assigned to an attribute and a method is bound to its `<KeyPress>` event. Note that we cannot bind to its `<KeyRelease>` event since that is already being handled by our `Highlighter` class.

After binding, the widget's content is set to just the number 1 and it is disabled as before.

The only method needed on this class is the one bound to our `Text` widget's class `<KeyPress>`:

```python
def on_key_press(self, event=None):
    final_index = str(self.text_widget.index(tk.END))
    num_of_lines = final_index.split('.')[0]
    line_numbers_string = "\n".join(str(no + 1) for no in
                          range(int(num_of_lines)))
    width = len(str(num_of_lines))

    self.configure(state='normal', width=width)
    self.delete(1.0, tk.END)
    self.insert(1.0, line_numbers_string)
    self.configure(state='disabled')
```

Whenever a character is added to our `Text` widget, we will need to find the final index inside it again. This will tell us the total amount of lines, since the first character of the index is the line number.

We gather this information by calling the `index` method of the `END` constant and casting the resulting index to a string. This string is then split on the full stop character and we take off the first number—our final line number.

This line number is passed to the `range` function, allowing us to get every previous number, which we `join` into a string on a newline character just like before.

We can use this line number to calculate the necessary width of our `LineNumbers` widget. Calling the `len` function on it gives us this number.

Now that we have all of the necessary information, we can begin configuring.

The state is changed back to `normal` to allow text updates, and the `width` is set to our calculated width. All current content is cleared and the new line numbers string is added in. Finally, the widget is disabled again so that the user cannot type into it.

Once again, we can make this module usable on its own if we want to try it out:

```python
if __name__ == '__main__':
    w = tk.Tk()
    t = tk.Text(w)
    l = LineNumbers(w, t, width=1)
    l.pack(side=tk.LEFT)
    t.pack(side=tk.LEFT, expand=1)
    w.mainloop()
```

Run this file as before and have a go at typing into it. You should see the line numbers change to always be in accordance with the amount of text in the accompanying Text widget.

With this class finished, we can begin using it within our TextEditor in a similar way to the Highlighter.

Using our LineNumbers class

Once again, we simply need to import the LineNumbers class at the top of our texteditor.py file:

```
from linenumbers import LineNumbers
```

With that taken care of, we just need to instantiate the class in our __init__ method. Since the code is already set up to apply our custom scrolling to an attribute named lne_numbers, let's delete all references to that attribute in __init__, except for the call to pack at the end, and replace them with this one line:

```
self.line_numbers = LineNumbers(self, self.text_area, bg="grey",
fg="white", width=1)
```

This ensures that our custom scrolling and event bindings will still apply to this newly created class.

Give the editor another whirl and check out the new dynamic line numbers.

There remains one more thing to take care of in this chapter, while the idea of indexing and tagging is fresh in our memories—the find/replace window.

At the end of the last chapter, we left this just as a pop-up box with no real functionality. It's time to bring it to life!

Integrating our FindWindow class

In order to integrate our FindWindow class with our TextArea, we will need to add some functionality to one of them. We can choose to keep the logic inside either class. For this example, I will put all of the searching logic into the TextArea instead of the FindWindow, but it could easily be kept in either one.

Bring back up your `textarea.py` file ready for editing. We are going to begin with one more `import` statement at the top:

```
import tkinter.messagebox as msg
```

We will be using the `messagebox` module to convey information to the user regarding the results of their searches. We have met this module already in Chapter 1, *Meet Tkinter*.

When the user enters text to be searched for in the find area, we will highlight it as yellow within our `TextArea` widget and scroll the view down to it. In order to do that, we will again take advantage of the tagging abilities of our `Text` widget.

As we know, a tag does nothing until we configure it. Within our __init__ method, we shall configure a tag and keep a reference to some variables as class attributes:

```
self.tag_configure('find_match', background="yellow")
self.find_match_index = None
self.find_search_starting_index = 1.0
```

We create a tag called `find_match` and tell our widget to color the background of any range tagged by this in yellow.

The `find_match_index` attribute will hold a reference to the last beginning index discovered by our `search` method, and the `find_search_starting_index` will hold an index at which we want to begin each subsequent search.

If you look back into your `FindWindow` class, you will see that it calls a method called `find` on its master. Let's implement this method in our `TextArea` class now:

```
def find(self, text_to_find):
    length = tk.IntVar()
    idx = self.search(text_to_find, self.find_search_starting_index,
                      stopindex=tk.END, count=length)

    if idx:
        self.tag_remove('find_match', 1.0, tk.END)

        end = f'{idx}+{length.get()}c'
        self.tag_add('find_match', idx, end)
        self.see(idx)

        self.find_search_starting_index = end
        self.find_match_index = idx
```

The method will take one argument—a string of text to search for.

Much like before, we create an `IntVar` to hold the length of a match and find the first occurrence with the `search` method.

Instead of the normal `while` loop, we instead use an `if` statement to handle the tagging. All matches we find are given our `find_match` tag and the range at which to match is calculated using the +nc capabilities we saw in our `Highlighter`.

Once the tag is added, we can use a method called `see` on our `TextArea` in order to scroll the match into view. This method takes an index as its argument and will scroll the `Text` widget until that index is viewable to the user. We pass the index of the beginning of our match to this method so that our user will instantly see their matches.

Now that the tagging and scrolling has been completed, we need to update our attributes which keep track of where we need to begin and end searching. This is because we don't want to find all matches in one go—we must wait for the user to press the `find` button once again before we do the next search attempt.

Once the search reaches the end of the widget and finds no more matches, we will inform the user using a message box:

```
    else:
        if self.find_match_index != 1.0:
            if msg.askyesno("No more results", "No further matches.
                           Repeat from the beginning?"):
                self.find_search_starting_index = 1.0
                self.find_match_index = None
                return self.find(text_to_find)
        else:
            msg.showinfo("No Matches", "No matching text found")
```

The message box will display different information depending on whether or not any matches were found. In order to detect this, we will call upon our `find_match_index` variable, since this kept a reference to the beginning index of a match. If this is still the initial value of 1.0, then we know that we did not find any matches.

If this attribute is a value other than 1.0, then a match occurred somewhere within the `Text` widget. We will ask the user if they wish to repeat the search from the beginning. This question is asked via an `askyesno` box.

Should the user wish to repeat the search, we need to reset the attributes, keeping track of search indexes to their default values and call the `find` method once again. Otherwise, we do not need to perform any action.

If no matches were found during the search, we will simply display this information to the user with a `showinfo` box.

That completes all of the logic necessary for the `find` button. Now, onto the `replace` button. Once again, checking our `findwindow.py` file, we can see that this calls a method called `replace_text` and passes it the contents of both `Entry` widgets. Let's create this functionality in our `TextArea` class:

```
def replace_text(self, target, replacement):
    if self.find_match_index:
        end = f"{self.find_match_index}+{len(target)}c"
        self.replace(self.find_match_index, end, replacement)
```

When replacing text, we must make sure that we have first found a match. If we have, then the value of our `find_match_index` will be set. We check for this before performing any logic.

Supposing we have a match, we need to get the range of its indexes, much like if we were adding a tag to it. Instead of adding a tag, however, we will be replacing its content with the replacement string.

We calculate the indexes of our needed range using the same method as always. Instead of having an `IntVar` with the length of the match, we instead need to call the `len` function on it. We add the length of the string to the `find_match_index` to calculate the end of the needed range.

The `replace` method of a `Text` widget will erase the content between the range of the first two arguments and insert the replacement text, given as the third argument, in its place. We can use this to easily replace a match with the provided replacement text.

Once a replacement has taken place, we need to adjust where the next call to the find method will begin its search, since the content of the `Text` widget has changed. A suitable place to resume searching from is the beginning of the line at which the replacement was made:

```
self.find_search_starting_index = f"{self.find_match_index} linestart"
self.find_match_index = None
```

To get this index, we just have to add the word `linestart` to the end of the index of our replacement. This value is then set as our `find_search_starting_index` attribute, to be used by our `find` method.

To prevent another attempt at replacement, we set our `find_match_index` back to `None` to avoid any more calls to `replace_text` from happening until another match is found.

The final thing to implement for our `FindWindow` is a method which will remove the `find_match` tags when the user closes the find/replace window. We will call this `cancel_find`:

```
def cancel_find(self):
    self.find_search_starting_index = 1.0
    self.find_match_index = None
    self.tag_remove('find_match', 1.0, tk.END)
```

All that needs to be done is resetting the attributes back to their default values and using the `tag_remove` method to remove all tags called `find_match` throughout the whole of the widget.

We will now need to update our `FindWindow` class to make it call this method. Open up `findwindow.py` and make the following changes:

```
self.cancel_button = ttk.Button(bottom_frame, text="Cancel",
command=self.on_cancel)

def on_cancel(self):
    self.master.cancel_find()
    self.destroy()
```

In the `__init__` method, we need to change the `command` attribute of the `cancel_button` from `self.destroy` to `self.on_cancel`.

The `on_cancel` method will call `cancel_find` on the `Text` widget before calling `self.destroy` as before.

Like with the others, we now need to add this class into our `TextEditor` in order to make it usable.

Using our FindWindow class

As you may have guessed, the `FindWindow` class needs to be imported at the beginning of the file:

```
from findwindow import FindWindow
```

Now, we need to create an instance whenever the user presses a key combination. Typically, a **Find and Replace** window appears on *Ctrl* and *F* or *Ctrl* and *R*. I will use *Ctrl* and *F* for this application:

```
def bind_events(self):
    ...
    self.bind('<Control-f>', self.show_find_window)

def show_find_window(self, event=None):
    FindWindow(self.text_area)
```

A method called `show_find_window` is created, which will be responsible for showing our `FindWindow` popup.

Inside this method, all we need to do is instantiate the `FindWindow` class, passing it our `TextArea` to act as its `master`. The `Toplevel` class which it inherits from will handle displaying the window itself.

That's everything for this chapter! Run this version of your text editor application and give the find/replace window a try. See how it highlights all matches in yellow and replaces words with others, even when they are of different lengths:

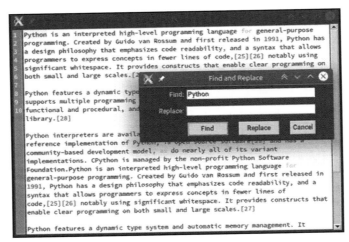

To try out automatic scrolling, enter (or paste) a large amount of text and search for a word which is not on display. You should see the widget automatically scroll down so that the highlighted match in yellow appears. Pretty cool, right?

Now that we have learned all about navigating Tkinter's powerful `Text` widget, we can move on to some more advanced parts of the application. These include menus and customization options.

Summary

In this chapter, we have learned all about Tkinter's indexing system. We know how to structure an index, combining the line number and character number with a full stop character to create an index such as `3.15`.

We then covered how this system is applied to provide greater functionality, including tags and searches.

Tags are Tkinter's way of adjusting the styling options of a certain range of text, marked by beginning and end indexes. We have seen a lot of different styling options which we can change using tags, including the text color, which allows us to achieve syntax highlighting. We know how to configure and remove tags as we need them.

Searching a `Text` widget using a loop is well-practiced. We know how to use Tkinter's special strings to very quickly create the ending indexes from the established beginning and length of the match. We can use these to apply tags or replace text with something else.

Along our journey, we also picked up some knowledge of YAML files and their syntax. We can now utilize YAML files to enable the user to adjust the styling of their syntax highlighting without having to dig into the underlying Python code at all.

Our text editor is now knowledgeable of the Python language, but why stop there? In the next chapter, we will be adding menus to our application. Along with the menus will come new functionalities, including the ability to load syntax for any language we wish to write a YAML file for. We will also be able to adjust the colors of our application window itself.

Not Just for Restaurants – All About Menus 7

To finish off our text editor, we will be adding menus. This includes a menu bar at the top of the application—the kind where you will find options such as file and edit—and a context menu, which typically appears when the user right-clicks.

Of course, along with the menus will come some new functionality. This includes the ability to control the styling of the application, the color scheme of the `TextArea` widget, the ability to open and save files, and more!

In this chapter, we will cover:

- The `Menu` widget
- Adding a menu to an application
- Creating submenus inside a menu
- Getting file information using the `filedialog` module
- Using the `colorchooser` widget to get a color choice

Let's start with a look over Tkinter's `Menu` widget, since this is the main new widget we will be focusing on in this chapter.

The Menu widget

As its name implies, the `Menu` widget is a widget that can hold many selectable options. Each option can be assigned a label, such as paste, and a command, which (like many other widgets) allows us to call a Python function when the user clicks on it.

We will be adding two different types of menus to our text editor in this chapter: a menu bar along the top of the window and a right-click context menu. Both are implemented using the same widget, but the way in which the widgets are added to the application differs.

Let's take some time to look at each method we will be using to add menus into our text editor, beginning with the top menu bar.

A menu bar

The top menu bar of an application usually just contains other menus, such as file and edit. These are known as "cascades" in Tkinter, and are essentially a menu inside a menu. This may be confusing at first, so let's begin with a very simple example to demonstrate the difference between a menu and a cascade.

Create a new Python file called menu.py and add the following code:

```
import tkinter as tk

win = tk.Tk()
win.geometry('400x300')

lab = tk.Label(win, text="Demo application")

menu = tk.Menu(win)
```

After importing Tkinter and creating a main window and Label, we make our first Menu widget. As with a lot of widgets, the first argument needed is the master, or parent, in which the widget will be drawn. We draw this menu in our main window as expected.

The menu won't actually do anything until we add some commands to it:

```
menu.add_command(label='Change Label Text', command=lambda:
lab.configure(text='Menu Item Clicked'))
menu.add_command(label='Change Window Size', command=lambda:
win.geometry('600x600'))
```

We create two commands to sit in this menu using the add_command method. This method takes two keyword arguments (in this case) called label and command. The label argument is the text to display (which the user will click on). The command argument is a function to be called when the menu item is clicked on, much like with a Button widget.

For our demo application we have two menu commands. The first of which says `Change Label Text` and when clicked will update the existing `Label` widget to say `Menu Item Clicked`. The second command says `Change Window Size` and will call the `geometry` method of our main window to increase its size.

Now that we have a `Menu` widget with some commands we need to draw it inside its parent. We use the `configure` method to achieve this:

```
win.configure(menu=menu)
```

A `Tk` widget, among others, can take a `menu` keyword argument, which tells it to draw a menu bar along the top. We use this argument to place our `Menu` widget into our main window. This is instead of using a geometry manager, such as `pack`, to handle inserting the widget.

Speaking of which, let's add our `Label` and finish off the demo script:

```
lab.pack(padx=50, pady=50)

win.mainloop()
```

Run this file and you should see a small window, which now contains a menu bar at the top:

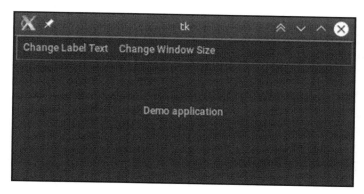

Give each option a click and see it execute the command assigned to it.

This is how commands within a menu work, in a nutshell. Now let's check out cascades and how they differ.

In the same `menu.py` file we are going to add a cascade to the beginning of our menu. A cascade can be thought of as a submenu, since it will also contain a `Menu` widget. Add this code between creating your `menu` variable and your calls to `add_command`:

```
cascade = tk.Menu(win)

cascade.add_command(label='Change Label color', command=lambda:
lab.configure(fg="blue4"))
cascade.add_command(label='Change Label Highlight', command=lambda:
lab.configure(bg="yellow"))

menu.add_cascade(label="Label colors", menu=cascade)
```

Another `Menu` widget is created, this time called `cascade`. We will be placing this menu inside our other `Menu` widget as a submenu.

As before, we add two commands to our `cascade` that will alter the styling of our `Label` using a `lambda`.

In order to place this menu into another the `add_cascade` method is used. Much like with `add_command`, this takes only keyword arguments. The `label` argument is the text that the user will see on the clickable area of the menu. The `menu` argument specifies which `Menu` widget we want to add as our cascade. We give this our `cascade` object so that this will become a submenu of our `menu` object.

Leave the rest of the code as it was and run this version of the file. You should see a new option as the left-most item in the window's menu bar. When you click this you will see the two commands we added to our `cascade` appear. Give each a try and see that it changes our `Label` just like the commands in the outer menu:

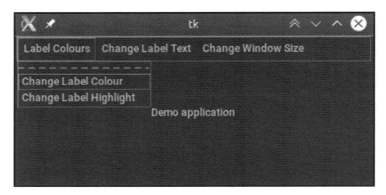

This is all there is to creating a menu bar along the top of an application. We simply need an instance of a Menu widget for each submenu, then one more to act as the top menu bar itself.

With the menu bar covered, let's have a look at adding a context menu that appears when the user right-clicks within the window.

A floating menu

In order to place a Menu at a specific location we can use the place method. The place method takes two arguments: x and y. As the names imply these are coordinates of the exact location at which to draw the menu.

Since we will be binding this menu's creation to the right-click of a mouse, we will have access to an event object inside the bound function. It may seem intuitive, therefore, to just pass the x and y attributes of the event object to the place method and assume this will put the menu where the mouse was clicked.

The problem with this, however, is that the event object's coordinates are relative to the widget that was bound, whereas the place system is relative to the user's screen. This means if the user is not running our application full-screen, the menu could be drawn somewhere completely outside the application!

In order to solve this problem we can use the winfo_x and winfo_y methods on the main window (our Tk widget). These will get the coordinates of our window relative to the user's screen, which we can then add to the x and y attributes of our event to get the location of the click.

To see all of this in action, open up your menu.py file and add in the following code between window.configure(menu=menu) and lab.pack(padx=50, pady=50):

```
context_menu = tk.Menu(win)
context_menu.add_command(label='close', command=win.destroy)

def on_right_click(event):
    x = win.winfo_x() + event.x
    y = win.winfo_y() + event.y

    context_menu.post(x, y)

win.bind('<Button-3>', on_right_click)
```

Once again we need a Menu widget to act as our right-click menu. We add a command called close, which calls the destroy method on our main window, exiting our application.

A function is defined that will be bound to the right-click event, which is <Button-3>.

This function does what was described previously in order to calculate the x and y positions at which we want to place our menu. We then call post with these coordinates to spawn our context menu.

Run this final version of our demo application and try right-clicking somewhere inside the window. You should see a menu come up with a close option. Click this to close the application again:

With knowledge of Tkinter's Menu widget fresh in our minds let's grab our text editor application and add in some menus.

Adding a menu bar to our text editor

Since the menu bar will sit directly in our Tk widget we can put all of the menu logic in our texteditor.py file. Open this file up and add the following into the __init__ method underneath the creation of our Highlighter:

```
self.menu = tk.Menu(self, bg="lightgrey", fg="black")
```

This line creates us a Menu widget, which we will store a reference to under a menu attribute. We configure the colors to specific values for now, but this will change later.

After the creation of our main `Menu` widget we could define several more here in the `__init__` method. However, this will quickly get very cluttered, not to mention it will require a lot of new code each time we want to add a new submenu into our menu bar.

Instead of this approach, we will write a method that automatically figures out what menu commands we want from just a list of strings representing the submenu labels:

```
sub_menu_items = ["file", "edit", "tools", "help"]
self.generate_sub_menus(sub_menu_items)
self.configure(menu=self.menu)
```

We decide in advance what menu options we want as cascades in our top menu bar. We then store a list of these in the variable `sub_menu_items`. These should look familiar to those of you who use graphical applications a lot.

This list is then passed to a method called `generate_sub_menus`, which will search our `TextEditor` class for methods that start with the given submenu name and add them in as commands to the relevant cascade.

Let's have a look at how this function will work:

```
def generate_sub_menus(self, sub_menu_items):
    window_methods = [method_name for method_name in dir(self)
                        if callable(getattr(self, method_name))]
    tkinter_methods = [method_name for method_name in dir(tk.Tk)
                        if callable(getattr(tk.Tk, method_name))]
```

We begin with two variables called `window_methods` and `tkinter_methods`. These are defined as list comprehensions, which may seem a little confusing. Allow me to break them down for clarity:

- `method_name for method_name in dir(self)`: The `dir` function, as we have seen when looking at imports, lists all available attributes. We use the `self` argument to get each attribute of our `TextEditor` instance instead of the whole application. This part will therefore return each attribute of our `TextEditor` instance and store it under `method_name`.
- `if callable(getattr(self, method_name))`: We want to filter only methods, not regular variable attributes, so we add an `if` statement to our list comprehension. Elements will only be returned if they are callable, which we check for using the `callable` function.

In order to get an attribute using a `string` variable, we need to pass the instance and the string to the `getattr` method. This attribute is then passed to the `callable` function to check that it is a method and not simply a variable.

We perform this list comprehension again, this time for the `Tk` widget itself. This gives us a list of everything available to a subclass of the `Tk` widget, since we want to ignore this when searching our `TextEditor` instance for methods to put in the menu:

```
my_methods = [method for method in set(window_methods) -
set(tkinter_methods)]
my_methods = sorted(my_methods)
```

To filter out only the methods that we have defined in this file we need to cast both lists to sets and then we can take the Tkinter methods away from our methods to get only the newly-defined ones. Again a list comprehension is used to cast this set back to a list.

To ensure that our commands will appear in the same order each time we call the `sorted` method on this newly returned list to ensure they are ordered alphabetically.

Now that we have all of the methods defined in this file we can begin building `Menus` and commands:

```
for item in sub_menu_items:
    sub_menu = tk.Menu(self.menu, tearoff=0, bg="lightgrey", fg="black")
    matching_methods = []
```

It is now time to iterate over our `sub_menu_items` list and create a new cascade for each one.

Each cascade has the main menu bar as its parent and the previously mentioned color scheme for its foreground and background (which again will change later).

The `tearoff` argument is used to indicate whether or not the user can grab the menu with their mouse and move it around the screen. We do not want this to happen, so we set it to 0 and prevent that behavior.

A list of all methods that begin with the word that defines our cascade now need to be found. We create a list called `matching_methods` to hold them. We now need to use a loop to search through our filtered `my_methods` and check to see if they belong in this particular cascade:

```
for method in my_methods:
    if method.startswith(item):
        matching_methods.append(method)
```

The `startswith` method of a string will allow us to check whether each of our methods begins with the relevant string of the cascade, for example, file.

If this method returns `True` then we append it to our list of `matching_methods`.

Once we have built up this list, we can convert each method to a command in our cascade. We can do this by adding another loop that runs after the `for method in my_methods` loop:

```
for match in matching_methods:
    actual_method = getattr(self, match)
    method_shortcut = actual_method.__doc__.strip()
    friendly_name = ' '.join(match.split('_')[1:])
        sub_menu.add_command(label=friendly_name.title(),
        command=actual_method, accelerator=method_shortcut)
```

The `getattr` function is once again used to get the actual attribute of our `TextEditor` instance to pass as the `command` argument when calling `add_command`.

Since most applications will display a keyboard shortcut for commands within their top menu, we are going to do the same in our text editor. Since there is no automatic way of achieving this we will set up a convention. The convention will be to put the keyboard shortcut as the `docstring` of each relevant method.

To parse this, we can use the __doc__ attribute of the found method to grab its `docstring`, calling `strip` to remove any excess whitespace.

The `label` for this command will be generated from the method name. This line does a few things in one go, so I will separate them to better explain each:

- The method name is `split` on an underscore to receive a list of each word
- We use a slice of `[1:]` to remove the first word from the list, since this word will be the cascade's label
- We re-join each piece on a space character

This process will convert a method name of `file_open_file` to `open file`, which is much nicer to read.

We pass these three variables to the `add_command` method on our cascade to complete the process. The `title` method is used on our `friendly_name` in order to capitalize each word for neatness.

The `accelerator` argument is responsible for displaying the keyboard shortcut next to a menu item.

 The accelerator only displays the keyboard shortcuts, it does not create them. They still need to be bound using the `bind` or `bind_all` methods that we have been using.

Now that our cascade has all of its commands added we just need to place it into the menu bar:

```
self.menu.add_cascade(label=item.title(), menu=sub_menu)
```

Again the `title` method is used for neatness.

That is all that we need to do in order to get our top menu into our application. Give this version of the code a run and check out our new menu:

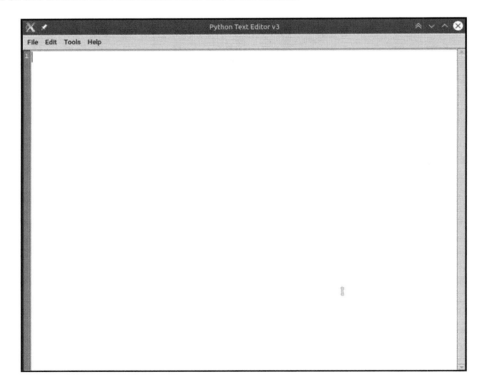

You will notice, however, that the menus are currently all blank. Don't worry, as we go through the chapter we will be adding methods which begin with one of our cascade words, and these will automatically appear in the relevant menu. By the end of this chapter each option will have some commands in it.

With one type of menu out of the way, let's move on to the context menu.

Adding a context menu to our text editor

Once again we will need to add some code to our __init__ method. Since there will only be one Menu needed for our context menu we can just define this directly instead of making another function. Type this code underneath the previous menu code:

```
self.right_click_menu = tk.Menu(self, bg="lightgrey", fg="black",
tearoff=0)
self.right_click_menu.add_command(label='Cut', command=self.edit_cut)
self.right_click_menu.add_command(label='Copy', command=self.edit_copy)
self.right_click_menu.add_command(label='Paste', command=self.edit_paste)
```

Another Menu widget is created using the same arguments as all of our cascades. We then add three commands to it—cut, copy, and paste. These will still do nothing at the moment, but first things first let's bind this menu to the right mouse button in our bind_events method:

```
def bind_events(self):
    ...
    self.text_area.bind("<Button-3>", self.show_right_click_menu)
```

Now let's define the methods that will allow our right-click context menu to function. We need three new methods named after the arguments to our add_command calls:

```
def edit_cut(self, event=None):
    """
    Ctrl+X
    """
    self.text_area.event_generate("<Control-x>")
    self.line_numbers.force_update()

def edit_paste(self, event=None):
    """
    Ctrl+V
    """
    self.text_area.event_generate("<Control-v>")
    self.line_numbers.force_update()
```

```
        self.highlighter.force_highlight()

    def edit_copy(self, event=None):
        """
        Ctrl+C
        """
        self.text_area.event_generate("<Control-c>")
```

Since these methods all start with the word *edit,* they will automatically be pulled into the edit cascade in our top menu. In order to fit in with our convention they require a docblock containing their keyboard shortcut.

Each method here has already been defined in our `TextArea` widget, so all we need to do is pass the `event` over to it with `event_generate`.

In the case of cut and paste, the line numbers and keywords are going to change, so we need to ensure both our `Highlighter` and `LineNumbers` class are told to update. We will need to add a method to each so that these methods do not error:

```
class Highlighter:
    ...
    def force_highlight(self):
        self.highlight()


class LineNumbers(tk.Text):
    ...
    def force_update(self):
        self.on_key_press()
```

No complex logic in either of these functions; they merely call the method, which is bound to a key event on our `TextArea` class.

With all of this added, go ahead and run your `texteditor.py` file. Check out the right-click menu, and make sure that the new methods have appeared in your **Edit** cascade, too:

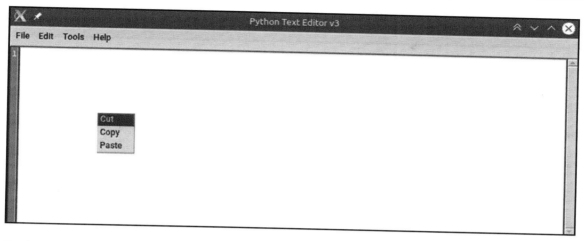

Both of our menus are now taken care of. If you want to add more functionality to your right-click menu at the end of this chapter, feel free to add more commands to it then. For now, we are going to move on to a new topic—handling files. This will allow us to add **New, Open**, and **Save** functionality to our file menu.

Handling files

We have already covered the usual handling of files in Python when parsing our yaml configurations. The basic syntax is as follows:

```
with open("path/to/file/", "r") as file:
    file.read()

with open("path/to/file", "w") as file:
    file.write("file contents")
```

This is very easy to do when we have a file path we are defining ourselves. The problem comes when we want the user to be able to open any file, and save a new file to any location on their computer. In this case we do not have the exact path, and it isn't very user-friendly to expect the user to be able to type in the full path either.

Luckily, Tkinter has a module that comes to our aid in this situation: `filedialog`. The `filedialog` module comes with a few different methods that allow us to easily get full paths to files, both for opening existing files and saving new ones, all with a user-friendly GUI.

We will be using two functions in this module for our text editor:

- `askopenfilename`: This asks the user for an existing file path on their computer. A window will open up displaying the contents of the current folder. The shown files can be filtered by using a keyword argument `filetypes`.
- `asksaveasfilename`: This displays a similar window to `askopenfilename` but does not enforce that the provided path already exists. If the user selects an existing file, an information box will appear telling the user that the path already exists, and asking them for confirmation to overwrite it.

Let's get straight into using this module in our text editor. Make sure you have the `texteditor.py` file open and add the import statement at the top:

```
from tkinter import filedialog
```

We will begin with the ability to open a file for editing. We want this functionality to appear under our file cascade, and the shortcut will be *Ctrl* and *O*:

```
def file_open(self, event=None):
    """
    Ctrl+O
    """
    file_to_open = filedialog.askopenfilename()
    if file_to_open:
        self.open_file = file_to_open

        self.text_area.display_file_contents(file_to_open)
        self.highlighter.force_highlight()
        self.line_numbers.force_update()
```

The method name will be `file_open`, since the `file_` prefix is needed to get this method to appear in our cascade.

When called by the `Menu` there will not be an event object passed, but if called by the keyboard shortcut there will be. To accommodate for this we accept an `event` argument but default it to `None`, since we do not actually need it.

The first thing we need to do is get the path to the file that the user wishes to open. We do this by calling the `askopenfilename` function from the `filedialog` module. This presents the user with a window showing their computer's files and allows them to click on the one they want.

This window also has a **Cancel** button, which will cause the function to return nothing. Because of this, we only want to perform the rest of the logic if the user actually chose a file, so the rest of this function will go inside an `if` statement, which checks if `askopenfilename` returned a non-empty string.

The path to the chosen file is stored as an attribute called `open_file`, before being passed over to a method of our `TextArea` widget called `display_file_contents`, which will handle writing the text contained in the file into itself.

As with some of our edit methods, since this method will change the contents of our `TextArea` we force the line numbers and syntax highlighting to update afterwards.

Let's hop on over to our `textarea.py` file and check out what needs to happen in `display_file_contents`:

```
def display_file_contents(self, filepath):
    with open(filepath, 'r') as file:
        self.delete(1.0, tk.END)
        self.insert(1.0, file.read())
```

To add the text from the supplied file path into our `TextArea`, we first need to open the file using the `open` method.

Inside this block we first delete the entire contents of the `TextArea` using the `delete` method. The range passed to this method is the beginning index (always `1.0`) and the `END` constant. This ensures that everything inside the widget will be deleted.

Now that the widget is empty we can write the contents of the opened file inside. We use the `insert` method to achieve this. The first argument is the beginning index, indicating that we want this content inserted at the beginning of our `TextArea`. The content to be written is the text within our `file`, which we extract using the `read` method.

You can now see the window created by the `askopenfilename` method by running `texteditor.py` and selecting the **Open** option from the **File** menu. Try opening the `texteditor.py` file itself inside the text editor application to see all of the syntax highlighting in action:

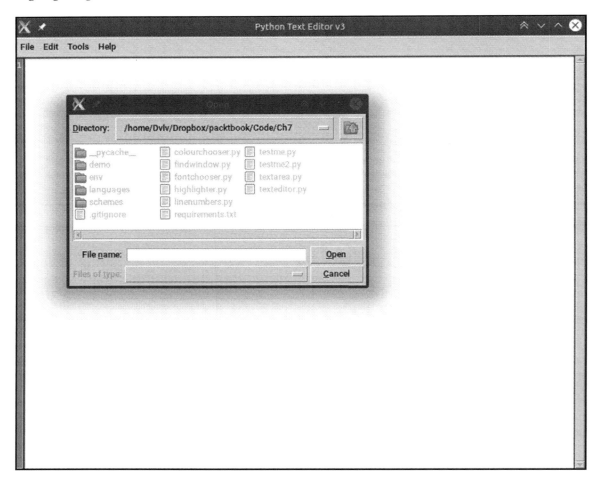

With opening a file sorted, the next thing to do is saving files. Once again we will define a method in our `texteditor.py` file to handle this:

```
def file_save(self, event=None):
    """
    Ctrl+S
    """
```

```
current_file = self.open_file if self.open_file else None
if not current_file:
    current_file = filedialog.asksaveasfilename()
if current_file:
    contents = self.text_area.get(1.0, tk.END)
    with open(current_file, 'w') as file:
        file.write(contents)
```

When saving a file, we need to know the location at which to write the new file contents. If we already have a file open, then our `open_file` attribute will be set and we can assume that the user is updating the same file. If not, we need to ask the user for the destination file path.

We get this information from the user with the `asksaveasfilename` method of the `filedialog` module. This will open a similar window to `askopenfilename` but with a **Save** button in place of the **Open** button.

Again, this window features a **Cancel** button, which will not return a file path, so we need to use an if statement to ensure the user did not cancel the operation.

If the user chose a destination, we need to open that path as a file handler and write the contents of our `TextArea` widget into it.

We get the contents of our `TextArea` using the `get` method, passing this the beginning index and `END` constant. This ensures that we have all of the content inside it.

The file handler is opened using the `open` function as before, but instead we pass `w` as the second argument to open the file in write mode. We then use the `write` method to insert the contents of our `TextArea` widget into this file.

That's all there is to saving a file. You can now run the `texteditor.py` file again and check out the **Save** option in your **File** menu. Try saving a new file, then try to save over it again afterwards. You should be presented with a confirmation message box. This is all built in to the `filedialog` module, we didn't need to do any of it ourselves!

Let's finish off the **File** menu with a **New** option, which will clear the currently open file from our `TextArea` and give the user a blank area to type into:

```
def file_new(self, event=None):
    """
    Ctrl+N
    """
    self.text_area.delete(1.0, tk.END)
    self.open_file = None
    self.line_numbers.force_update()
```

This method should be self-explanatory, since each line has been encountered recently. We simply delete the entirety of our `TextArea` widget, remove any reference to our `open_file` attribute (so that the save option does not overwrite it), and force the line numbers to update.

With that, all options from our **File** menu are now complete.

We can also quickly add a couple more methods to our **Edit** menu and finish that off too:

```
def edit_select_all(self, event=None):
    """
    Ctrl+A
    """
    self.text_area.event_generate("<Control-a>")

def edit_find_and_replace(self, event=None):
    """
    Ctrl+F
    """
    self.show_find_window()
```

Since we have defined select all functionality in our `TextArea` widget we may as well add this to our **Edit** menu. We just need to pass along the `event` like we have done with cut, copy, and paste.

Since find/replace windows usually exist in the **Edit** menu of other text editors, we can also add a menu option for this in our text editor. The method just needs to call the same method as is bound to *Control + F* already.

With this, two of our four cascade menus are now filled. The next one to focus on is the **Tools** menu, which will contain functions that allow the user to customize the editor to their liking, including loading different syntax highlighting files.

Changing the syntax highlighting

As you may remember from the previous chapter, syntax highlighting is defined in a `.yaml` file stored in a folder named `languages`. We want to allow the user to easily define their own syntax highlighting keywords and schemes by simply creating another `.yaml` file.

To experiment with this feature, create yourself a `.yaml` file in the `languages` folder. Ensure it contains numbers, strings, and any other category of keywords you like.

If you want to, you can copy this small example for SQL:

```
categories:
  keywords:
    color: orange
    matches: [select, where, and, from, order, by, group]

  dangerous:
    color: red4
    matches: [set, update, drop, replace]

numbers:
  color: purple

strings:
  color: red
```

Now that we have another syntax highlighting file to test with we can write a method to load it:

```
def load_syntax_highlighting_file(self):
    syntax_file = filedialog.askopenfilename(filetypes=[("YAML file",
                        ("*.yaml", "*.yml"))])
    if syntax_file:
        self.highlighter.clear_highlight()
        self.highlighter = Highlighter(self.text_area, syntax_file)
        self.highlighter.force_highlight()
```

Once again we need the path to the new `.yaml` file. We get this from the user with the `askopenfilename` function. This time we want to ensure that the user only chooses a `.yaml` file, so we let them know by using the `filetypes` keyword argument.

The `filetypes` argument needs a list of available file types. This list should contain a tuple for each type. This tuple should contain a string to tell the user what the file type should be, followed by a string (or tuple of strings if there are more than one), which indicates the file extension of any allowed files.

For our example, we want to enable any `.yaml` file, which could be indicated by a `.yml` or `.yaml` file extension. The strings to represent these are `"*.yml"` and `"*.yaml"`. We then signal the file types to the user with the string `"YAML file"`. We combine these two arguments into a tuple of `("YAML file", ("*.yaml", "*.yml"))`. Since the only file type we want to allow is `.yaml` files, our list will only contain this one item.

This function will now show the usual GUI window but will only allow the user to select files that end with `.yml` or `.yaml`.

If the user does not cancel the operation, we need to create a new instance of our `Highlighter` class, which uses the selected `.yaml` file.

We first clear the current highlighting from our `TextArea`, create a new instance of the `Highlighter` class with the chosen file path, then re-highlight the `TextArea`'s contents with the new scheme.

Now that we have this method available we can add it to our **Tools** menu by wrapping it in another function:

```
def tools_change_syntax_highlighting(self, event=None):
    """
    Ctrl+M
    """
    self.load_syntax_highlighting_file()
```

The last thing to address is the `clear_highlight` method in our `Highlighter` class:

```
def clear_highlight(self):
    for category in self.categories:
        self.text_widget.tag_remove(category, 1.0, tk.END)
```

In this method we just loop through each category for our keywords and remove the associated tags. We can leave the numbers and strings since they will be used by any other syntax file, and the tags will be reconfigured to use the new colors when our new `Highlighter` instance is created.

With that added, we can now switch syntax to a different language. Run your editor and type some code in the language that you created a `.yaml` file for. Now open the tools menu and select `Change Syntax Highlighting` and open your `.yaml` file. You should see the keywords of your language change color.

Now that this feature has been added our editor is no longer strictly a Python editor. If you prefer another language, you can change the `.yaml` file opened in the ___init___ method of your `texteditor.py` file to point to that language instead.

Now that the user has some control over what language they wish to work in, we should also give them some choices over how the editor looks. Let's add the ability for them to change the font of their editor, then afterwards we can allow them to set their own colors, too.

Changing the editor's font

As we saw from our blackjack game, fonts in Tkinter are usually handled by a `font` argument against a widget. The `Text` widget is no exception, this takes the same argument in the same format—a tuple of (family, size, styles).

To change the font in our text editor, we could decide ourselves what font the editor should be in and hard-code that into the declaration of our `TextArea` instance. However, we cannot guarantee that the user has that font installed, nor can we assume that they like writing in that font! We also cannot assume what font size the user can read best. The only solution is to allow the user to choose their own font settings and find a way of saving their chosen configuration for the next time they open our application.

Since `.yaml` files are working out so well, we shall just use these for persistent storage.

 Other options for persistent storage include plain text files, pickle, shelve or SQLite (which will be covered in a later chapter of this book).

To keep the interface of our text editor clean, we will use a second `Toplevel` window to display the font choosing screen. Go ahead and create a file named `fontchooser.py` in the same folder as the rest of your Python code:

```
import tkinter as tk
import tkinter.ttk as ttk
from tkinter.font import families
```

For this class we will be using a new module called `font`. This is a module that handles some font-related logic. In particular we only need one function from it—`families`. This function returns all available font families on the user's system. We can use this to build a list of available fonts for the user to choose from, and we know that they will definitely be installed.

As mentioned, this class will inherit from the `Toplevel` class, much like our `FindWindow`:

```
class FontChooser(tk.Toplevel):
    def __init__(self, master, **kwargs):
        super().__init__(**kwargs)
        self.master = master

        self.transient(self.master)
        self.geometry('500x250')
        self.title('Choose font and size')
```

Most of this code should look familiar. We initialize the Toplevel superclass with all of our keyword arguments, set a reference to the master widget, assign this window as a transient of its master, adjust its default size, and give the window a title of "`Choose font and size`".

We now need to find a way of displaying all of the available fonts to the user. We haven't really met a widget that will do this in a particularly friendly way yet, but one does exist—the `Listbox` widget.

The Listbox widget

The `Listbox` widget displays a large scrollable box with vertically-stacked options. Depending on the configuration, the user can select either one or multiple items from within the widget.

Methods that act on the `Listbox` widget may seem familiar from our work with the `Text` widget. These include `insert`, `delete`, and `get`. The indexing system is simpler, however, being just an integer representing how many items down the list the indicated entry is (for example, the third entry in the box has index 3).

Let's create a `Listbox` widget to hold our choices of font family:

```
self.font_list = tk.Listbox(self, exportselection=False)

self.available_fonts = sorted(families())

for family in self.available_fonts:
    self.font_list.insert(tk.END, family)
```

We create a `Listbox` widget and store a reference to it under an attribute named `font_list`. As always, the first argument to a widget is its parent, and we use the keyword argument `exportselection=False` to prevent the `Listbox` from losing its selected option when the widget loses focus.

The font families are `sorted` so they appear in alphabetical order, then we loop over them and use the `insert` method to add them into our `Listbox`. The `END` constant is used to ensure that each new item is pushed to the end of the listbox, keeping the alphabetical order.

We now need to select the currently chosen font in our `Listbox` so that the user can see what font they are currently writing in. This information will be available in the `TextEditor` class later, but we can refer to it by the `font_family` attribute in this class:

```
current_selection_index =
self.available_fonts.index(self.master.font_family)
if current_selection_index:
    self.font_list.select_set(current_selection_index)
    self.font_list.see(current_selection_index)
```

To get the location of the currently set font, we just need to pass the font family (as a `string`) to the `index` method, which returns us an integer representing its index. Since our master will have a reference to the chosen font family, we can pass this to the `index` method to get its index.

If we have received an index, we can use the `select_set` method to automatically select the currently set font family in our `Listbox`. The `see` method can also be used to scroll the chosen family into view.

That's it for our `Listbox` widget. We now have an easy to use interface for the user to select a font family that is installed on their system.

We now need to allow them to set the font size. To do this we could use a simple `Entry` widget, but we would have to write validation to prevent them from submitting any letters, since the font size should only contain numbers.

Thankfully, Tkinter provides a number-only input widget called a `Spinbox`.

The Spinbox widget

The `Spinbox` widget is a widget that allows the programmer to set specified values, either as a single tuple of choices or two keyword arguments that specify the beginning and end of a range.

Since we want to force the font size to be an integer, and we can assume that nobody will want a font size under 5 or over 99, we can use these things to form our `Spinbox`:

```
self.size_input = tk.Spinbox(self, from_=5, to=99,
value=self.master.font_size)
```

We create a `Spinbox` widget, passing the parent widget as normal.

The `from_` keyword argument is used to specify the minimum selectable value. The argument requires a trailing underscore because the word `from` is a keyword in Python. Likewise, the `to` argument specifies the maximum value.

To specify the default value we can supply a `value` argument. Again this will be stored in our `TextEditor` class as the `font_size` attribute, so we pass this over to the `value` argument.

This finishes off the two pieces of information that we need to get from our user, so we just need a way to save this information permanently.

Saving the user's choices

To ensure the user is able to save their choices, we need a **Save** button:

```
self.save_button = ttk.Button(self, text="Save", command=self.save)
```

Now we can finish off our __init__ method by packing all of our widgets:

```
self.save_button.pack(side=tk.BOTTOM, fill=tk.X, expand=1, padx=40)
self.font_list.pack(side=tk.LEFT, fill=tk.Y, expand=1)
self.size_input.pack(side=tk.BOTTOM, fill=tk.X, expand=1)
```

Since our **Save** button calls a method called `save`, let's define this now.

```
def save(self):
    font_family = self.font_list.get(self.font_list.curselection()[0])
    font_size = self.size_input.get()
    yaml_file_contents = f"family: {font_family}\n" \
                       + f"size: {font_size}"

    with open('schemes/font.yaml', 'w') as file:
        file.write(yaml_file_contents)

    self.master.update_font()
```

When saving our user's choices, we first need to extract them from their respective widgets.

The `curselection` method of a `Listbox` returns a tuple of all selected indexes. Since we are only allowing for the selection of one item (the default behavior) we will always want the first entry in this tuple. We can then pass this to the `get` method to obtain the string at this index, which will be the chosen font family.

The font size can be obtained by simply calling the `get` method on our `Spinbox`.

Now that we have these two choices we can write them into a `.yaml` file to ensure they remain persistent. We use formatted strings to construct the contents of the `.yaml` file, open a file handle (which will be stored in `schemes/font.yaml`), and use the `write` method to put that string in the file.

With the storage taken care of we now need to pass over to the `TextEditor` widget to update the styling of our `TextArea`. We call a method named `update_font`, which we will write now:

```
class TextEditor(tk.Tk):
    ...
    def update_font(self):
        self.load_font_file('schemes/font.yaml')
        self.text_area.configure(font=(self.font_family, self.font_size))
```

The `update_font` method will pass over to another method that handles loading the `.yaml` file which we just created. It then configures the `text_area` widget, passing its attributes to the `font` argument.

Let's now look at the `load_font_file` method:

```
def load_font_file(self, file_path):
    with open(file_path, 'r') as stream:
        try:
            config = yaml.load(stream)
        except yaml.YAMLError as error:
            print(error)
            return

    self.font_family = config['family']
    self.font_size = config['size']
```

This method looks very similar to all of our other methods that load and parse a `.yaml` file. We simply extract the `family` and `size` variables from the provided `.yaml` file and assign them to our `font_family` and `font_size` attributes.

With this all finished, our `FontChooser` is now fully functioning. The last thing to do is to create the method that will be responsible for placing it into our **Tools** menu. We will also need to import the class before we can begin to use it:

```
from fontchooser import FontChooser

class TextEditor(tk.Tk):
    ...
    def change_font(self):
        FontChooser()

    def tools_change_font(self, event=None):
        """
        Ctrl+L
        """
        self.change_font()
```

After writing these two methods, we can now try out our font selection window. First create a folder named `schemes` alongside your `languages` folder, then run your `texteditor.py` file and type some text (or open a file). Choose `Change Font` from the **Tools** menu, and try changing the font and size from this window:

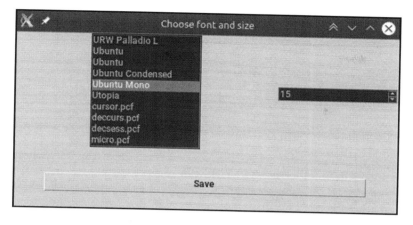

Now that we can change the font family and size, we should allow the user to change the editor's colors. We can approach this in a similar way to how we handled the font by making a new window that writes some options to a .yaml file for persistence.

Changing the editor's color scheme

Begin with a new file named colorchooser.py in the same directory as the rest of your Python files. In this file, we will be creating another Toplevel window, which gives the user the ability to set some color variables.

Once again, we have the problem of needing to get some information from a user in a specified format. Luckily, Tkinter is on our side once again, and has provided a colorchooser module that allows us to collect color choices from the user. We again need only one function from this module, called askcolor:

```
import tkinter as tk
import tkinter.ttk as ttk
from tkinter.colorchooser import askcolor
```

We begin this file by importing this function from the colorchooser module found within Tkinter. We can now begin creating our class:

```
class colorChooser(tk.Toplevel):
    def __init__(self, master, **kwargs):
        super().__init__(**kwargs)
        self.master = master

        self.transient(self.master)
```

```
        self.geometry('400x300')
        self.title('color Scheme')
```

This class begins in almost exactly the same way as our `FontChooser`, so it should not need explaining:

```
    self.chosen_background_color = tk.StringVar()
    self.chosen_foreground_color = tk.StringVar()
    self.chosen_text_background_color = tk.StringVar()
    self.chosen_text_foreground_color = tk.StringVar()
```

Four `StringVars` are created. These will hold the following:

- The background color of the `TextEditor` (and all secondary `Toplevel` windows)
- The foreground color of the `TextEditor` (and all secondary `Toplevel` windows)
- The background color of the `TextArea` widget
- The foreground color of the `TextArea` widget

The four `StringVars` are defaulted to attributes that will be stored in the `TextEditor` class. We will add these later:

```
    self.chosen_background_color.set(self.master.background)
    self.chosen_foreground_color.set(self.master.foreground)
    self.chosen_text_background_color.set(self.master.text_background)
    self.chosen_text_foreground_color.set(self.master.text_foreground)
```

To lay out the window we will need a few different `Frame` widgets:

```
    window_frame = tk.Frame(self, bg=self.master.background)
    window_foreground_frame = tk.Frame(window_frame, bg=self.master.background)
    window_background_frame = tk.Frame(window_frame, bg=self.master.background)

    text_frame = tk.Frame(self, bg=self.master.background)
    text_foreground_frame = tk.Frame(text_frame, bg=self.master.background)
    text_background_frame = tk.Frame(text_frame, bg=self.master.background)

    self.all_frames = [window_frame, window_foreground_frame,
                       window_background_frame, text_frame,
                       text_foreground_frame, text_background_frame]
```

We create two main `Frame` instances, one for the window settings and one for the text settings. Each of these then contain a `Frame` for the foreground settings and one for the background settings.

Each of these `Frame` instances has its background color set to the `background` attribute of the `TextEditor`.

Since we want to be changing the color of these frames as the user updates them, we keep a reference to all of them as an `all_frames` attribute. That way we can easily loop over this list and `configure` them to the new color.

Now that we have our layout elements in place we can start adding widgets.

For each configurable option we will need:

- A `Label` to indicate what the user is changing
- A way for the user to choose a color
- A preview of the chosen option

To achieve this, we will be using two `Label` widgets for the textual information, and a `Button` which will utilize the `askcolor` function to display a color chooser to the user.

We also require a `Label` to indicate whether the color changes will impact the application window or the `TextArea`.

Let's begin by adding some `Label` widgets into our window:

```
window_label = ttk.Label(window_frame, text="Window:", anchor=tk.W,
style="editor.TLabel")
foreground_label = ttk.Label(window_foreground_frame, text="Foreground:",
anchor=tk.E, style="editor.TLabel")
background_label = ttk.Label(window_background_frame, text="Background:",
anchor=tk.E, style="editor.TLabel")
```

The first group handles the window subtitle and both of the indicator labels. Each `Label` in this class will have a style of `editor.TLabel`. This will be configured by the `TextEditor` class once we are finished on this window:

```
text_label = ttk.Label(text_frame, text="Editor:", anchor=tk.W,
style="editor.TLabel")

text_foreground_label = ttk.Label(text_foreground_frame,
text="Foreground:", anchor=tk.E, style="editor.TLabel")
text_background_label = ttk.Label(text_background_frame,
text="Background:", anchor=tk.E, style="editor.TLabel")
```

The second group does the same but for the text area configurations.

Now that we have our indication Label widgets in place we can get on with the actual functionality—the color chooser:

```
foreground_color_chooser = ttk.Button(window_foreground_frame, text="Change
Foreground color", width=26,   style="editor.TButton", command=lambda
sv=self.chosen_foreground_color: self.set_color(sv))

background_color_chooser = ttk.Button(window_background_frame, text="Change
Background color", width=26, style="editor.TButton", command=lambda
sv=self.chosen_background_color: self.set_color(sv))

text_foreground_color_chooser = ttk.Button(text_foreground_frame,
text="Change Text Foreground color", width=26, style="editor.TButton",
command=lambda sv=self.chosen_text_foreground_color: self.set_color(sv))

text_background_color_chooser = ttk.Button(text_background_frame,
text="Change Text Background color", width=26, style="editor.TButton",
command=lambda sv=self.chosen_text_background_color: self.set_color(sv))
```

Four Button widgets are created. Each is essentially the same, the differences are which Frame is the parent and which StringVar we want to store the color choice in. Just like our Label widgets, all Button widgets in our application will need a style named editor.TButton.

To get a feel of how the Button widgets will function let's jump to the method they are all calling: set_color:

```
def set_color(self, sv):
    choice = askcolor()[1]
    sv.set(choice)
```

This function takes a StringVar argument, calls the askcolor function, parses the second return value from it, and stores the result in the StringVar.

The askcolor function pops up a window with three color sliders—red, green, and blue. The user can then slide each primary color to create the color they are after. There is also an Entry in which they can enter the hex value of their color choice if they know it:

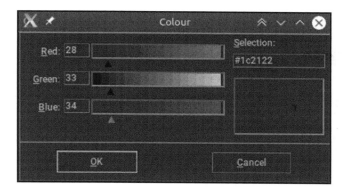

This function returns a tuple of two items. The first is another tuple of the chosen red, green, and blue amounts as floating point numbers. The second is the hex string of their chosen color. Since Tkinter works with hex strings by default, we can disregard the tuple of floats and just grab the hex string.

With this covered we can return to the __init__ method and continue setting up our widgets:

```
foreground_color_preview = ttk.Label(window_foreground_frame,
textvar=self.chosen_foreground_color, style="editor.TLabel")

background_color_preview = ttk.Label(window_background_frame,
textvar=self.chosen_background_color, style="editor.TLabel")

text_foreground_color_preview = ttk.Label(text_foreground_frame,
textvar=self.chosen_text_foreground_color, style="editor.TLabel")

text_background_color_preview = ttk.Label(text_background_frame,
textvar=self.chosen_text_background_color, style="editor.TLabel")
```

Four more Label widgets will show the user their choice of color next to each Button. Since the chosen colors are stored in each StringVar, we just need to set these Label widgets to display the StringVar's value.

Just one more widget to define now—a **Save** button. This will write the user's choices to a .yaml file once again, so that each time they open the editor it is in the same color scheme as when they closed it:

```
save_button = ttk.Button(self, text="save", command=self.save,
style="editor.TButton")
```

That's it for the widgets! We will finish off our __init__ method with some calls to pack:

```
window_frame.pack(side=tk.TOP, fill=tk.X, expand=1)
window_label.pack(side=tk.TOP, fill=tk.X)

window_foreground_frame.pack(side=tk.TOP, fill=tk.X, expand=1)
window_background_frame.pack(side=tk.TOP, fill=tk.X, expand=1)

foreground_label.pack(side=tk.LEFT, padx=30, pady=10)
foreground_color_chooser.pack(side=tk.LEFT)
foreground_color_preview.pack(side=tk.LEFT, expand=1, fill=tk.X, padx=(15,
0))

background_label.pack(side=tk.LEFT, fill=tk.X, padx=(30, 27))
background_color_chooser.pack(side=tk.LEFT)
background_color_preview.pack(side=tk.LEFT, expand=1, fill=tk.X, padx=(15,
0))
```

Begin by packing our application settings. We first pack the Frame widgets, then our three widgets for the foreground, and finally our three widgets for the background:

```
text_frame.pack(side=tk.TOP, fill=tk.X, expand=1)
text_label.pack(side=tk.TOP, fill=tk.X)

text_foreground_frame.pack(side=tk.TOP, fill=tk.X, expand=1)
text_background_frame.pack(side=tk.TOP, fill=tk.X, expand=1)

text_foreground_label.pack(side=tk.LEFT, padx=30, pady=10)
text_foreground_color_chooser.pack(side=tk.LEFT)
text_foreground_color_preview.pack(side=tk.LEFT, expand=1, fill=tk.X,
padx=(15, 0))

text_background_label.pack(side=tk.LEFT, fill=tk.X, padx=(30, 27))
text_background_color_chooser.pack(side=tk.LEFT)
text_background_color_preview.pack(side=tk.LEFT, expand=1, fill=tk.X,
padx=(15, 0))
```

The same is repeated for the TextArea widgets.

Finally, just our **Save** button left to pack:

```
save_button.pack(side=tk.BOTTOM, pady=(0, 20))
```

That's our huge __init__ method completed! If you want to preview it, add an if __name__ == '__main__' block and give this file a run.

Otherwise, we'll finish off this class by writing our save method, which will write a .yaml file for persistent storage:

```
def save(self):
    yaml_file_contents = f"background:
'{self.chosen_background_color.get()}'\n" \
                       + f"foreground:
'{self.chosen_foreground_color.get()}'\n" \
                       + f"text_background:
'{self.chosen_text_background_color.get()}'\n" \
                       + f"text_foreground:
'{self.chosen_text_foreground_color.get()}'\n"

    with open("schemes/default.yaml", "w") as yaml_file:
        yaml_file.write(yaml_file_contents)
```

The .yaml file will contain our user's four choices. We use a formatted string to inject the values of our StringVars into a basic .yaml syntax. Be sure to notice that each injected variable should be wrapped in a string, since the # character will be in our values and this constitutes a comment in .yaml.

We then open a .yaml file stored in our schemes folder and write the contents of our string into that file.

Now that we have saved the user's choices, we need to pass over to our TextEditor class and tell it to recolor the application:

```
self.master.apply_color_scheme(self.chosen_foreground_color.get(),
                               self.chosen_background_color.get(),
                               self.chosen_text_foreground_color.get(),
                               self.chosen_text_background_color.get())
```

A method called apply_color_scheme is called and we pass the four StringVar's values as arguments.

To finish off our `save` method we also need to update the `colorChooser` window itself, so we need to configure the visible widgets. This is where our `all_frames` list comes in handy:

```
for frame in self.all_frames:
    frame.configure(bg=self.chosen_background_color.get())

self.configure(bg=self.chosen_background_color.get())
```

We loop through all of our `Frame` widgets and configure their background to the value of the relevant `StringVar`. The window itself is also configured to use the new background color.

All of the `Label` and `Button` widgets are handled by the `TextEditor` class (using the `style` argument mentioned earlier). Let's write this code now:

```
class TextEditor(tk.Tk):
    ...
    def __init__(self):
        ...
        self.background = 'lightgrey'
        self.foreground = 'black'
        self.all_menus = [self.menu, self.right_click_menu]
        ...
    def generate_sub_menus(self, sub_menu_items):
        ...
        self.all_menus.append(sub_menu)
    def apply_color_scheme(self, foreground, background,
                           text_foreground, text_background):
        self.background = background
        self.foreground = foreground
        self.text_area.configure(fg=text_foreground, bg=text_background)
        for menu in self.all_menus:
            menu.configure(bg=self.background, fg=self.foreground)
        self.configure_ttk_elements()
```

Inside `apply_color_scheme` the user's chosen values from the `colorChooser` window are now saved as attributes of the `TextEditor` class so that they can be sent around to any other windows that may need them.

The `TextArea` widget is configured to use the foreground and background, which were passed to this function. This is all we need to do for this widget.

In order to change all of our menus we will need to loop through them. This requires a list of them, much like we did with the `Frame` widgets back in our `colorChooser` class. This list is defined in our `__init__` method after creating the menu bar and right-click menu, then appended to at the end of each loop in our `generate_sub_menus` method.

Once all of the `configure` calls are done we still need to update our `ttk` widgets. The `configure_ttk_elements` method lets us do this:

```
def configure_ttk_elements(self):
    style = ttk.Style()
    style.configure('editor.TLabel', foreground=self.foreground,
background=self.background)
    style.configure('editor.TButton', foreground=self.foreground,
background=self.background)
```

A `Style` object is created, which is how the application will handle `ttk` element styling. The `Style` then configures the two style strings, which we saw in our `colorChooser`—`editor.TLabel` and `editor.TButton`. These have their foreground set to the value in our `foreground` attribute, and their background set to the value of our `background` attribute.

To ensure the new colors are applied when the application loads, make sure you change every hard-coded `bg='lightgrey'` to `bg=self.background` and every `fg='black'` to `fg=self.foreground`. These should be at the creation of `self.menu`, the creation of each submenu in `generate_sub_menus`, and the creation of our right-click context menu.

You can now go ahead and run the `texteditor.py` file to see the `colorChooser` in action. Go ahead and change some of the colors and watch how the editor reacts:

There are now some tweaks we need to make to the other classes to make sure they use the chosen color scheme.

In the `FontChooser`'s `__init__` method, we need to set its background color to that of the application. The **Save** button also needs to take the `editor.TButton` style:

```
class FontChooser(tk.Toplevel):
    def __init__(self, master, **kwargs):
        ...
        self.configure(bg=self.master.background)
```

```
    ...
    self.save_button = ttk.Button(self, text="Save",
                        style="editor.TButton", command=self.save)
```

Similarly, our `FindWindow` now needs to be updated. The three `Button` widgets should get our `editor.TButton` style, the `Label` widgets need to become `ttk Label` widgets with our `editor.TLabel` style, and all `Frame` and window colors need to reflect the application's.

Since the `master` widget of our `FindWindow` is actually the `TextArea`, we need to use `self.master.master` to refer to our `TextEditor`:

```
class FindWindow(tk.Toplevel):
    def __init__(self, master, **kwargs):
        ...
        self.configure(bg=self.master.master.background)
        ...
        top_frame = tk.Frame(self, bg=self.master.master.background)
        middle_frame = tk.Frame(self, bg=self.master.master.background)
        bottom_frame = tk.Frame(self, bg=self.master.master.background)
        ...
        find_entry_label = ttk.Label(top_frame, text="Find: ",
                        style="editor.TLabel")
        ...
        replace_entry_label = ttk.Label(middle_frame, text="Replace: ",
                            style="editor.TLabel")
        ...
        self.find_button = ttk.Button(bottom_frame, text="Find",
                            command=self.on_find, style="editor.TButton")
        self.replace_button = ttk.Button(bottom_frame, text="Replace",
                        command=self.on_replace, style="editor.TButton")
        self.cancel_button = ttk.Button(bottom_frame, text="Cancel",
                        command=self.on_cancel, style="editor.TButton")
```

And with that we are finished with our color changing code! All we need to do is wrap it in a function, which will add it to the **Tools** menu:

```
def change_color_scheme(self):
    colorChooser(self)

def tools_change_color_scheme(self, event=None):
    """
    Ctrl+G
    """
    self.change_color_scheme()
```

This also marks the end of the **Tools** menu. That leaves us with just one more submenu to add something to—the **Help** menu.

In the **Help** menu we can just add some information about our application. If you would like, you can add some detail and images here. For the sake of this example I will just keep it simple:

```python
import tkinter.messagebox as msg

def show_about_page(self):
    msg.showinfo("About", "My text editor, version 3, written in
                Python3.6 using tkinter!")

def help_about(self, event=None):
    """
    Ctrl+H
    """
    self.show_about_page()
```

A simple `showinfo` box displays some information to the user about the version number and technologies of the application.

All of the functionality of our editor is now finished.

The last thing to do to fully complete the application is to bind all of the keys that are displayed in our submenus, since unfortunately they do not bind automatically:

```python
def bind_events(self):
    ...
    self.bind('<Control-n>', self.file_new)
    self.bind('<Control-o>', self.file_open)
    self.bind('<Control-s>', self.file_save)

    self.bind('<Control-h>', self.help_about)

    self.bind('<Control-m>', self.tools_change_syntax_highlighting)
    self.bind('<Control-g>', self.tools_change_color_scheme)
    self.bind('<Control-l>', self.tools_change_font)
```

With that our text editor application is complete! We have now created a functioning text editor which boasts:

- A working menu bar and right-click context menu
- The ability to open and save files
- Keyboard shortcuts and context menu items to cut, copy, and paste text
- The ability to choose the font and font size
- Syntax highlighting for any file type we can write a `.yaml` file for
- A customizable color scheme for both the application and the text area
- A functioning find/replace window

This is where we shall leave this project. If you feel that there is some functionality that another text editor has which you like, feel free to try and implement it into this project as an exercise.

The third and final application we will move on to will be an online instant messaging program. We may even see our old friend the `Text` widget there!

Summary

In this chapter we have learned all about menus. There are many different ways in which the flexible `Menu` widget can be utilized, and we have practiced three.

We first created a main menu bar along the top of our application where we could provide access to functions of the editor. Afterwards we added menus into this bar by creating a cascade. This gave us **File, Edit, Tools**, and **Help** menus sitting at the top of our editor. We also looked at a solution that allows these items to auto-populate with functions and keyboard shortcuts providing we follow a naming convention for our editor's methods.

Finally, we created a separate right-click context menu. This allows the user to manipulate the text in our `TextArea` widget without having to know the keyboard shortcuts or move the mouse all the way to the top of the screen.

In order to create these `Menus` we learned about the two main ways of adding items—`add_command` and `add_cascade`. We saw that `add_cascade` allows us to create a submenu inside another menu by passing the `label` as the text to show and `menu` as the `Menu` widget to insert, and `add_command` allows us to call a function when the user clicks this entry, provided we pass that function to the `command` argument.

Creating the file menu allowed us to make use of the `filedialog` module. We made use of two functions from this module—`askopenfilename` and `asksaveasfilename`. We now know just how simple Tkinter makes it to get file path choices from a user who may not know how to build a full path to a file, since with this module they don't have to! We also got a glimpse of how to force a file type when asking the user to open a file, meaning they should not be able to pick an incorrect file and have the application behave in an unexpected way.

Additional `Toplevel` windows were added to our application and configured to share the color scheme of the `TextEditor` class itself. This also allowed us to see a practical example of how `ttk`'s `Style` object allows for very easy application-wide styling of the widgets it includes, such as `Label` and `Button` widgets.

The `colorchooser` and `font` modules were briefly looked at, and we learned how to make use of one function in each—`families` and `askcolor`. We saw that the `families` function makes it super easy to get a tuple of all fonts available on the user's system, making font selection worry-free. Getting a color choice from a user was also made incredibly simple via the `askcolor` function—providing the user with sliders and a hex code entry so that they can see exactly what color they are selecting.

In the next chapter, we shall be moving on to an online chat application. Here we will be making use of the ever-powerful `Canvas` widget, as well as the `Text` widget we have learned a lot about from this project. We will eventually set up a chat server using the simple yet powerful `flask` module and maintain a list of friends using `sqlite` for permanent storage.

8
Talk Python to Me – a Chat Application

The next project we will undertake is an online instant messaging application. This will allow us to manage a list of friends who we can chat to. When chatting, a user will have access to a list of smileys to add character to their messages.

In this chapter, we will cover:

- Creating a scrollable `Frame`
- Using the `grid` geometry manager
- Positioning a `Toplevel` window relative to its parent
- Embedding images into a `Text` widget

Creating a scrollable frame

There will come a time when writing applications with Tkinter when you will want to add a `Scrollbar` to the application as a whole, rather than an individual widget (such as the `Text` widget, which we have already covered). This is not a trivial task, since Tkinter will usually expand itself to show all of its containing widgets, or if the geometry is already set, will simply hide them underneath the bottom border of the window.

Let's take a look at what I mean. Open a new Python script and type the following short snippet:

```python
import tkinter as tk

win = tk.Tk()

for _ in range(30):
    tk.Label(win, text="big label").pack(pady=20)

win.mainloop()
```

If you run this file you should see a very tall window open up. You will see a certain number of Label widgets (depending on your monitor's resolution) but will likely not see all 30.

If you have the ability to move the window above the top of your screen (on my Linux machine I can hold *Alt* and drag the middle of the window upwards) you can then expose the bottom of the window. Drag the bottom of the window downwards (thus increasing the window's height) and you will see more Label widgets lie underneath:

To solve this problem, we obviously just need a `Scrollbar`! Let's try adding one:

```python
import tkinter as tk

win = tk.Tk()
f = tk.Frame(win)
for _ in range(30):
    tk.Label(win, text="big label").pack(pady=20)

scroll = tk.Scrollbar(win, orient='vertical', command=win.yview)
scroll.pack(side=tk.RIGHT, fill=tk.Y)

win.mainloop()
```

This code should allow us to scroll the window with the `Scrollbar`. However, if you try executing this file you will be shown the following error:

```
Traceback (most recent call last):
  File "demo/demo.py", line 8, in <module>
    scroll = tk.Scrollbar(win, orient='vertical', command=win.yview)
  File "/usr/lib64/python3.6/tkinter/__init__.py", line 2095, in
__getattr__
    return getattr(self.tk, attr)
AttributeError: '_tkinter.tkapp' object has no attribute 'yview'
```

How about a `Frame` widget instead?

```
Traceback (most recent call last):
  File "demo/demo.py", line 8, in <module>
    scroll = tk.Scrollbar(win, orient='vertical', command=f.yview)
AttributeError: 'Frame' object has no attribute 'yview'
```

No, that didn't work either. There must be some way we can get our window to scroll though, right?

The solution is to use the `Canvas` widget to embed a `Frame` widget as a window. Since the `Canvas` widget can handle scrolling, we can use this trick to get ourselves a scrollable `Frame`:

```python
import tkinter as tk

win = tk.Tk()
canvas = tk.Canvas(win)
frame = tk.Frame(canvas)

scroll = tk.Scrollbar(win, orient='vertical', command=canvas.yview)
scroll.pack(side=tk.RIGHT, fill=tk.Y)

canvas.configure(yscrollcommand=scroll.set)
canvas.pack(fill=tk.BOTH, expand=1)
canvas.create_window((0, 0), window=frame, anchor='nw')

for _ in range(30):
    tk.Label(frame, text="big label").pack(pady=20)

win.mainloop()
```

This time we create a `Canvas` first, then a `Frame` inside it. Our `Scrollbar`'s command can then be set to the `yview` of our `Canvas`.

To create the `Frame` widget as a window inside our `Canvas`, the `create_window` method is used. The first argument to this method is the coordinates within the `Canvas` at which to place this window. `(0, 0)` puts the window at the upper-left corner of the `Canvas`. Next, the `window` argument is what we want to draw as the window, so we pass this our `Frame`. Finally, the `anchor` allows us to align the window, and we use `nw` to keep everything aligned in the upper-left corner.

> When using the `create_window` method, do not also use a geometry manager (such as `pack`) on the widget that you are using as a window. This will prevent the widget from displaying at all!

Now that our window is created, we can add our 30 `Label` widgets to it.

Give this version of the code a try. You should now see we have a normal-sized window with a scrollbar. However, the scrollbar still doesn't seem to work!

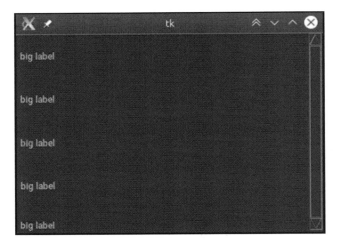

In order to make the `Frame` widget inside the `Canvas` scrollable we have one final thing left to do—configure its `scrollregion`. As the name suggests, this defines where in the `Canvas` can be scrolled.

Add this function and binding to your code and give it another try:

```
def on_frame_resized(self, event=None):
    canvas.configure(scrollregion=canvas.bbox("all"))


win.bind('<Configure>', on_frame_resized)
```

The `on_frame_resized` function will configure the `scrollregion` of the `Canvas`. The `bbox("all")` grabs the bounding box coordinates of the whole `Canvas`, and we pass this as the `scrollregion` to allow us to scroll the entire `Canvas`.

This function is bound to the `<Configure>` event, which is called when the window is created and resized. This ensures that, as our `Canvas` grows and shrinks along with the main window, we will still be able to scroll all of it.

If you run this version of the code, you should now be presented with a completely scrollable window.

This is the basic recipe for creating a window that can be scrolled via a `Scrollbar`. You can also use the mouse wheel bindings we have practiced in previous chapters to allow the window to be scrolled using the mouse wheel.

Now that we know how to make a scrollable window, let's begin by creating one. We will be using this to create our friends list window, which will feature information about all of the people we are able to chat to.

Creating our FriendsList class

Begin with a new folder, which will hold all of the code for our chat application. Inside this folder, create a file called `friendslist.py`. In this file, we will begin writing our `FriendsList` class:

```python
import tkinter as tk
import tkinter.ttk as ttk


class FriendsList(tk.Tk):
    def __init__(self, **kwargs):
        super().__init__(**kwargs)

        self.title('Tk Chat')
        self.geometry('700x500')

        self.canvas = tk.Canvas(self, bg="white")
        self.canvas_frame = tk.Frame(self.canvas)

        self.scrollbar = ttk.Scrollbar(self, orient="vertical",
                                command=self.canvas.yview)
        self.canvas.configure(yscrollcommand=self.scrollbar.set)

        self.scrollbar.pack(side=tk.LEFT, fill=tk.Y)
        self.canvas.pack(side=tk.LEFT, expand=1, fill=tk.BOTH)

        self.friends_area = self.canvas.create_window((0, 0),
                        window=self.canvas_frame, anchor="nw")

        self.bind_events()

        self.load_friends()
```

Hopefully everything here looks very familiar. We import the usual `tkinter` and `ttk` modules, set a few window properties, then get straight into creating the components for our scrollable window.

After the `Scrollbar`, `Canvas`, and `Frame` are all taken care of, we call `bind_events` to handle binding of our necessary functions, followed by `load_friends` to populate the window with all of our added friends:

```python
def bind_events(self):
    self.bind('<Configure>', self.on_frame_resized)

def on_frame_resized(self, event=None):
    self.canvas.configure(scrollregion=self.canvas.bbox("all"))
```

In `bind_events` we bind a method to our window's `<Configure>` event, which takes care of setting up the `scrollregion` of our `Canvas`, as we saw with the previous demo.

To add friends to our window, we will first create all of the necessary widgets inside their own `Frame` then add this to the `canvas_frame`, which is inside our `Canvas`:

```python
def load_friends(self):
    friend_frame = ttk.Frame(self.canvas_frame)

    profile_photo = tk.PhotoImage(file="images/avatar.png")
    profile_photo_label = ttk.Label(friend_frame, image=profile_photo)
    profile_photo_label.image = profile_photo

    friend_name = ttk.Label(friend_frame, text="Jaden Corebyn",
                            anchor=tk.W)

    message_button = ttk.Button(friend_frame, text="Chat",
                                command=self.open_chat_window)

    profile_photo_label.pack(side=tk.LEFT)
    friend_name.pack(side=tk.LEFT)
    message_button.pack(side=tk.RIGHT)

    friend_frame.pack(fill=tk.X, expand=1)
```

Each friend will consist of three widgets:

1. A `PhotoImage` holding their avatar of choice.
2. A `Label` showing their name.
3. A `Button` that opens up their chat window.

Since there will be no server-side code in this iteration, I will be using placeholder information in this method. At a later point we will be able to pull this information from a database.

We can now run this initial version of the window. You should see a wide window with a small section containing the friend information:

This doesn't look very nice; we should make the friends span the entire window width. In order to do this we just need one more binding:

```
def bind_events(self):
    ...
    self.canvas.bind('<Configure>', self.friends_width)

def friends_width(self, event):
    canvas_width = event.width
    self.canvas.itemconfig(self.friends_area, width=canvas_width)
```

This time we bind to our `Canvas'` `<Configure>` event. Whenever our `Canvas` is resized, we grab its new width from the `event` object and apply it to the window within. In order to access the window in our `Canvas`, we use the `itemconfig` method. This method is like `configure` but it references items that have been created inside another widget, such as windows or images.

We pass this method our `friends_area` attribute, which holds the result of our `create_window` call, and the new width we want it to be set to.

Run this updated version of the file and you should see the friend will span the entire window width now. It will also stay at full width as you resize the window:

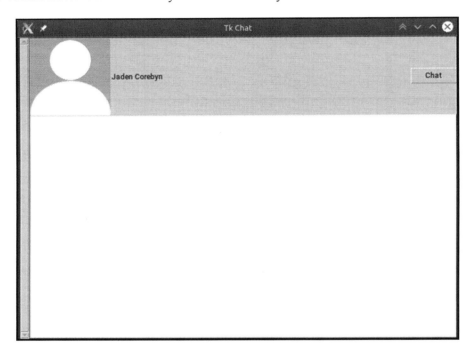

The last thing to do is create the ability to add a new friend. We can use our knowledge of the `Menu` widget to present this feature:

```
def __init__(self, **kwargs):
    ...
    self.menu = tk.Menu(self, bg="lightgrey", fg="black", tearoff=0)

    self.friends_menu = tk.Menu(self.menu, fg="black", bg="lightgrey",
                                tearoff=0)
```

```
    self.friends_menu.add_command(label="Add Friend",
                              command=self.add_friend)
    self.menu.add_cascade(label="Friends", menu=self.friends_menu)

    self.configure(menu=self.menu)
```

We can create a `Menu` in our `__init__` method, which contains a `Friends` submenu. Inside here will be an `Add Friend` option.

Since we have no way of getting friend information yet, we can just call our `load_friends` method to act as a placeholder:

```
def add_friend(self):
    self.load_friends()
```

One final method remains now—`open_chat_window`. This will require us to create a new class that will act as the chat window. Create a new file in your folder called `chatwindow.py`, then add this code to finish off your `friendslist.py` file:

```
from chatwindow import ChatWindow

...

    def open_chat_window(self):
        cw = ChatWindow(self, 'Jaden Corebyn', 'images/avatar.png')
```

With this done we can move on to our `ChatWindow` class.

Creating our ChatWindow class

Before we begin coding our `ChatWindow`, let's have a brief overview of the design.

The window will contain the following elements:

- A messages area, showing all messages sent by you to this friend, and sent by this friend to you
- A scrollbar that allows you to scroll up to view older messages
- A text area for you to type a message to send to this friend
- A button that sends the contents of your message to your friend, then clears the text area

- A button that lets the user pick a smiley to include in their message
- Your avatar
- This friend's avatar

From a layout point of view, the message area is the primary part of the application, so it will take up the most space within the window, and be central.

The text area and buttons will be placed below the messages area so that they are nearby but do not draw the eye away from the messages area.

The avatars will be off to the right-hand side of the window, with your friend's image above yours. This keeps your avatar near your message input, and again prevents stealing focus from the message area.

From this information we can begin to figure out what widgets we will need to achieve this design.

The messages area could be achieved by a few different means, but in this case the best option is a disabled `Text` widget. We know exactly how to dynamically update these from our text editor application, and we will soon look at how we can add images into one as well.

The scrollbar can be handled by the normal `Scrollbar` widget, which we have used to control a `Text` widget in the past.

The user's messages will be typed into a second `Text` widget, allowing them to send messages longer than the one line allowed by an `Entry` widget.

The buttons can be handled by the normal `Button` widget. These can display both text and images, as we will see shortly.

Finally, the avatars will be handled with a `PhotoImage` and displayed using a `Label` widget.

With regard to structuring the layout, we have three distinct areas, which can be separated like so:

We can represent each area with its own `Frame`. This allows us to control the layout very easily.

With these decisions in mind we can begin structuring the `ChatWindow` class.

Since the `FriendsList` class inherits from the `Tk` widget, and we want to be able to have multiple chat windows open at once, the `ChatWindow` will need to inherit from the `Toplevel` widget:

```
import tkinter as tk
import tkinter.ttk as ttk

class ChatWindow(tk.Toplevel):
    def __init__(self, master, friend_name, friend_avatar, **kwargs):
        super().__init__(**kwargs)
        self.master = master
        self.title(friend_name)
        self.geometry('540x640')
        self.minsize(540, 640)

        self.right_frame = tk.Frame(self)
        self.left_frame = tk.Frame(self)
        self.bottom_frame = tk.Frame(self.left_frame)
```

The minimum information each `ChatWindow` will need passed from the `FriendsList` is the friend's name and avatar image. We also accept the standard `master` argument, and any further keyword arguments, which will be passed back to the `Toplevel` base class.

The `minsize` method is used to prevent the user from shrinking the window too small, making their conversations unreadable. This method takes two numbers: the first is the minimum width, and the second is the minimum height. You will notice that these match the default size passed to the `geometry` method.

We begin our layout by creating three `Frame` widgets. The `right_frame` will hold our avatars, the `left_frame` our messages area, and the `bottom_frame` our text input and buttons:

```
    self.messages_area = tk.Text(self.left_frame, bg="white", fg="black",
wrap=tk.WORD, width=30)
    self.scrollbar = ttk.Scrollbar(self.left_frame, orient='vertical',
command=self.messages_area.yview)
    self.messages_area.configure(yscrollcommand=self.scrollbar.set)
```

The first widgets we create are those that handle reading messages. Our messages area, as mentioned, will be a `Text` widget. As well as some color information, we initialize this with the `wrap` argument set to the `WORD` constant, meaning the messages will not break up words as a message reaches the edge of the widget, and the `width` argument to `30`, setting the default size of the widget.

Alongside our `messages_area` we create a `Scrollbar` as normal and set it up to affect the `messages_area` with the usual `yview` and `yscrollcommand` arguments:

```
self.text_area = tk.Text(self.bottom_frame, bg="white", fg="black",
height=3, width=30)
self.send_button = ttk.Button(self.bottom_frame, text="Send",
command=self.send_message, style="send.TButton")
```

The widgets that will sit in our `bottom_frame` come next. Another `Text` widget is created for the user to type their message into, and a `Button` is made, which will send their message when clicked:

```
self.profile_picture = tk.PhotoImage(file="images/avatar.png")
self.friend_profile_picture = tk.PhotoImage(file=friend_avatar)

self.profile_picture_area = tk.Label(self.right_frame,
image=self.profile_picture, relief=tk.RIDGE)
self.friend_profile_picture_area = tk.Label(self.right_frame,
image=self.friend_profile_picture, relief=tk.RIDGE)
```

To finish off our widgets, we create the two images that will act as avatars in our `right_frame`. As we have seen before, we begin by creating `PhotoImage` objects that Tkinter can use, then we use a `Label` widget in order to display them.

In order to display a `PhotoImage` using a `Label`, all we need to do is pass it as the `image` argument. We also set the `relief` argument to the `RIDGE` constant as a way of placing a small border around the image.

Now that all of our widgets have been defined we can begin packing them into the window:

```
self.left_frame.pack(side=tk.LEFT, fill=tk.BOTH, expand=1)
self.scrollbar.pack(side=tk.LEFT, fill=tk.Y)
self.messages_area.pack(side=tk.TOP, fill=tk.BOTH, expand=1)
self.messages_area.configure(state='disabled')
```

The `left_frame` is packed into the window and its widgets are packed into it. The `messages_area` is then disabled using the `state` argument:

```
self.right_frame.pack(side=tk.LEFT, fill=tk.Y)
self.profile_picture_area.pack(side=tk.BOTTOM)
self.friend_profile_picture_area.pack(side=tk.TOP)
```

The `right_frame` then follows suit. The user's avatar is added to the bottom of the `Frame` widget, and the friend's at the top:

```
self.bottom_frame.pack(side=tk.BOTTOM, fill=tk.X)
self.text_area.pack(side=tk.LEFT, fill=tk.X, expand=1, pady=5)
self.send_button.pack(side=tk.RIGHT, pady=5)
```

We finish packing with the `bottom_frame` and its widgets. Some padding around them is added with the `pady` argument for aesthetics:

```
self.configure_styles()
self.bind_events()
```

The `__init__` method is finished off by configuring the styles of our `ttk` widgets and binding any necessary events.

We'll start the `bind_events` method by allowing the user to send their message with the *Return/Enter* key as well as by clicking the button:

```
def bind_events():
    self.bind("<Return>", self.send_message)
    self.text_area.bind("<Return>", self.send_message)
```

Now that we are all set up to send our messages, let's write the `send_message` method to get things going:

```
def send_message(self, event=None):
    message = self.text_area.get(1.0, tk.END)

    if message.strip():
        message = "Me: " + message
        self.messages_area.configure(state='normal')
        self.messages_area.insert(tk.END, message)
        self.messages_area.configure(state='disabled')

        self.text_area.delete(1.0, tk.END)

    return "break"
```

Since we can call this method from an event binding, we need to catch the `event` object as a parameter.

The message is extracted from the `text_area` using its `get` method. To avoid sending empty messages of just spaces, we first use the strip method on the message, then check that it still has content.

If it does, we add the word `Me:` to the beginning to indicate that the message was written by us, then enable the `messages_area`, add our message, and disable it again.

The `text_area` is then cleared out so that the user does not have to manually delete their last message.

The string `break` is returned to avoid the default behavior of the *Return/Enter* key.

One last thing we should do before previewing our `ChatWindow` is handle adjusting the `ttk` styling:

```
def configure_styles(self):
    style = ttk.Style()
    style.configure("send.TButton", background='#dddddd',
foreground="black", padding=16)
```

This method only affects our `send_button` at the moment. It gives the button a light gray background with black text, and adds some padding to make it the same height as the `text_area`.

Now that this is in place, we can take a look at our `ChatWindow` in action. Add this small block to the bottom of the file and run it:

```
if __name__ == '__main__':
    w = tk.Tk()
    c = ChatWindow(w, 'friend', 'images/avatar.png')
    c.protocol("WM_DELETE_WINDOW", w.destroy)
    w.mainloop()
```

You should now have a chat window appear. Go ahead and type some messages and send them. You should see them appear in the messages area:

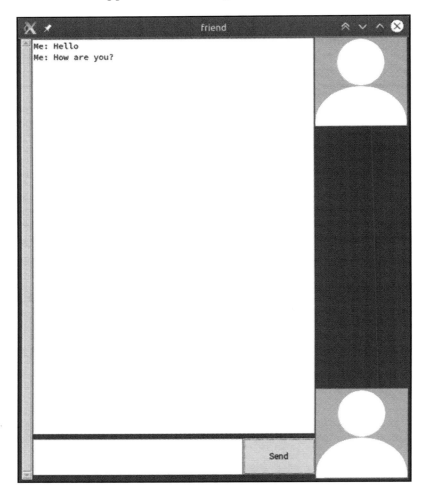

While sending text messages is nice, people often want to send images known as smileys or emojis. Luckily, the `Text` widget we are using to display messages can support images.

Before we add these to our `ChatWindow` class, we should create a user-friendly way for the user to select their choice of smiley.

Creating our SmilieSelect class

We are going to pop up a small window that contains all available smileys as buttons. When the user clicks on one of these smiley buttons, the image will be inserted into their `text_area`.

Create a new Python file in your folder called `smilieselect.py`. In that file, begin with the following code:

```
import os
import tkinter as tk
import tkinter.ttk as ttk

class SmilieSelect(tk.Toplevel):
    smilies_dir = os.path.abspath(os.path.join(os.path.dirname(__file__),
                                              'smilies/'))
```

Our application needs to keep track of where these images are stored on the filesystem, since multiple classes will need to access them. We achieve this by setting a class variable on the SmilieSelect window called `smilies_dir`.

The smiley images will be stored in a folder named `smilies`, which will live in the folder holding the rest of our scripts. Go ahead and create this folder now:

```
def __init__(self, master, **kwargs):
    super().__init__(**kwargs)
    self.master = master
    self.transient(master)
    self.position_window()
```

Our __init__ method begins by setting the window to a transient of its master, then calls a method called `position_window`. This will allow us to place the smiley window relative to the chat window every time. Let's jump to this method now:

```
def position_window(self):
    master_pos_x = self.master.winfo_x()
    master_pos_y = self.master.winfo_y()

    master_width = self.master.winfo_width()
    master_height = self.master.winfo_height()

    my_width = 100
    my_height = 100

    pos_x = (master_pos_x + (master_width // 2)) - (my_width // 2)
    pos_y = (master_pos_y + (master_height // 2)) - (my_height // 2)
```

```
geometry = f"{my_width}x{my_height}+{pos_x}+{pos_y}"
self.geometry(geometry)
```

In order to place our smiley window in the center of the chat window, we need to know three things:

- The chat window's position on the user's screen
- The chat window's width and height
- The smiley window's width and height

We can obtain the chat window's position by calling its `winfo_x` and `winfo_y` methods. Its width and height are accessed with `winfo_width` and `winfo_height` respectively. Finally, we define the smiley window's size as 100 x 100.

We can then use these numbers to calculate the *x* and *y* position to place the window at, which we store as `pos_x` and `pos_y`.

The geometry method can control not only the default size of a window, but its position as well. It does this when you pass its argument in the following format: `width`, `x`, `height`, `+`, `x_coordinate`, `+`, and `y_coordinate`.

Or, in Python terms:

```
"{}x{}+{}+{}".format(width, height, x_coordinate, y_coordinate)
```

We can see this in action in the call to the `geometry` method of our `position_window` code, except using the formatted string syntax, which is available in Python version 3.6.

With this method written we can go back and finish off the __init__ method, which is where the bulk of our logic lies:

```
def __init__(self, master, **kwargs):
    ...
    smilie_files = [file for file in os.listdir(self.smilies_dir) if
file.endswith(".png")]

    self.smilie_images = []

    for file in smilie_files:
        full_path = os.path.join(self.smilies_dir, file)
        image = tk.PhotoImage(file=full_path)
        self.smilie_images.append(image)
```

This class needs to hold a list of all available smiley images. This will take a few steps to accomplish.

We create a list of the filenames using the `listdir` method of the `os` module. This method simply performs a directory listing of the supplied folder. We provide this method our `smilies_dir` and filter out for files that don't have the `.png` extension.

 In order for this code to function you will need some `.png` files inside your `smilies` directory. The ones I have used in my implementation are available on the Open Game Art website at `https://opengameart.org/content/mikulka%E2%80%99s-smile`. Due to permissive licensing, they are available on this book's GitHub repository as well.

Now that we have the filenames of our smileys, we need to turn them into `PhotoImage` objects, which Tkinter can utilize.

In order to do this, we loop over our list of smiley files and use the `os.path.join` method to join the file name to the `smilies_dir` location. This gives us the full path to our image files, which we can use to create a `PhotoImage` object. We then append this to our `smilie_images` list for later use.

With a full list of `PhotoImage` objects, we can now create `Button` widgets, which will allow the user to select that particular smiley for inclusion in their message.

The most logical way to display these buttons is in a grid. Since I will be using seven images in my implementation of this application, I will be using a 3 x 3 grid. If you have more smiley images available, feel free to adjust the numbers for a more suitable grid.

As the name suggests, the `grid` geometry manager makes creating grid layouts very easy, so we will be using this (instead of `pack`) to put our `Button` widgets into the window:

```
for index, file in enumerate(self.smilie_images):
    row, col = divmod(index, 3)
    button = ttk.Button(self, image=file,
                    command=lambda s=file: self.insert_smilie(s))
    button.grid(row=row, column=col, sticky='nsew')
```

When adding our `smilie` buttons to the window, we loop over our list of `PhotoImages` using the `enumerate` function, which keeps track of the index within the list. We can use that index to figure out which cell to place the `Button` in via the `divmod` function. This function takes a number to be divided as the first argument, and a number to divide that number by as its second. We supply our `index` value as the to-be-divided number, and 3 (the number of rows and columns in our resultant grid) as the to-be-divided-by number. The `divmod` function returns a 2-tuple containing the amount of times the first number can be wholly divided by the second, and the remainder.

For example, since the number 4 can be divided by 3 once, with a remainder of 1, the result of divmod(4, 3) will be (1, 1). The result of divmod(6, 3) would be (2, 0) since the number 6 is divided by 3 twice with no remainder.

We can use this tuple to decide the row and column at which to place each Button.

A Button widget is created using the PhotoImage as the image argument to display the smiley. This Button is then put into the window with the grid geometry manager, passing the nsew string to the sticky argument, causing each button to expand as the window's grid expands.

In order to make the window's grid expand when the window changes size, we need to set the weight of each cell to the same value:

```
for i in range(3):
    tk.Grid.columnconfigure(self, i, weight=1)
    tk.Grid.rowconfigure(self, i, weight=1)
```

To adjust the weight of each cell, we need to use the columnconfigure and rowconfigure methods of the Grid class itself. Since we have 3 columns and 3 rows, we loop over the range of 3 and pass each value to this method, along with weight=1 to set each to the same weight.

With that, our __init__ method is finished. Now we need to write the method that each smilie button will call to add its image to the text_area of the chat window:

```
def insert_smilie(self, smilie):
    self.master.add_smilie(smilie)
    self.destroy()
```

This method is provided the PhotoImage of the clicked button, and simply passes this along to the add_smilie method of the master widget, which will be our ChatWindow.

That completes all of the functionality needed for our SmilieSelect class.

To test our SmilieSelect window, all we need to do now is add an if __name__ == "__main__" block:

```
if __name__ == '__main__':
    w = tk.Tk()
    s = SmilieSelect(w)
    w.mainloop()
```

Give your `smilieselect.py` file a run and check out your grid of available smileys. Note that the buttons will not function, since the plain `Tk` widget we are using as its master has no `add_smilie` method:

Now we just need to link this window back to our `ChatWindow` to start sending smileys in our messages. Go back to your `chatwindow.py` file and create the `add_smilie` method:

```
def __init__(self, master, friend_name, friend_avatar, **kwargs):
    ...
    self.text_area.smilies = []

def add_smilie(self, smilie):
    smilie_index = self.text_area.index(self.text_area.image_create(tk.END,
image=smilie))
    self.text_area.smilies.append((smilie_index, smilie))
```

In order to link smileys back to our `text_area`, we will need to add an attribute to it named `smilies`. This will be a list of 2-tuples containing the index at which the image should be added and the `PhotoImage` instance that was used.

Of course, we also need a way to bring up the smiley window from within the `ChatWindow`:

```
from smilieselect import SmilieSelect

def __init__(self, master, friend_name, friend_avatar, **kwargs):
    ...
    self.smilies_image = tk.PhotoImage(file="smilies/mikulka-smile-
cool.png")
    self.smilie_button = ttk.Button(self.bottom_frame,
            image=self.smilies_image, command=self.smilie_chooser,
            style="smilie.TButton")
    ...
    self.bottom_frame.pack(side=tk.BOTTOM, fill=tk.X)
    self.smilie_button.pack(side=tk.LEFT, pady=5)
    self.text_area.pack(side=tk.LEFT, fill=tk.X, expand=1, pady=5)
```

```
        self.send_button.pack(side=tk.RIGHT, pady=5)

    def smilie_chooser(self, event=None):
        SmilieSelect(self)
```

The `SmilieSelect` class is imported and a method named `smilie_chooser` is created, which simply instantiates the class.

In our `__init__` method, we make a button that will spawn this window. The button will feature one of the smileys itself, so a `PhotoImage` with one of them is created and passed to the `image` argument of the `Button`. This `Button` is then packed on the left of the `text_area`.

Running this file will show us a message window that allows us to pick a smiley from the menu and have it appear in our message. However, when we send the message it will disappear:

To get the image to appear in our `messages_area`, we will have to adjust our `send_message` method:

```
def send_message(self, event=None):
    message = self.text_area.get(1.0, tk.END)

    if message.strip() or len(self.text_area.smilies):
        message = "Me: " + message
        self.messages_area.configure(state='normal')
        self.messages_area.insert(tk.END, message)
```

The first change we need is to check for the presence of any smileys in our message, since there's no need to add images if none were selected. The logic for adding the text content of our message is unchanged.

If we do have some smileys in the message then we will have two pieces of information about each—the index at which they were inserted and the `PhotoImage` instance that represents them. Since we never know how many lines will already be in our `messages_area`, we can ignore the line number portion of the index and just get the character number from it.

To know where to place the image in our `messages_area`, we need to get the last line number from it. We can then join that to the character number from the smiley index and create the index at which we need to insert the image:

```
if len(self.text_area.smilies):
    last_line_no = self.messages_area.index(tk.END)
    last_line_no = str(last_line_no).split('.')[0]
    last_line_no = str(int(last_line_no) - 2)
```

The line with our previous message in it is calculated by getting the index of the end of the `Text` widget and taking off 2 from the line number to accommodate for newline characters:

```
for index, file in self.text_area.smilies:
    char_index = str(index).split('.')[1]
    char_index = str(int(char_index) + 4)
    smilile_index = last_line_no + '.' + char_index
    self.messages_area.image_create(smilile_index, image=file)

self.text_area.smilies = []
```

Now that we have the correct line number, we can loop through any smileys added by the submitted message and find their character number. Note that we need to add 4 to this to take into account the `Me:` which has been added to the beginning of our message.

This character number is then joined to our calculated line number with a full stop character to create a Tkinter index, and we give this to the `image_create` method to add our smiley image.

Once we have added all of the chosen smileys to the `messages_area`, we need to clear the `smilies` attribute of our `text_area`, so that the smileys that were added in this message are not sent along with the next message as well:

```
self.text_area.delete(1.0, tk.END)

return "break"
```

The method is finished off in the same way as before, by removing the contents of the `text_area` and returning the `break` string to prevent any default behaviors.

Give this file a run now and see your messages get sent along with any smileys you included!

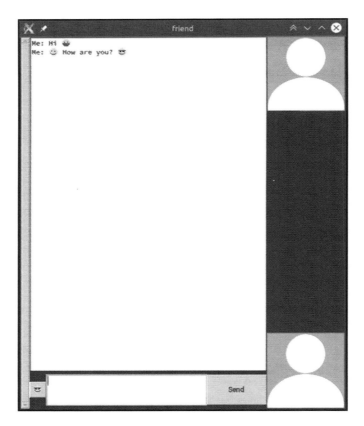

That is where we will finish off this chapter. We have now laid out some components of a chat system that we are ready to connect to the internet. Soon, our application will send its messages to a server as well as update the window itself, and our friends will be able to see our messages and talk back, too!

Summary

In this chapter, we covered something that inevitably comes up when making GUI applications—scrolling a window.

We saw that in order to scroll a window we need to use a widget that supports it, such as a Canvas widget. The advantage of the Canvas widget is that we can use the create_window method to insert other widgets inside of it to act as windows. These windows function as their regular widget, and are then able to be scrolled.

Speaking of creating widgets inside others, we also learned how to add images inside a Text widget by using the image_create method. This method only needs the index at which to create the image and a PhotoImage instance.

The design implementation for our chat application has been considered, and the necessary windows and widgets are all in place and ready to connect.

We have now practiced using one of the alternate geometry managers—grid. We have seen how easily this allows us to lay out our widgets in an even grid, and we also saw how to make the grid expand when the window is resized using columnconfigure and rowconfigure.

In the next chapter, we will get our application online! We will be using the flask module to write a simple web server that our application can connect to. This server will handle sending messages from us to our friends, and vice versa. We will also be able to create user accounts so that actual friends can be added and removed.

Connecting – Getting Our Chat Client Online

9

In this chapter, we will be connecting our chat application to a web service written using the flask microframework. We will learn how to write a small flask application that handles HTTP requests and updates a sqlite database in the process. We will then take advantage of the `requests` module to allow for easy communication between a graphical application and a web service.

In this chapter, we will cover the following topics:

- Using the `flask` module to create a web service
- Handling both GET and POST requests in flask
- Using a sqlite database for persistent storage
- Making HTTP requests using the `requests` module

Let's begin by having a look at flask. We'll take a tour of what it is and how it works before using it to create a web service that can handle which users exist in our chat application and who is allowed to talk to whom.

Introduction to flask

The `flask` module provides a microframework for creating web applications with Python. It makes heavy use of decorators to make handling HTTP requests very simple. It also keeps a lot of the internals away from your code, making what you write very easy to read, even with little knowledge of flask itself.

Since this book teaches by example, let's get right into setting up a flask server.

Our first web page

The first step is to install flask. As usual, we can install flask using `pip` inside a virtual environment.

Using the command line, navigate to the folder where you have been writing your chat application and enter the following commands:

```
python3 -m venv env

source env/bin/activate

pip install flask
```

Pip should take care of installing flask, along with its dependencies, inside your new virtual environment.

Once this has finished, create a folder named `server` alongside your Python files for the previous chapter. This is where we will be placing our web service for the chat application.

Inside this folder, create a file named `server.py` and place the following code inside:

```python
from flask import Flask

app = Flask(__name__)
app.config.from_object(__name__)

@app.route("/")
def index():
    return "This is a flask website!"


if __name__ == '__main__':
    app.run(debug=True)
```

With these few lines of code, we now have a functioning web server. We just need to run it before we can visit it in a web browser.

If you have closed your terminal session from earlier, open a new one and navigate into your root directory for this project. Load the virtual environment with `source env/bin/activate`, move into the `server` folder, and run `python3 server.py`. Your terminal should respond with something like this:

```
* Running on http://127.0.0.1:5000/ (Press CTRL+C to quit)
* Restarting with stat
* Debugger is active!
* Debugger PIN: 143-718-128
```

Head on over to `http://127.0.0.1:5000/` in a web browser and see your web page in action:

You should be able to see the string that was returned in your index function appear in your web browser. So, how did this happen? Let's break down the code sample:

```
from flask import Flask

app = Flask(__name__)
app.config.from_object(__name__)
```

The first three lines are very standard flask setup. You will likely see every flask application include these three.

In order to use flask, we obviously need to import it. The main class which handles a flask application is called `Flask`.

It is convention for your instance of the `Flask` class to be named `app`. The next two lines simply handle creating the `flask` instance and configuring it.

After our application is configured, we need to assign some URLs to it. We do this using decorators:

```
@app.route("/")
def index():
    return "This is a flask website!"
```

One particular decorator we can use is the `@app.route` decorator. This adds a route to your application using the specified string as the path.

In this example, we used the string /, which means the root of your URL.

To experiment with this, try changing this parameter to /hello, then visiting `http://127.0.0.1:5000/`. Since there is no longer a route at your root URL, this will result in a 404 error. If you instead visit `http://127.0.0.1:5000/hello`, you will once again see your message appear.

Once all of our routes are configured, we just need to run the application. Luckily, flask provides an easy way to achieve that:

```
if __name__ == '__main__':
    app.run(debug=True)
```

We simply need to call the `run` method on our `app` to get our server running. We pass `debug=True` while developing, as this gives us a very detailed stack trace if any errors occur.

Now we know how to return a simple web page from a flask application. However, we won't be dealing with web pages in our chat application. Instead, we just want raw data.

In order to receive this data from a web service, we can return something called **JavaScript Object Notation (JSON)**. It provides a nice way of sending data over the internet, and is very similar to a Python dictionary. So similar, in fact, that JSON data is written as a dictionary and read back into one too.

Using JSON

Let's modify our simple example to return JSON instead of a web page:

```
from flask import Flask, jsonify

...
@app.route("/")
def index():
```

```
data = {
    "cats": 5,
    "people": 8,
    "dogs": 4
}

return jsonify(data)
```

. . .

Flask comes with a module called `jsonify`, which translates a dictionary into JSON and returns it as the response. This makes handling JSON data very easy.

In this example, we create a dictionary with some example values. In a proper application, this could instead be data which has been pulled from a database and manipulated in some way.

This data is then passed to the `jsonify` function and given to the requesting application in JSON format.

Make sure your web server is running (run `python3 server.py` if it isn't), then open up a web browser and go over to `http://127.0.0.1:5000` again. This time, you should see your response laid out differently. The exact format will depend on the web browser you are using. This screenshot shows how the response looks in Firefox version 60:

So, now that we have JSON coming from our web service, how do we use it in practice?

This question leads us nicely to the next topic—the `requests` module.

The requests module

Requests was written to make HTTP requests very simple and human-readable. In simple terms, it lets us visit a web address directly in Python code instead of having to use a browser. This also gives us back the data returned from the server, meaning we can make use of it in our Python code.

We can use requests to grab data back from our flask web service and use it in some Python code. We will begin with a small demo script which will make use of the data which is being returned from our `index` function.

First things first; we need to install the `requests` module via `pip`. Make sure your virtual environment is sourced and run `pip install requests` in your command line.

Sending a GET request

A GET request allows the requester (often called a **client**) to receive some information from a server. We can use a GET request to ask our server for some data in JSON format, which we can then use in the rest of the script.

Ensure your flask server is still running, then, open up a new Python file. Add the following content:

```
import requests

r = requests.get("http://127.0.0.1:5000")
data = r.json()

print(f"There are {data['people']} people. {data['cats']} of them have a
cat, and {data['dogs']} of them have a dog")
```

In this example, we import the `requests` module and use it to send a GET request to our server using its `get` method.

Since our server returns JSON, we can use the `json` method to parse the result into a Python dictionary, which we call `data`.

This `data` dictionary is then available to be used as a regular Python dictionary, which is demonstrated by using its attributes in a call to `print`.

Run the example and you should see the following output:

```
> python3 demo/req.py
There are 8 people. 5 of them have a cat, and 4 of them have a dog
```

From this, you can see that the content of our `data` dictionary on the server was transferred successfully to this new script.

So, we've seen that we can get data from a server into an arbitrary script easily using the `requests` module, but what about sending data from our script to the server?

Thankfully, requests allows us to do that too, using an HTTP POST request.

Sending a POST request

A POST request allows us to send data over to the server which it can then process as it needs to. It is a common method for saving or updating data that is stored in a database on the server machine.

Let's try this out now; open up your server and add a new endpoint as follows:

```
from flask import Flask, jsonify, request
...
@app.route("/send_me_data", methods=["POST"])
def send_me_data():
    data = request.form
    for key, value in data.items():
        print("received", key, "with value", value)

    return "Thanks"
...
```

This function includes a second argument in the route decorator called `methods`. This argument specifies the HTTP methods, which are allowed to be sent to this endpoint. Since we want to send data using a POST request, we set this value to a list containing just the string POST.

To access the data sent over a POST request, the `request` object itself must be first imported from the `flask` module. `flask` module then provides an `ImmutableDict` class which can be found in the `request.form` object. We can loop over this dictionary and do whatever we need to do with its data. In this case, we just print everything received to the command-line window.

To ensure the requester receives a response, we return the string `Thanks`.

Now, let's adjust our requesting script to use this new endpoint:

```
import requests

data = {
    "pens": 12,
    "pencils": "eight",
}

r = requests.post("http://127.0.0.1:5000/send_me_data", data=data)
print(r.text)
```

We now create some data in our script and use the `post` method of the `requests` module to send this to our new endpoint. The `data` argument of this method is a dictionary of data to send over.

Since our endpoint is no longer returning JSON, we can print `r.text` to display its response.

Give this script a run and you should see `Thanks` come back from the server:

```
> python3 demo/req.py
Thanks
```

If you then check on your server, you should see, amongst some of the normal output of `flask`, that the data that was sent over has also been printed:

```
Restarting with inotify reloader
* Debugger is active!
* Debugger PIN: 232-123-067
received pens with value 12
received pencils with value eight
127.0.0.1 - - [27/Feb/2018 16:39:47] "POST /send_me_data HTTP/1.1" 200 -
```

This means that our sending of data from the requester to the server was successful!

That's the basics of sending and receiving data over HTTP covered. It's now time to make some of the data meaningful and introduce some form of permanent storage.

The sqlite3 module

SQLite is a database technology which comes included with Python, via the `sqlite3` module. It works by creating a file on the user's filesystem which is then altered using basic SQL syntax.

Since data stored in a SQLite database is stored on disk, it can be used as a form of permanent storage for web and GUI applications.

Using sqlite in Python is as easy as importing the built-in `sqlite3` module and then sending it several SQL queries.

We will be using sqlite to store some data about our chat application on the server. Let's have an introduction to sqlite by creating data storage for the users of our chat application.

Creating a database and table

Inside your `server` folder, create a new Python file named `create_database.py` and add the following code:

```python
import sqlite3

database = sqlite3.connect("chat.db")
cursor = database.cursor()

create_users_sql = "CREATE TABLE users (username TEXT, real_name TEXT)"
cursor.execute(create_users_sql)

database.commit()
database.close()
```

After importing the `sqlite3` module, we connect to a database named `chat.db`. This database will become a file inside our `server` folder once the code has run.

We use this connection to receive a `cursor`, which is able to perform SQL queries over a database.

The SQL query to create a table inside our database comes next. It is customary to write the keywords of SQL in capital letters to easily distinguish your databases, tables, and columns from the rest of the query. We create a table named `users`, which will hold two columns—`username` and `real_name`.

We can then pass this query to our `cursor` and use its `execute` method to carry out the query. This will create our table inside the database.

SQL relies on things called **transactions**, which allow for a user to roll back any updates which they may not want to keep. This is useful if a database is updated at one point in a script but, later on, an error occurs, which means we no longer want to keep that update.

In order to tell our transaction that we do indeed want to make it persist, we call the `commit` method. This makes our `users` table permanent.

Once we are done with a database connection, we can then close it to free up resources. This is achieved with the `close` method.

Run this file and your database should be created! You will see a file named `chat.db` has appeared in your `server` folder which holds the database and its `users` table.

Now that we have this prepared and ready, it's time to begin adding data to it.

Adding data to a SQLite database

In order to add data to our SQLite database, we need to use an `insert` statement. We provide the insert statement with the name of the table we are updating and the values we wish to add to this table. We can then execute this as a query in the same way as before.

The insert syntax is as follows:

```
INSERT INTO table (column1, column2) VALUES (value1, value2);
```

So, for our `users` table, we could use the following:

```
INSERT INTO users (username, real_name) VALUES ("davidlove", "David Love");
```

Since we are going to be doing this from various flask endpoints, we should establish a method of doing this easily. To achieve this, make a file in your `server` folder, called `database.py` and add the following code:

```
import sqlite3

def add_user(username, real_name):
    sql = "INSERT INTO users (username, real_name) VALUES (?, ?)"
    query_params = (username, real_name)

    perform_insert(sql, query_params)
```

This function will allow us to easily add new users by just providing their `username` and `real_name` as strings.

You may notice that our query contains question marks. When using variables as part of a database query there is the potential for abuse, known as **SQL injection**, which could allow someone with malicious intent to gain unauthorized access to data.

To mitigate this, database-related libraries typically allow the user to enter question marks in place of variables within a query, then pass in the variable to insert as a second parameter. The library will then take care of sanitizing the user's input and building the full query to execute.

In this example, the question marks take the place of the provided `username` and `real_name`, which are instead stored as a tuple named `query_params` and passed to the `perform_insert` function.

This function will then take care of running a query with the given arguments:

```
def perform_insert(sql, params):
    conn = sqlite3.connect('chat.db')
    cursor = conn.cursor()
    cursor.execute(sql, params)
    conn.commit()
    conn.close()
```

This function should look familiar, as it does a lot of what we did in order to create the database.

It opens a connection to the `chat.db` file, gets a cursor from it, executes the SQL query (along with the given parameters), commits, and, finally, closes the connection.

Since we need to perform these steps every time we want to run a query, we have separated this piece of code into a function, avoiding repetition, and making the other functions smaller and easier to understand.

Now that we have the ability to enter some users, let's try it out from the REPL:

```
Python 3.6.4 (default, Jan 03 2018, 13:52:55) [GCC] on linux
Type "help", "copyright", "credits" or "license" for more information.
>>> import database
>>> database.add_user("davidlove", "David Love")
>>>
```

Well, it looks like we added a user, but there's no actual feedback. How can we check which users we have now?

In order to see the content of a database, we need to perform a `select` statement.

Selecting data from a SQLite database

A `select` statement needs to know the table being read and the fields which the user wants returned. The basic syntax is as follows:

```
SELECT field1, field2 FROM table;
```

So, to read the users from our `users` table, we can do the following:

```
SELECT username, real_name from users;
```

Again, as we will be doing this repeatedly, writing a function that will do it for us is a good idea.

Add the following to `database.py`:

```
def get_all_users():
    sql = "SELECT username, real_name FROM users"
    params = []

    return perform_select(sql, params)
```

Here, we provide the basic `select` statement as the `sql` variable and an empty list as the `params` variable, since we do not need to include any user-supplied data.

Once again, everything which handles the database connection has been separated into a new function, this time named `perform_select`:

```
def perform_select(sql, params):
    conn = sqlite3.connect('chat.db')
    cursor = conn.cursor()
    cursor.execute(sql, params)
    results = cursor.fetchall()
    conn.close()

    return results
```

This function, unlike `perform_insert`, does not modify the data inside our database. This means we do not need to call `commit` as there are no changes.

Instead, we need to call `fetchall`, which will return a list of all results which are returned by the query. After closing the connection, we return this list.

Now that we have implemented this, we can head back to our REPL and check whether our insert was successful:

```
Python 3.6.4 (default, Jan 03 2018, 13:52:55) [GCC] on linux
Type "help", "copyright", "credits" or "license" for more information.
>>> import database
>>> database.get_all_users()
[('davidlove', 'David Love')]
```

Great! Looks like our `insert` statement was successful and we have our user inside the `users` table.

That covers the basics of using sqlite. We will learn some more advanced features while developing our chat application, but the basics are in place for now.

Now that our database is in place, we can hook it up to the web service we have running. This will allow us to use `flask` and `requests` to query the database from within a Tkinter GUI, such as our chat application.

Linking flask and sqlite

We now need to import and use our database module inside our server module. In order to make this easier, we should first wrap all of our functions in a class.

Update your `database.py` file, creating a class named `Database` and adding the necessary `self` instances to your methods. We can also move the database name out to an attribute in the `__init__` method:

```
import sqlite3

class Database:
    def __init__(self):
        self.database = "chat.db"

    def perform_insert(self, sql, params):
        conn = sqlite3.connect(self.database)
        ...
```

```
def perform_select(self, sql, params):
    conn = sqlite3.connect(self.database)
    ...

# update the rest of your methods to include self where necessary
```

Now that we have that done, we can import and instantiate the database in our `server.py` file:

```
...
from database import Database
...
database = Database()
...
```

With our database in place, we can go ahead and turn the `get_all_users` method into an endpoint available via our flask server.

Get rid of the testing endpoints and add this one in their place:

```
@app.route("/get_all_users")
def get_all_users():
    all_users = database.get_all_users()

    return jsonify(all_users)
```

This will simply call the method from our `Database` class with the same name and return the results as JSON.

Visit `http://1227.0.0.1:5000/get_all_users` in your web browser and view the results. You should see the user you created has appeared on screen. You will notice, however, that the data is not labeled in any way. It would be much more useful if we could have this as a dictionary instead.

To make this change, we shall go back to our `Database` class and modify the `perform_select` method to return a list of dictionaries instead of a list of tuples:

```
def perform_select(self, sql, params):
    conn = sqlite3.connect(self.database)
    conn.row_factory = sqlite3.Row
    cursor = conn.cursor()
    cursor.execute(sql, params)
    results = [dict(row) for row in cursor.fetchall()]
    conn.close()

    return results
```

We can pass the Row class from `sqlite3` as the `row_factory` attribute of our connection to receive Row instances instead of tuples as the result of our `select` statement.

These Row instances are similar to dictionaries, but are not compatible with JSON. To ensure that our results can be returned as JSON, we need to explicitly convert them to dictionaries. We do this using the `dict` method inside a list comprehension, so that the `results` we return will definitely be a list of dictionaries.

Head back to your web browser and refresh the page. You should now see dictionary results come back from your endpoint:

```
[
  {
    "real_name": "David Love",
    "username": "davidlove"
  }
]
```

We now can simply visit a server endpoint to perform a select query! How about an insert?

To perform an insert, we would need to send data to our web server from our Python application, then have flask store it in sqlite. To try this out, let's write an endpoint that will create new users:

```
@app.route("/add_user")
def add_user():
    data = request.form
    username = data["username"]
    real_name = data["real_name"]
    database.add_user(username, real_name)

    return jsonify(
        "User Created"
    )
```

As before, we use `request.form` to access POST data, then extract values from it like a normal dictionary. We grab the `username` and `real_name` values and pass them over to our `Database`'s add_user method.

We need to return something for the requester to see; so, we just return the string User Created.

One last endpoint to make is to check whether a user already exists. After that, we can go ahead and begin linking our chat application to our web server:

```
@app.route("/user_exists", methods=["POST"])
def user_exists():
    username = request.form.get("username")
    exists = database.user_exists(username)

    return jsonify({
        "exists": exists
    })
```

This endpoint will return JSON with one key—exists. The requester can then extract the value of this key to tell whether or not the username is already in the database.

Of course, we need a method of the same name in our Database class now:

```
def user_exists(self, username):
    sql = "SELECT username FROM users WHERE username = ?"
    params = (username,)

    results = self.perform_select(sql, params)

    if len(results):
        return True

    return False
```

The SQL used by this method uses a new element of a select query—the where clause. As you may be able to tell, this is a way of filtering the results to include only those which match certain criteria. In this case, we want to return records which have a username which matches a provided variable. To achieve this, we add WHERE username = ? to the end of our select statement. Recall that the question mark will be replaced with our username variable when executing the query.

Since we do not actually want the returned record, merely to check for its existence, we can use len(results) to check how many records were returned. If this function returns any number above 0, the username must exist; so, we return True. Otherwise, the username is not in our database and we can return False.

With the setup finished, we can finally go back to our chat application and begin utilizing our web service.

Updating our FriendsList class

The first thing we can do with our `FriendList` class is provide some sort of login system. Since each user has a unique username and real name, we can use these credentials to identify the user who runs the application. Normally, a system would also require a password, but we can skip that for this implementation.

In order to display the login screen to the user, we will need to take away the default behavior of showing the friends list straight away and instead display some widgets for the user to enter their details.

Open your `friendist.py` file again and begin by extracting parts of the __init__ method to a new one. Your new __init__ will look like this:

```
class FriendsList(tk.Tk):
    def __init__(self, **kwargs):
        super().__init__(**kwargs)

        self.title('Tk Chat')
        self.geometry('700x500')

        self.menu = tk.Menu(self, bg="lightgrey", fg="black", tearoff=0)

        self.friends_menu = tk.Menu(self.menu, fg="black",
                                    bg="lightgrey", tearoff=0)
        self.friends_menu.add_command(label="Add Friend",
                                      command=self.add_friend)

        self.menu.add_cascade(label="Friends", menu=self.friends_menu)

        self.show_login_screen()
```

The code which has been removed from here will go into a method called `show_friends`, as follows:

```
    def show_friends(self):
        self.configure(menu=self.menu)
        self.login_frame.pack_forget()

        self.canvas = tk.Canvas(self, bg="white")
        self.canvas_frame = tk.Frame(self.canvas)

        self.scrollbar = ttk.Scrollbar(self, orient="vertical",
                                       command=self.canvas.yview)
        self.canvas.configure(yscrollcommand=self.scrollbar.set)
```

```
        self.scrollbar.pack(side=tk.LEFT, fill=tk.Y)
        self.canvas.pack(side=tk.LEFT, expand=1, fill=tk.BOTH)

        self.friends_area = self.canvas.create_window((0, 0),
                    window=self.canvas_frame, anchor="nw")

        self.bind_events()
        self.load_friends()
```

Looking over our new __init__, you will see that, once the normal variables are set and the menu is created, we go off to a method called `show_login_screen`. This will put a `Frame` in the window, which contains `Entry` widgets for the user to enter their username and real name, and buttons to either log in or create a new account:

```
    def show_login_screen(self):
        self.login_frame = ttk.Frame(self)
        username_label = ttk.Label(self.login_frame, text="Username")
        self.username_entry = ttk.Entry(self.login_frame)

        real_name_label = ttk.Label(self.login_frame, text="Real Name")
        self.real_name_entry = ttk.Entry(self.login_frame)
```

We begin by making a `Frame` to hold all of our widgets. Since the layout will represent a grid, we will be using the `grid` geometry manager in this frame, meaning there will be no need to add additional `Frame` widgets inside of it.

As we want the user to be able to enter their username and real name, we will need two `Entry` widgets for them to type in, as well as two `Label` widgets to indicate what information goes into each.

The `Entry` widgets will need to be attributes, so that we can get their values in other methods, but the rest will not need to be referenced, so they can be regular variables:

```
    login_button = ttk.Button(self.login_frame, text="Login",
    command=self.login)
    create_account_button = ttk.Button(self.login_frame, text="Create Account",
    command=self.create_account)
```

We also have two Button widgets, which will let the user have the ability to either log in with the provided credentials or use them to create a new account:

```
username_label.grid(row=0, column=0, sticky='e')
self.username_entry.grid(row=0, column=1)

real_name_label.grid(row=1, column=0, sticky='e')
self.real_name_entry.grid(row=1, column=1)

login_button.grid(row=2, column=0, sticky='e')
create_account_button.grid(row=2, column=1)
```

With all of our widgets defined, we can begin adding them to our Frame. We use grid to create a 2 x 3 grid inside the Frame:

```
for i in range(3):
    tk.Grid.rowconfigure(self.login_frame, i, weight=1)
    tk.Grid.columnconfigure(self.login_frame, i, weight=1)

self.login_frame.pack(fill=tk.BOTH, expand=1)
```

We again loop over each cell and set them to an equal weight, allowing our layout to persist as the user resizes their window.

Finally, we use pack to add our login_frame to the window, telling it to fill both directions and expand to the full size.

Before we can see this in action, we will need to define the two methods called by the new buttons. We can just use placeholder methods for now:

```
def login(self):
    pass

def create_account(self):
    pass
```

You should now be able to run your `friendslist.py` file and see your new login screen, as follows:

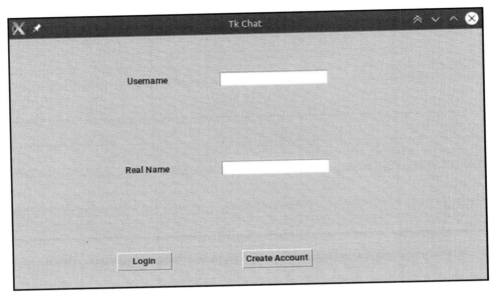

To actually complete the methods that these buttons will call, we are going to need to connect our `FriendsList` class up to our web service. In order to keep the logic nicely contained, we will be creating a new class to handle all of this.

Creating the Requester class

Make yourself a new file in the same folder as your `friendslist.py` file named `requester.py`:

```
import json
import requests

class Requester:
    def __init__(self):
        self.url = "http://127.0.0.1:5000"
```

As the name implies, the `Requester` class will be making use of the `requests` module to communicate with our web service. We will also need to use the `json` module to read any data which is returned.

In our __init__, we just need to keep a reference to the URL at which our web service operates. Keeping it here means that, if we change it for any reason, we only have one place in this class to update.

Since our web service uses both GET and POST endpoints, we can generalize our requesting by extracting it to a method:

```
def request(self, method, endpoint, params=None):
    url = self.url + endpoint

    if method == "GET":
    r = requests.get(url, params=params)
        return r.text
    else:
        r = requests.post(url, data=params)

        return r.json()
```

This method will take the `request` method (GET or POST), the `endpoint` (which should match that in the relevant `app.route` decorator in our server file) and any parameters which need to be passed.

Based on the `request` method, it will send our parameters using a different keyword argument to the method provided by `requests` and return different parts of the response.

If it was a GET request, we will return `r.text`, which contains any text returned from the server. If it was a POST request instead, our server will have returned JSON, so we need to use the `json` method to convert it to a Python dictionary.

Now that we have this method in place, we can begin implementing our login and account creation calls.

When logging in, we just need to check that the provided username and real name exist in our database, so we have to call the `/user_exists` endpoint:

```
def login(self, username, real_name):
    endpoint = "/user_exists"
    params = {"username": username}

    user_exists = self.request("POST", endpoint, params)

    return user_exists["exists"]
```

We pass the endpoint the provided `username` and return the value of the `exists` key in the JSON returned by the server.

When creating an account, we should also first check whether the user exists and only create the account if they do not:

```
def create_account(self, username, real_name):
    endpoint = "/user_exists"
    params = {"username": username}
    exists = self.request("POST", endpoint, params)

    if exists["exists"]:
        return False

    endpoint = "/add_user"
    params["real_name"] = real_name

    self.request("POST", endpoint, params)

    return True
```

Here, we see much the same code as before, except if the user does already exist, we want to return `False`. If they do not, we then call the `/add_user` endpoint, providing the real name as well, then return `True`.

Now that our `Requester` is in place, we can import it in our `FriendsList` and connect it to the web service.

Connecting our FriendsList to our web service

To get our `FriendsList` talking to our web service, we first need an instance of our new `Requester`. We will also import `messagebox`, so that we can show some pop-up windows if there are any errors:

```
import tkinter.messagebox as msg
from requester import Requester
...
    def __init__(self, **kwargs):
        ...
        self.requester = Requester()
        ...
```

With this in place, we can write the actual `login` and `create_account` methods:

```
def login(self):
    username = self.username_entry.get()
    real_name = self.real_name_entry.get()

    if self.requester.login(username, real_name):
        self.username = username
        self.real_name = real_name

        self.show_friends()
    else:
        msg.showerror("Failed", f"Could not log in as {username}")
```

To log in, we first use the `get` method to retrieve the text inside our two `Entry` widgets, then pass them to the `login` method of our `requester`.

If the call to the web service is successful, we set the current `username` and `real_name` to attributes of this class, then call the `show_friends` method, which will display our test friend as before.

If the provided details do not exist in our database, we will receive a negative response from our web service. We will show this to the user using a message box, letting them know they were not able to log in.

If they instead pick the `Create Account` button, we will call this method:

```
def create_account(self):
    username = self.username_entry.get()
    real_name = self.real_name_entry.get()

    if self.requester.create_account(username, real_name):
        self.username = username
        self.real_name = real_name

        self.show_friends()
    else:
        msg.showerror("Failed", "Account already exists!")
```

This method is very similar to the `login` method, but calls the `create_account` method of our `requester` and displays a different message if the call to the web service returned a negative response.

You can now run your `friendslist.py` file and try creating an account and logging in.

Once logged in, you will still see the placeholder friend which we set up last chapter. Since we have a database full of accounts now, we can go ahead and replace this with the other people in our database.

To make our `FriendsList` display existing users, we need to create a method in our `Requester` which will fetch them all:

```
def get_all_users(self):
    endpoint = "/get_all_users"
    users = self.request("GET", endpoint)

    return json.loads(users)
```

The endpoint to fetch all users is a GET endpoint which takes no parameters; so, we only need to specify the `endpoint` argument in order to make this request.

As our web service returns a JSON object with no particular key, we can just parse it using the `json` module's `loads` method and return it to our `FriendsList`.

Now, we can loop over the returned users and display them in our application:

```
def load_friends(self):
    all_users = self.requester.get_all_users()

    for user in all_users:
        if user['username'] != self.username:
            friend_frame = ttk.Frame(self.canvas_frame)
```

We call the `get_all_users` method we just wrote, then use a `for` loop to iterate over each user. This user will be a dictionary containing their username and real name.

Since we don't need to be able to talk to ourselves, we can ignore a user who has a username matching the one we have set as our `username` attribute.

For each user, we will create a `Frame` to hold their related widgets. These widgets will be the same as they were before:

```
profile_photo = tk.PhotoImage(file="images/avatar.png")
profile_photo_label = ttk.Label(friend_frame, image=profile_photo)
profile_photo_label.image = profile_photo

friend_name = ttk.Label(friend_frame, text=user['real_name'], anchor=tk.W)

message_this_friend = partial(self.open_chat_window,
```

```
        username=user["username"], real_name=user["real_name"])
    message_button = ttk.Button(friend_frame, text="Chat",
    command=message_this_friend)
```

There are two main changes we have made to the widgets this time – the `friend_name` `Label` now contains the `real_name` attribute from the `user` dictionary, and each `Chat` button will now need to open a specific conversation window (which we will make adjustments for next).

In order to create a different function for each user in our dictionary, we will be using a `partial` function. This allows us to freeze the arguments of a provided function. Here, we have given the `open_chat_window` method and frozen the `username` and `real_name` arguments as those from our dictionary.

We then finish off the method by packing our widgets, as normal:

```
    profile_photo_label.pack(side=tk.LEFT)
    friend_name.pack(side=tk.LEFT)
    message_button.pack(side=tk.RIGHT)

    friend_frame.pack(fill=tk.X, expand=1)
```

With this method updated, we now need to adjust our `open_chat_window` method to accept the `username` and `real_name` arguments and do something with them:

```
    def open_chat_window(self, username, real_name):
        cw = ChatWindow(self, real_name, username, 'images/avatar.png')
```

As this method just instantiates the `ChatWindow` class, all we need to do is pass the `username` and `real_name` values over to it. We now need to implement these variables in this class, too.

Connecting our ChatWindow

The first thing to do with our `ChatWindow` is allow it to receive the `username` variable:

```
    class ChatWindow(tk.Toplevel):
        def __init__(self, master, friend_name, friend_username, friend_avatar,
    **kwargs):
            ...
            self.friend_username = friend_username
```

You may be wondering why we need this variable here. The reason we will be requiring it is to help keep track of the conversation history.

There will be a separate database holding conversations between you and each individual friend, to make for very easy retrieval of the conversation history. This will, of course, require changes to our web service and, of course, our `Requester` will need to be updated too.

Let's begin with the necessary server adjustments to facilitate the conversation databases.

Updating our server to store conversations

As mentioned, each conversation will be contained to its own SQLite database. For easy organization, go ahead and create a folder named `conversations` inside your `server` folder to hold each of these.

We will use a clever naming convention, which ensures that the same database is accessed by both users involved in the conversation, thus avoiding data duplication.

Creating the Conversation class

Inside your `server` folder (not the new `conversations` folder), create a file named `conversation.py`. This will hold a class of the same name, which handles the sqlite side of creating and interacting with these databases:

```
import sqlite3

class Conversation:
    def __init__(self, database):
        self.database = database
```

This looks much like the `__init__` method of our `Database` class, but it will have its SQLite database filename passed to it, allowing this class to work with multiple different conversation databases.

The first method we will need to write is one that will create the table inside the database:

```
def initialise_table(self):
    sql = "CREATE TABLE conversation (author text, message text, date_sent
text)"
    conn = sqlite3.connect(self.database)
    cursor = conn.cursor()
    cursor.execute(sql)
    conn.commit()
    conn.close()
```

From the `create` statement, we can see that each database will hold a single table called `conversation`. This table will hold three pieces of information about each entry—the author (who sent the message), the message text itself, and the date when the message was sent.

 Sqlite does not have a data type to represent a date, so we will just be using text to store this.

After the creation of the `sql` statement follows all of the connection handling code we have seen before. If you wish to extract this to a method again, feel free.

Now that we have the tables created, we can write a method to read the data from them:

```
def get_history(self):
    sql = "SELECT * FROM conversation"
    conn = sqlite3.connect(self.database)
    conn.row_factory = sqlite3.Row
    cursor = conn.cursor()
    cursor.execute(sql)
    results = [dict(row) for row in cursor.fetchall()]
    conn.close()

    return results
```

This method creates a query which extracts all information from the database and returns it as a dictionary. If you have not seen the `select *` statement before, this simply tells the database to return all columns. This saves the need to type out each column individually and update the query if a new column is added at a later point.

Returning data is nice, but there's no point if we cannot add data too!

```
def add_message(self, author, message, date_sent):
    sql = "INSERT INTO conversation VALUES (?, ?, ?)"
    params = (author, message, date_sent)
    conn = sqlite3.connect(self.database)
    cursor = conn.cursor()
    cursor.execute(sql, params)
    conn.commit()
    conn.close()
```

With this final method, we can now add data to our table. The `author`, `message`, and `date_sent` passed to this method are stored in the relevant column of our `conversation` table.

That finishes off our `Conversation` class. We can now update our web service to communicate with it.

Using the Conversation class in our server

To integrate the `Conversation` class with our flask server, we need to create some endpoints that will call its methods. Since the `Conversation` class needs a database passed in, we will also have to deduce which database we are writing to in our endpoints.

The following naming conventions will be used for our databases:

- Take the username of the author
- Take the username of the person receiving the message
- Arrange them alphabetically
- Join them with an underscore
- Add `.db` as the file extension

When we name our database as such, we will only have one database per two people conversing. Arranging the names alphabetically when determining the database to use ensures that it doesn't matter which user opens the conversation; they will always refer to the same database.

Since we are requiring usernames to be unique, we shouldn't ever have a clash of database names, either.

Let's create the method which determines the database file from two provided usernames. Since this is just a helper function, it does not need its own route:

```
...
from conversation import Conversation
...
conversations_dir = os.path.abspath(os.path.join(os.path.dirname(__file__),
'conversations/'))
...

def get_conversation_db_path_for_users(data):
    user_one = data["user_one"]
    user_two = data["user_two"]
    users_in_order = sorted([user_one, user_two])
    users_in_order = "_".join(users_in_order)
    conversation_db = users_in_order + ".db"
    conversation_db_path = os.path.join(conversations_dir, conversation_db)
    return conversation_db_path
```

Since our conversation databases will all be kept in the `conversations` folder, we create an absolute path to this directory and save it in a variable named `conversations_dir`. We can then use this to keep the location of all the databases consistent.

Our `get_conversation_db_path_for_users` will take a dictionary, which should have `user_one` and `user_two` as keys. These will contain the two usernames of the people who are talking.

As mentioned, these will be ordered alphabetically and joined with an underscore, before `.db` is added on to create the full filename. The database filename is then joined to the `conversations_dir` to create the full path to the file.

Now that we are able to determine the database file from two usernames, we can write the endpoints which use this function.

The first endpoint will initialize the database with its table if it does not already exist:

```
@app.route("/create_conversation_db", methods=["POST"])
def create_conversation_db():
    conversation_db_path = get_conversation_db_path_for_users(request.form)

    if not os.path.exists(conversation_db_path):
        conversation = Conversation(conversation_db_path)
        conversation.initialise_table()

    return jsonify({
        "success": True,
    })
```

This method begins by figuring out the conversation database file path from the supplied POST parameters. If this does not correspond to an existing file, we initialize an instance of our `Conversation` class and tell it to initialize the table.

We don't need any feedback from this endpoint, so, we can just return a simple JSON object.

Now, we can write an endpoint which obtains the conversation history between two users:

```
@app.route("/get_message_history", methods=["POST"])
def get_message_history():
    conversation_db_path = get_conversation_db_path_for_users(request.form)
    conversation = Conversation(conversation_db_path)
    history = conversation.get_history()

    return jsonify({
        "history": history
    })
```

We again use the POST parameters to get the conversation database, and then use this to create an instance of our `Conversation` class.

The history is obtained with the `get_history` method of the `Conversation` instance and this is returned as JSON to the requester.

Finally, we need an endpoint to add messages to the conversation database, which can be called by our `ChatWindow`:

```
import arrow
...

@app.route("/send_message/<username>", methods=["POST"])
def send_message(username):
    data = request.form
    author = data["author"]
    message = data["message"]
    date_sent = arrow.now().timestamp

    conversation_db_path = get_conversation_db_path_for_users({"user_one":
author, "user_two": username})
    conversation = Conversation(conversation_db_path)
    conversation.add_message(author, message, date_sent)

    return jsonify({
        "success": True
    })
```

This endpoint shows some syntax, which we have not yet come across. In order to extract a part of a URL as a variable, we can wrap it in pointy brackets inside the `route` string, then include it as an argument with the decorated function. In the preceding example, we have done this with the `username` variable.

This now means that, if we visit `http://127.0.0.1:5000/send_message/James`, our `username` variable will be `James`.

Along with the receiver's username, we also extract the author and message from the POST data. Our `date_sent` will be set to the current timestamp.

I have used the arrow library to handle the timestamp, which can be installed with `pip install arrow`. You could also use the `datetime` module to get the timestamp if you would prefer.

We can construct the necessary parameters for our `get_db_path_for_users` function by putting the `author` and `username` variables into a dictionary. This then gives us the path to the conversation database, which we can use to create a `Conversation` instance and use its `add_message` method to insert our message.

Again, we shouldn't need any feedback from this endpoint, so we can just return JSON, which lets the requester know that it has completed.

Our server is now equipped to update the relevant conversation database in response to some web requests. The next thing to do is to update our `Requester` to send them.

Adding the new endpoints to our Requester

When the user opens up a chat window with a friend, our `Requester` will need to contact the web server to retrieve the conversation history. If there is no conversation history to be obtained, then we will want to initialize the database to prevent errors.

Since initializing the database when it already exists will do nothing, we are safe to call the endpoint even if a database already exists.

We can take advantage of this in our `Requester`, so that we can skip adding a separate method for initialization and, instead, handle it all when getting the history:

```
def prepare_conversation(self, user_one, user_two):
    endpoint = "/create_conversation_db"
    params = {"user_one": user_one, "user_two": user_two}

    self.request("POST", endpoint, params)

    endpoint = "/get_message_history"
    history = self.request("POST", endpoint, params)

    return history
```

The first method to add to our `Requester` is `prepare_conversation`. We can call this each time the user opens a new `ChatWindow` instance. It will create a conversation database if one does not already exist and get the content if it does.

The JSON returned from the web service will just be returned so that the `calling` class has access to it.

We will also need a method to add a message to the database:

```
def send_message(self, author, friend_name, message):
    endpoint = f"/send_message/{friend_name}"
    params = {
        "author": author,
        "message": message,
    }

    self.request("POST", endpoint, params)

    return True
```

The `send_message` method will take the author name, friend name, and message, and then send the appropriate POST request to our web service. Since we don't have any useful information returned from the web service, we can just return `True` here.

Since the username of the person we are messaging is extracted from the URL, we use a format string to insert the `friend_name` variable into the `endpoint` URL.

That concludes the changes we need to make to our `Requester`. Now, everything is finally set up ready for us to connect our `ChatWindow` class!

Updating our ChatWindow class to send requests to the server

With all of the heavy lifting passed over to our other classes, the changes required to our `ChatWindow` class should be very simple.

Firstly, let's update it so that the messages we send are sent to the web service and stored in a conversation database:

```
def send_message(self, event=None):
    message = self.text_area.get(1.0, tk.END)

    if message.strip() or len(self.text_area.smilies):
        self.master.requester.send_message(
            self.master.username,
            self.friend_username,
            message,
```

```
)
    message = "Me: " + message
    self.messages_area.configure(state='normal')
    self.messages_area.insert(tk.END, message)
    ...
```

Before adding the `Me` : and incorporating the smileys into our `messages_area`, we fire off a request to the web service containing our username, the friend's username, and the unaltered message. We can access our username by referring to the `username` attribute of the `FriendsList` class, which will be our `master` widget.

Likewise, instead of creating a `requester` per `ChatWindow`, we can just use the one from our `master` widget.

The rest of this method remains unchanged.

Yes, that's really all that we need to do here to get our `ChatWindow` class connected!

The last thing to add is the conversation history when the user opens up the chat window. For this, we will need two new methods.

We will add a method which updates the `messages_area` with a message without sending it back to the `requester`:

```
def receive_message(self, author, message):
    self.messages_area.configure(state='normal')

    if author == self.master.username:
        author = "Me"

    message_with_author = author + ": " + message

    self.messages_area.insert(tk.END, message_with_author)
    self.messages_area.configure(state='disabled')
```

This method looks like a very abridged version of `send_message`, since it will just receive a message and its author, swap the author's name to `Me` if the author matches the stored username, and then add it to our `messages_area`.

With that in place, we can grab the conversation history from our web service and add it to the `messages_area` with this method:

```
def __init__(self, master, friend_name, friend_username, friend_avatar,
**kwargs):
    ...
```

```
        self.load_history()

    def load_history(self):
        history =
    self.master.requester.prepare_conversation(self.master.username,
    self.friend_username)

        if len(history['history']):
            for message in history['history']:
                self.receive_message(message['author'], message['message'])
```

When the `ChatWindow` is first loaded, we want to prepare it with the chat history or by initializing the conversation database if it does not already exist. We use the `prepare_conversation` method of the `requester` to achieve this.

Once we have the history, we loop over each message and pass the information to our `receive_message` method to add it to our `messages_area`.

That's it, our `ChatWindow` is now connected! Run your `friendslist.py` file, log in and open up a chat window with someone. Send them a few messages, then close the window. When you open it again, you should see your old messages are still there!

With that, this chapter comes to an end. Our `FriendsList` and `ChatWindow` are now both connected to our web service via the `Requester` class.

The current implementation works fine if two people want to close and re-open their chat window between each method, but this is obviously not very user-friendly. In the next chapter, we will look at getting messages to send in the background.

Summary

In this chapter, we have learned a lot about some non-Tkinter technologies which can be used to supplement a GUI application.

We learned how to set up a very basic web service using the `flask` module. We know how to create URL routes using the `app.route` decorator and have learned how to handle both GET and POST requests. We also had an introduction to JSON as a portable way of sending information back to a client.

The SQLite database technology has been explored and we know how to create databases in our filesystem. We have practiced querying them and seen some basic SQL statement syntax. We have learned both how to put information into a database table and how to retrieve it again. We also saw that we can use the `Row` class to get information as a dictionary, which is often preferable to the standard tuple responses.

We have looked at sending GET and POST requests using the `requests` module. We have seen how to send data over to an endpoint, as well as parse the response with either `r.text` or `r.json()`. We have also created a generic class wrapper around this module which makes code from other classes much more succinct and readable.

After all of that knowledge was practiced, we then utilized it to get both our `FriendsList` and `ChatWindow` classes communicating with the new web service via `requests`, which called a `flask` endpoint to communicate with an `sqlite3` database.

Our `FriendsList` class now knows what users exist on the server and the `ChatWindow` is able to keep and display a history of sent messages between two users.

In the next chapter, we will polish off our chat application by getting messages to update in the background while the user has the window open. We will also sort out the ability for each account to have its own avatar image and block other users from contacting them.

Making Friends – Finishing Our Chat Application

10

We will be finishing off our chat application by using threads to get it listening for incoming messages in the background. We will explore the motivation for incorporating threads in a GUI application, then learn how they can be implemented.

Once our application is listening for new messages, we will polish things off by making the user-chosen avatars function properly and we will learn how to handle manipulating images in Python.

We'll finish up by allowing users to add each other as friends and block friends if they no longer wish to talk to them.

In this chapter, we will cover the following topics:

- Why we may need to use threads when making a GUI application
- How to create and use a thread in Python
- Manipulating images using **Python Imaging Library** (PIL)
- Uploading images to a web service

Using threads

When writing a Python application, all of the code will run in a single thread by default. This means that, as you read down a file, each line will be carried out one at a time. A piece of code cannot run if there is another piece above it which is executing a large task.

If we wanted to carry out multiple tasks at the same time, there are a couple of different ways we could go about doing so. One way is the use of a thread. When using a thread, the operating system will be able to quickly switch between two running pieces of code so quickly that it appears as if they are being executed at the same time. This means that if you have a function which takes a lot of processing, you are able to do multiple smaller tasks in the time it would take for that function to execute, thereby speeding up the overall process.

Why use a thread with a GUI application?

Graphical applications tend to execute everything in the main thread. This means that updates to its widgets happen in line with all other code that is currently executing.

As a result of this, any slow processing will often block the updating of the GUI. We can demonstrate this with a small example:

```
import tkinter as tk
import time

win = tk.Tk()
win.geometry("200x150")

counter = tk.IntVar()
label = tk.Label(win, text="Ready to Work")
counter_label = tk.Label(win, textvar=counter)
```

The example starts with a window which will contain a `Label` displaying the value of an `IntVar`.

We will be creating a button that increases the value stored in the `IntVar`, as well as another button which will simulate a very heavy processing task (using `time.sleep`).

Before we can create the buttons, we will need the functions they will call:

```
def increase_counter():
    counter.set(counter.get() + 1)

def work():
    label.configure(text="Doing work")
    time.sleep(5)
    label.configure(text="Finished")
```

With these functions defined, we can finish the example off by creating the buttons and then packing all of our widgets:

```
counter_button = tk.Button(win, text="Increase Counter",
command=increase_counter)
work_button = tk.Button(win, text="Work", command=work)

label.pack()
counter_label.pack()

counter_button.pack()
work_button.pack()

win.mainloop()
```

Save and run this file and you should see a small window appear:

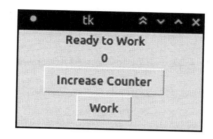

Click the **Increase Counter** button a few times and notice how it will add one to the number above it.

Now, click the **Work** button and observe how it appears to get stuck in the pressed state. While it is like this, the rest of the program doesn't appear to respond.

Once it has finished and the label shows **Finished**, try pressing it once more. While it is stuck down, click the **Increase Counter** button a few times, then wait for it to finish once again.

You should then notice that even though the **Increase Counter** button did not appear to respond to your clicks, the number above it will increase as the other task completes.

Finally, press the **Work** button one more time, then close the window. You should see that the window will not close until the five second sleep has finished.

This behavior is very undesirable. When a large task needs to execute, if the GUI elements stop responding, a user may click something multiple times thinking it is not working, only to realize that it was indeed functioning and they have now performed an action more times than they intended.

We also do not want to prevent the user from closing an application for a long period of time, since they may end up force-closing it, which can lead to problems such as loss of data.

So, how do we perform a large task without locking up the GUI? One possible solution is to use a separate thread.

Using a thread

In order to use a thread in Python, we can import a module named threading and subclass its Thread class. Inside our new class, we need to overwrite the run method and perform our logic in there. Once we have done this, we can call the start method on an instance of our class to execute its task in a separate thread.

Let's update our demo application to use a thread. We'll begin by importing the threading module and creating a subclass of Thread:

```
import tkinter as tk
import time
import threading

class WorkThread(threading.Thread):
    def run(self):
        label.configure(text="Doing work")
        time.sleep(5)
        label.configure(text="Finished")

        return
...
```

Our old work function has been moved to the run method of our Thread subclass. This allows it to run in a separate thread when its start method is called.

Speaking of which, we now need to adjust our old work function to make use of this class:

```
def work():
    thread = WorkThread()
    thread.start()
```

In this function, we just make an instance of our `WorkThread` class and call its `start` method.

With these changes made, we are now ready to try out our new multithreaded application.

Run this file once again and make sure the **Increase Counter** button still works. Now, click the **Work** button and notice how it does not stay pressed in. This time, you will be able to click the **Increase Counter** button while the application is still working and see the number above increase.

That's how easy it is to integrate a separate thread in a GUI application.

With our new knowledge of how to run a task in the background, we can begin implementing a background task which listens for new messages being sent by a friend in our chat application.

Adding a Thread to our ChatWindow

To get our `ChatWindow` class listening for new messages, we will use a thread to repeatedly poll our web service for messages which we haven't seen yet.

In order to determine what we have and have not already received, we will be using the `date_sent` column in our conversation table.

Before we can implement a threaded solution, some modifications need to be made to our database, server, and requester.

Creating new endpoints

The first thing we will need is the ability to select new messages from our conversation databases. We will need to provide the current user's username and the last time when we checked for messages. Our database will then return all new messages by a different author since the last time we checked for messages.

Open up your `conversation.py` file and add the following method to it:

```
def get_new_messages(self, timestamp, username):
    sql = "SELECT author, message FROM conversation WHERE date_sent > ? AND
author <> ?"
    params = (timestamp, username)
```

```
conn = sqlite3.connect(self.database)
conn.row_factory = sqlite3.Row
cursor = conn.cursor()
cursor.execute(sql, params)
results = [dict(row) for row in cursor.fetchall()]
conn.close()

return results
```

Our SQL query grabs the author's name and message for any record matching the aforementioned criteria. The <> in SQL is a *not equal to* operator.

With this in place, we can update our server.py file to add a matching endpoint:

```
@app.route("/get_new_messages", methods=["POST"])
def get_new_messages():
    data = request.form
    conversation_db_path = get_conversation_db_path_for_users(data)
    conversation_db = Conversation(conversation_db_path)

    timestamp = data["timestamp"]
    requester_username = data["user_one"]

    new_messages = conversation_db.get_new_messages(timestamp,
requester_username)

    return jsonify({
        "messages": new_messages
    })
```

After constructing the path to the relevant conversation database, we pull the author's username and the timestamp of the last check out of the POST parameters, then pass these over to our new method.

Any messages returned from the database are then provided back to the requester in JSON format.

Speaking of which, we will need a matching method in our Requester class to call this new endpoint:

```
def get_new_messages(self, timestamp, user_one, user_two):
    """ user_one is the author's username, and user_two is the friend's """
    endpoint = "/get_new_messages"
    params = {
        "timestamp": timestamp,
        "user_one": user_one,
        "user_two": user_two,
```

```
    }

    new_messages = self.request("POST", endpoint, params)

    return new_messages
```

This method takes a timestamp of the last request, the author's username (as `user_one`), and the friend's username (as `user_two`).

It then sends this data over to the server, via POST request, and returns the response.

Now that the web service work has been done, we can utilize the new endpoints inside a thread. To keep things neat, we will be making a new file to hold our thread class. Go ahead and create a file called `listeningthread.py` alongside your `chatwindow.py` file.

The ListeningThread class

Our `ListeningThread` class will need to inherit from `threading.Thread` and contain a `run` method, which can happen in the background.

Since we want to be always checking for new messages until the user closes their `ChatWindow`, we shall put our request inside a loop which the `ChatWindow` will be able to end when closed.

Let's begin our `ListeningThread` class, as follows:

```
import arrow
import threading
import time

from requester import Requester
```

Our class will be making use of the following modules:

- `arrow`: This is used to create the timestamps
- `threading`: This is used to run in the background
- `time`: This is used to sleep for two seconds between requests
- `requester`: This is used to contact our web service

With the imports taken care of, we can begin writing the class.

```
class ListeningThread(threading.Thread):
    def __init__(self, master, user_one, user_two):
        super().__init__()
        self.master = master
        self.user_one = user_one
        self.user_two = user_two
        self.requester = Requester()
        self.running = True
        self.last_checked_time = arrow.now().timestamp
```

Our __init__ method will create a few attributes. These do the following:

- master: This refers to our ChatWindow widget and will be used later to handle stopping the thread's infinite loop when the window is closed
- user_one: The logged-in user of the application
- user_two: The friend they are messaging
- requester: Our Requester object
- running: A variable which is used to begin and end the loop
- last_checked_time: The timestamp sent to our web service to determine what messages we have and have not seen

We are now prepared to write the run method, which will be called when this class is started:

```
def run(self):
    while self.running:
        new_messages = 
self.requester.get_new_messages(self.last_checked_time, self.user_one, 
self.user_two)
        self.last_checked_time = arrow.now().timestamp
        for message in new_messages['messages']:
            self.master.receive_message(message["author"],
                                        message["message"])

        time.sleep(2)

    del self.master.listening_thread

    return
```

In order to run in a constant loop, we use a `while` loop combined with our `running` attribute. This way, in order to cancel the loop, we just need to set the thread instance's `running` attribute to `False`.

When in the loop, the thread is calling the `get_new_messages` endpoint, updating its `last_checked_time`, then passing any returned messages over to the `ChatWindow`'s `receive_message` method.

After each iteration, the thread will wait for two seconds before repeating.

When the loop is stopped, the thread will delete the `listening_thread` attribute from our `ChatWindow` class, then `return` to exit the method. We will see why this happens shortly.

This completes our `ListeningThread` class. We can now import and implement it in our `ChatWindow` to get new messages coming in.

Implementing the ListeningThread class in our ChatWindow

To make use of our new `ListeningThread`, we just need to import it and call its `start` method:

```
...
from listeningthread import ListeningThread
...
def __init__(self, master, friend_name, friend_username, friend_avatar,
**kwargs):
    ...
    self.listening_thread = None
    self.listen()
```

After importing the class, we add a `listening_thread` attribute to our `__init__` method, then call the `listen` method to get our `ListeningThread` running:

```
def listen(self):
    self.listening_thread = ListeningThread(self, self.master.username,
                                            self.friend_username)
    self.listening_thread.start()
```

We set our `listening_thread` attribute to an instance of the `ListeningThread` class, passing it our `username` and `friend_username`. We then call its `start` method to begin its loop in the background of our application.

When our `ChatWindow` is closed, we need to terminate the loop in our thread so that the user will not need to force-close each window. To do that, we need to set the `running` attribute of our `listening_thread` to `False`.

In order to hook an event to happen when the user closes a window, we can utilize the `protocol` method of a widget, allowing us to execute a function when certain events happen. The string `WM_DELETE_WINDOW` will correspond to the closing of a window.

Add the following to the __init__ method, just before creating our `listening_thread` attribute, to hook the necessary event:

```
self.protocol("WM_DELETE_WINDOW", self.close)
```

This allows us to run our `close` method, when the user closes the window:

```
def close(self):
    if hasattr(self, "listening_thread"):
        self.listening_thread.running = False
        self.after(100, self.close)
    else:
        self.destroy()
```

In our `close` method, we check for the presence of our `listening_thread` attribute. If we still have it, this means our thread is still running. We update its `running` attribute to `False`, so that it will break out of its loop, then schedule this same function to run again after `100` milliseconds.

Since the `ListeningThread` class will delete its master's `listening_thread` attribute when it breaks from its loop, when our `close` function runs again and sees we no longer have this attribute, we will know that the thread has finished and we are safe to use the `destroy` method to close our `ChatWindow`.

Our application now has the ability to listen for incoming messages without locking up the GUI. To test this out, run two instances of the `friendslist.py` file, and one of the `server.py`. Log into different accounts on each and open up a conversation with the other.

When you type a message into one window, you should see it appear in the second shortly after:

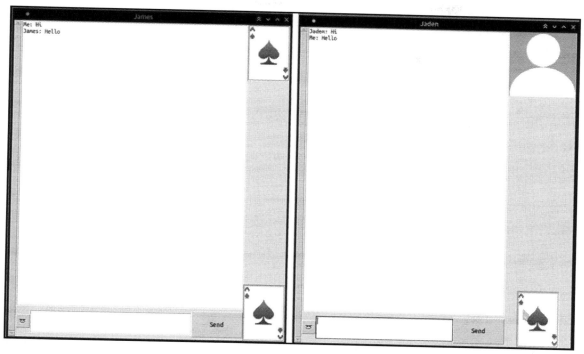

Everybody having the default orange avatar can get a little bit confusing. We should allow the users to upload their own avatar to use, instead.

Allowing users to upload avatars

To create the ability for a user to upload their choice of avatar, we will need a new place for them to do so. Let's create another `Toplevel` window, which will contain the necessary widgets and functionality.

The AvatarWindow class

Make a new file alongside your `friendslist.py` file named `avatarwindow.py`:

```
import base64
import os
import tkinter as tk
import tkinter.ttk as ttk
from tkinter import filedialog

avatar_file_path = os.path.abspath(os.path.join(os.path.dirname(__file__),
"images/avatar.png"))
```

Our user's avatar will sit in a predefined file. This will be named `avatar.png` and will sit in the `images` folder. We create a variable named `avatar_file_path` to hold the absolute path to this file.

In order to store our image data in our database, we will be `base64` encoding the content of the file. To do this, we will need to import the `base64` module:

```
class AvatarWindow(tk.Toplevel):
    def __init__(self, master):
        super().__init__()

        self.master = master
        self.transient(master)

        self.title("Change Avatar")
        self.geometry("350x200")

        self.image_file_types = [
            ("Png Images", ("*.png", "*.PNG")),
        ]
```

After defining some usual features of the window, we create an attribute called
`image_file_types`, which will hold the possible file types which the user can use as their
avatar. Since we have already defined that our avatar will be a `.png` image, we will restrict
the user to only being able to upload `.png` files:

```
self.current_avatar_image = tk.PhotoImage(file=avatar_file_path)

self.current_avatar = ttk.Label(self, image=self.current_avatar_image)
choose_file_button = ttk.Button(self, text="Choose File",
command=self.choose_image)

self.current_avatar.pack()
choose_file_button.pack()
```

We display two widgets in this window: a `Label` showing the currently-set avatar image
and a `Button` which will open up a file picker for the user to choose their new avatar
image.

We bind the button to a method named `choose_image`:

```
def choose_image(self):
    image_file =
filedialog.askopenfilename(filetypes=self.image_file_types)

    if image_file:
        img_contents = ""
        img_b64 = ""
        with open(avatar_file_path, "rb") as img:
            img_contents = img.read()
            img_b64 = base64.urlsafe_b64encode(img_contents)

        self.master.requester.update_avatar(self.master.username, img_b64)
        self.current_avatar_image = tk.PhotoImage(file=avatar_file_path)
        self.current_avatar.configure(image=self.current_avatar_image)
```

The first thing to do in this method is to get the user to choose the path to an image file. We
use the `askopenfilename` method of the `filedialog` module in order to do this. We pass
our `image_file_types` over as the `filetypes` argument to ensure that the user chooses
only `.png` images.

If the user chooses an image file, then we will `base64` encode its content to send over to our
web service. After opening the chosen file, we use the `urlsafe_b64encode` method to do
this, since we will be sending the encoded content over HTTP.

To send this content over to our database, we call upon the `update_avatar` method of our `Requester` (which we will write next), passing it our username and encoded avatar data.

To finish off, we create a new `PhotoImage` object of the user's new avatar and update our `Label` to display it.

If we want to try this window out, without integrating it back into our `FriendsList` class, we will need an `if __name__ == "__main__"` block:

```
if __name__ == "__main__":
    win = tk.Tk()
    aw = AvatarWindow(win)
    win.mainloop()
```

Before we can get this working, we will need to update our database and web service to handle avatars, since there is currently nowhere to store them.

Adjusting the database

To store an avatar against a particular user, we will need to add a column to our `users` database. We can do this via the Python REPL from our `server` folder, as follows:

```
Python 3.6.4 (default, Jan 03 2018, 13:52:55) [GCC] on linux
Type "help", "copyright", "credits" or "license" for more information.
>>> import database
>>> d = database.Database()
>>> sql = "ALTER TABLE users ADD avatar text"
>>> params = []
>>> d.perform_insert(sql, params)
>>>
```

In order to add a column to an existing table, we use an `alter table` command. We then specify the table name, new column name, and new column type.

With the preceding statement, we have added a column named `avatar` of the `text` type. This is the column which we will use to hold our avatar image.

We can now add some methods to the `Database` class which will allow us to both store and retrieve avatar data for a particular user:

```
def update_avatar(self, username, img_b64):
    sql = "UPDATE users SET avatar=? WHERE username=?"
    params = (img_b64, username)

    return self.perform_insert(sql, params)
```

In order to alter an existing record without creating a new one, we can use an `update` statement. We supply this statement with the table name, the columns to update, and the `where` condition on which to filter the relevant records.

Since we want to update the `avatar` column for a record matching a supplied username, we use `SET avatar=?` to mark the avatar column for updating and provide `WHERE username=?` to say that we only want to update records which match a given username value.

This handles updating the avatars, but we will also want to be able to retrieve an avatar for a given user:

```
def get_user_avatar(self, username):
    sql = "SELECT avatar FROM users WHERE username=?"
    params = (username,)

    return self.perform_select(sql, params)
```

Selecting a user's avatar requires just a simple `select` statement, featuring a `where` clause to specify the provided username.

Now that we have taken care of the database, we can create some server endpoints to allow the use of this new column.

Adding server endpoints

We will need two endpoints to make full use of our avatars – one to upload a new one, and one to fetch an avatar for a particular user.

Open up `server.py` and add the following functions:

```
@app.route("/update_avatar/<username>", methods=["POST"])
def update_avatar(username):
    img_b64 = request.form.get("img_b64")
    database.update_avatar(username, img_b64)
```

```
        return jsonify({
            "success": True
        })
```

This first endpoint will store the `base64` encoded image data in the database against the username provided in the URL:

```
@app.route("/get_user_avatar/<username>")
def get_avatar(username):

    avatar_b64 = database.get_user_avatar(username)['avatar']

    return jsonify({
        "avatar": avatar_b64
    })
```

The second endpoint will get the user's `base64` encoded avatar from the database and return it in JSON format.

With the web service all set up, our `AvatarWindow` should be ready to upload new avatars! However, since it relies on the `requester` instance of our `FriendsList`, it will not function fully until we integrate it.

Let's finish off our `AvatarWindow` by creating a menu option for it in the `FriendsList` class.

Updating the FriendsList class

We still have a `Friends` menu at the top of our `FriendsList` class, but this doesn't make much sense as a place to put our avatar uploading functionality. Instead, we can create a new submenu called `avatar`:

```
...
from avatarwindow import AvatarWindow
...
def __init__(self, **kwargs):
    ...
    self.avatar_menu = tk.Menu(self.menu, fg="black",
                            bg="lightgrey", tearoff=0)
    self.avatar_menu.add_command(label="Change Avatar",
                            command=self.change_avatar)

    self.menu.add_cascade(label="Friends", menu=self.friends_menu)
    self.menu.add_cascade(label="Avatar", menu=self.avatar_menu)
```

After importing our new class, we create a menu called `avatar_menu` to hold a `Change Avatar` function. This will call a method named `change_avatar`:

```
def change_avatar(self):
    AvatarWindow(self)
```

All that our `change_avatar` method needs to do is spawn an instance of our `AvatarWindow`, since everything else is contained in that class.

With this finished, we can now spawn the `AvatarWindow` and upload an image to serve as our avatar. Go ahead and run your `friendslist.py` file, log in, and then pick **Avatar | Change Avatar** from the top-menu:

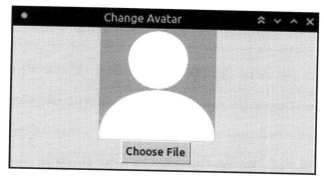

Allowing the user to choose any image could lead to problems with our layout if a user chooses a very large one, since Tkinter itself cannot resize images. Try opening a very big image and see how it does not properly fit into the `AvatarWindow`. To handle this, we will need to use a library called **Python Imaging Library** (**PIL**) to scale down the chosen image.

Manipulating images with PIL

In order to use PIL, we will first need to install it. The version which I will be using is available on `pip` and can be installed with the following command:

```
pip install pillow
```

PIL provides multiple ways of resizing an image. Two possible methods we could use in our application are `resize` and `thumbnail`.

The `resize` method will alter an image to be the exact size provided to the method (as a two-tuple of width and height). On the other hand, the `thumbnail` method will preserve the aspect ratio of an image, preventing skew, resizing the larger dimension of the image to the provided maximum size, and keeping the smaller dimension at the same ratio.

 For my implementation of this application, I will be using the `thumbnail` method to resize avatars, as it will make any rectangular images look nicer when scaled down. If you would prefer to keep images as squares, you may replace the calls to `thumbnail` with `resize` to achieve this.

With `PIL` installed, head back over to your `avatarwindow.py` file and edit the `choose_image` function, as follows:

```
from PIL import Image
...

def choose_image(self):
    image_file =
filedialog.askopenfilename(filetypes=self.image_file_types)

    if image_file:
        avatar = Image.open(image_file)
        avatar.thumbnail((128, 128))
        avatar.save(avatar_file_path, "PNG")

        img_contents = ""
```

After the user selects their image file, we want to overwrite the file stored at our `avatar_file_path` with a scaled-down version. To do this, we use the `open` method of PIL's `Image` class, passing it the path to their chosen image file.

Once we have this image, we use the thumbnail method to scale it down, passing it a two-tuple of `(128, 128)` to act as the maximum width and height of the new image.

To save this scaled image over the one in our `avatar_file_path`, we call the `save` method. We pass this method the path at which to save the image and the format, in our case, `PNG`.

The rest of the method then continues as normal.

Run your application once again, open the avatar window, and choose a large image. You should now see that your chosen avatar fits nicely inside the window.

The last thing we need to address with our chat application is the management of users. Currently, every user of the system is available to chat with every other user. This is not ideal, since people will be able to talk to complete strangers. We need to add a way for users to add other users as `friends`, thus giving them the ability to talk to one another.

While we are at it, we should also allow users to block other users, should they wish to cease contact.

Adding and blocking other users

To implement adding and blocking users, we are going to be creating a new table in our chat database. This table will be called `friends` and will contain information about each pairing of friends and whether or not communication between them has been blocked.

New database table

Once again, we can use the Python REPL to create a new table. Access your `server` folder and run a Python shell:

```
Python 3.6.4 (default, Jan 03 2018, 13:52:55) [GCC] on linux
Type "help", "copyright", "credits" or "license" for more information.
>>> import database
>>> d = database.Database()
>>> sql = "CREATE TABLE friends (user_one text, user_two text, blocked
integer)"
>>> params = []
>>> d.perform_insert(sql, params)
>>>
```

Our database will contain two users, called `user_one` and `user_two`, as well as an integer representing whether communication has been blocked. This integer will be treated as a Boolean, where 0 represents no blocking and 1 represents the conversation being blocked.

We now need to write some new methods in our `Database` class to query and update this table:

```
def add_friend(self, user_one, user_two):
    sql = "INSERT INTO friends (user_one, user_two, blocked) VALUES
(?,?,0)"
    query_params = (user_one, user_two)

    self.perform_insert(sql, query_params)
```

When adding a friend pairing, we will assume that they wish to talk to each other, so we will insert the blocked flag as a 0 by default.

This handles the ability to add a friend. We now will need to be able to get all friends of a user for when they log into the ChatWindow:

```
def get_friends(self, username):
    all_friends = []
    sql = "SELECT user_two FROM friends WHERE user_one=? AND blocked=0"
    params = (username,)
    friends = self.perform_select(sql, params)

    sql = "SELECT user_one FROM friends WHERE user_two=? AND blocked=0"
    friends2 = self.perform_select(sql, params)

    for friend in friends:
        all_friends.append(friend["user_two"])
    for friend in friends2:
        all_friends.append(friend["user_one"])

    return all_friends
```

Since we do not know which column the querying user's username will be in, we need to select records from both columns and then merge the results into one list.

We first select records where our specified username is user_one, then user_two. We loop over the returned lists of dictionaries and merge the records into our all_friends list.

This method gives us all usernames of friends added by a supplied user, but to display them on our FriendsList window, we need their avatar and real name, too. This will require one more method:

```
def get_users_by_usernames(self, usernames):
    question_marks = ','.join(['?' for user in usernames])
    sql = f"SELECT * FROM users WHERE username IN ({question_marks})"
    params = [user for user in usernames]

    friends = self.perform_select(sql, params)

    return friends
```

Since we do not know how many usernames we got back from the previous query, we don't know how many question marks to put into this one. For this reason, we use a string `join` to create a list of question marks, providing one per username with a list comprehension. We then use string formatting to put this list of question marks into our query.

With SQL, in order to check whether a record is inside a list, we use an `IN` clause, then provide every possible value in regular brackets separated by a comma. For example, to select the first three users, we could do `SELECT * FROM users WHERE id IN (1, 2, 3)`.

That takes care of adding and retrieving friends in our `Database` class.

When it comes to blocking users, we need to find the record which contains the two usernames and flip the `blocked` column to a `1`:

```
def block_friend(self, username, contact_to_block):
    sql = "UPDATE friends SET blocked=1 WHERE (user_one = ? AND user_two =
?) OR (user_two = ? AND user_one = ?)"
    query_params = (username, contact_to_block, username, contact_to_block)

    self.perform_insert(sql, query_params)
```

Since we don't know which friend will be in which user column, we can use an `OR` clause to specify that we want either one of the two provided conditions to be true.

That's it for our `Database` now. As usual, we will now need to add server endpoints to interact with these new methods.

Creating the server endpoints

Our web service will need three new endpoints—one to add a friend, one to block a friend, and one to grab all friends of a user.

Let's start with the endpoint to add a friend:

```
@app.route("/add_friend", methods=["POST"])
def add_friend():
    data = request.form
    user_one = data['user_one']
    user_two = data['user_two']

    if database.user_exists(user_two) and database.user_exists(user_one):
        database.add_friend(user_one, user_two)
        success = True
```

```
    else:
        success = False

    return jsonify({
        "success": success
    })
```

This endpoint will be supplied with the two usernames that we want added to the `friends` table. Before we can add them, we need to check that they both exist in the `users` table already.

If they do, we call our database's `add_friend` method and return a successful response. If not, we will not add them to the `friends` table and, instead, we will return a negative success response.

Now onto retrieving a user's friends:

```
@app.route("/get_friends/<username>")
def get_friends(username):
    friends = database.get_friends(username)

    if len(friends):
        all_friends = database.get_users_by_usernames(friends)
    else:
        all_friends = []

    return jsonify({
        "friends": all_friends
    })
```

This method requires a username, then passes that over to the database's `get_friends` method. If we have any results come back, we pass them over to the `get_users_by_usernames` method in order to grab their real name and avatar. Otherwise, we return an empty list:

```
@app.route("/block_friend", methods=["POST"])
def block_friend():
    data = request.form
    user_one = data['user_one']
    user_two = data['user_two']

    database.block_friend(user_one, user_two)

    return jsonify({
        "success": True
    })
```

Finally, when blocking a user, we pass the two usernames over to the database's
`block_friend` method and return `True`.

With the endpoints taken care of, we now need to update our `Requester` to pass them
data:

```
def add_friend(self, user_one, user_two):
    endpoint = "/add_friend"
    params = {
        "user_one": user_one,
        "user_two": user_two,
    }

    success = self.request("POST", endpoint, params)
```

When adding a friend, we POST the two usernames over to our endpoint and let it take care
of the rest:

```
def get_friends(self, username):
    endpoint = f"/get_friends/{username}"

    friends = self.request("GET", endpoint)

    return json.loads(friends)
```

When retrieving friends, we send a GET request to the relevant endpoint, then use `loads` to
parse the returned JSON as a dictionary:

```
def block_friend(self, user_one, user_two):
    endpoint = "/block_friend"
    params = {
        "user_one": user_one,
        "user_two": user_two,
    }

    self.request("POST", endpoint, params)

    return True
```

Much like adding a friend, we can just supply the two usernames to the endpoint when
blocking a friend.

That's all of the groundwork taken care of. Now, we can tie this new functionality back into
our chat application.

Tying it all together

Let's begin with the ability to add a friend, since we need this to make the rest of our changes work properly.

We already have a Friends menu in the top menu bar of our FriendsList class containing an Add Friend command, which seems appropriate for this functionality. We'll replace the placeholder method with a functioning one:

```
def __init__(self, **kwargs):
    ...
    self.friends_menu.add_command(label="Add Friend",
command=self.show_add_friend_window)
    ...

def show_add_friend_window(self):
    AddFriendWindow(self)
```

In order to take the information, we need to add a friend and we will require a new Toplevel window. Go ahead and create a file named addfriendwindow.py alongside your friendslist.py file:

```
import tkinter as tk
import tkinter.ttk as ttk

class AddFriendWindow(tk.Toplevel):
    def __init__(self, master):
        super().__init__()
        self.master = master

        self.transient(master)
        self.geometry("250x100")
        self.title("Add a Friend")
```

This class will be a fairly standard Toplevel subclass. It needs to contain an Entry widget for gathering the friend's username and a Button widget to submit the data:

```
main_frame = ttk.Frame(self)

username_label = ttk.Label(main_frame, text="Username")
self.username_entry = ttk.Entry(main_frame)

add_button = ttk.Button(main_frame, text="Add", command=self.add_friend)

username_label.grid(row=0, column=0)
self.username_entry.grid(row=0, column=1)
```

```
self.username_entry.focus_force()
```

As well as the `Entry` and `Button` widgets, we will also use a `Label` widget to signal to the user what they need to type into the `Entry` widget.

When the window opens, we will force the focus to the `username_entry`. This means the user will not have to click inside the widget in order to begin typing into it:

```
add_button.grid(row=1, column=0, columnspan=2)

for i in range(2):
    tk.Grid.columnconfigure(main_frame, i, weight=1)
    tk.Grid.rowconfigure(main_frame, i, weight=1)

main_frame.pack(fill=tk.BOTH, expand=1)
```

We are using the `grid` geometry manager to add the widgets to their `Frame`, and then `pack` to add the frame to the window. As before, we use `columnconfigure` and `rowconfigure` to set all cells to the same `weight`:

```
def add_friend(self):
    username = self.username_entry.get()

    if username:
        if self.master.add_friend(username):
            self.username_entry.delete(0, tk.END)
```

When adding a friend, we first need to get the value of our `Entry` widget. If there is something typed into it, we will pass it over to the `add_friend` method of the `FriendsList` class. Should this return a positive response, we will clear the `Entry` widget, so that more friends can quickly be added if necessary.

This completes the functionality of this class. We can now move back to our `FriendsList` class and implement its `add_friend` method:

```
def add_friend(self, username):
    if self.requester.add_friend(self.username, username):
        msg.showinfo("Friend Added", "Friend Added")
        success = True
        self.reload_friends()
    else:
        msg.showerror("Add Failed", "Friend was not found")
        success = False

    return success
```

If our friend was successfully added, we use a `showinfo` box to alert the user, then reload our friends list to show them in it.

If the added user does not exist, we will receive a negative response from our `Requester`. We will relay this message to the user with a `showerror` box:

```
def reload_friends(self):
    for child in self.canvas_frame.winfo_children():
        child.pack_forget()
    self.load_friends()
```

In order to reload our friends list, we first need to loop over all of the frames we have added to our scrollable window and remove them.

To get the children of a widget in Tkinter, we can use the `winfo_children` method. This will return an iterable of all widgets that have been added to that widget via a geometry manager.

Once we have the child widgets, we need to remove them to avoid duplicates. We do this using the `pack_forget` method. This method is a way of undoing a call to `pack` and will remove them from display.

With our `canvas_frame` emptied, we now need to put back the list of friends. We do this by calling the `load_friends` method once again, which will now include any new friends.

On the topic of our `load_friends` method, we need to change this to call the new endpoint we have written to get all friends who are not blocked:

```
def load_friends(self):
    my_friends = self.requester.get_friends(self.username)
    for user in my_friends["friends"]:
        if user['username'] != self.username:
            friend_frame = ttk.Frame(self.canvas_frame)
            ...
            block_this_friend = partial(self.block_friend,
                                        username=user["username"])
            block_button = ttk.Button(friend_frame, text="Block",
                                       command=block_this_friend)
            ...
            profile_photo_label.pack(side=tk.LEFT)
            friend_name.pack(side=tk.LEFT)
            message_button.pack(side=tk.RIGHT)
            block_button.pack(side=tk.RIGHT, padx=(0, 30))
            ...
```

At the beginning of this method, we call the `get_friends` method of our `Requester`, passing it our `username` attribute. This will then return any friends we have added and not blocked. We then loop over them as before, creating a `Frame` for each.

Included in our widgets now is a second button which we can use to block a friend. We again use a partial function to freeze the `username` argument for each friend, and map it to the `block_friend` method.

We pack the button to the right after packing our message button, so that it appears to the left of our `Chat` button.

The final update we need to do to this class is to create the `block_friend` method:

```
def block_friend(self, username):
    self.requester.block_friend(self.username, username)
    self.reload_friends()
```

This method passes our username and the friend's username to the `block_friend` method of our `Requester`, then reloads the friends list to remove them.

That wraps up everything for our `FriendsList` class. Give it a run and check out its new functionality. Try creating multiple accounts and adding, and then blocking, some friends:

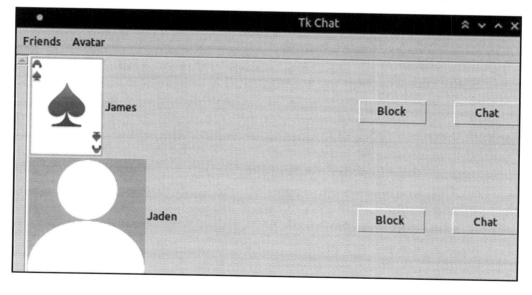

This is where we will leave our chat application. We have now written a server, which handles matching people to their friends and allowing them to send messages back and forth, as well as choosing their own avatars for all of their friends to see.

Our GUI has been updated to make requests to our server and offer a nice interface to each new endpoint. We also have a separate thread running, which will continually fetch new messages very shortly after they have been sent.

Upon finishing this chapter, you can now boast that you have written three different GUI applications using Python and Tkinter. The first was a game of blackjack featuring animated images and text. The second was a powerful text editor with syntax highlighting and dynamic line numbers. Now, you have also added a chat application to your arsenal, as well as some knowledge on how to hook a GUI application up to a web service to create the ability to share information with others.

In the final chapter of this book, we will learn how to package these applications up for others to install. Currently, running our applications on a new machine requires installing Python and executing scripts from the command line. For non-programmers, this is a barrier to entry for our applications and we can benefit from learning some tools which remove this need.

Summary

In this chapter, we have learned why using a second thread within a GUI application can be beneficial. We have seen that large tasks can make the GUI look as if it has stopped responding, which can confuse users. After introducing a separate thread, we then eliminated this problem and made the application behave as a user would likely expect.

Using our new knowledge of threads, we then improved our chat application by allowing it to pull in new messages in the background, without disabling the GUI itself while doing so.

Afterwards, we increased the quality of our application by allowing the user to choose their own avatars. We learned how we can use the `PIL` module to resize and save images, removing any restrictions on the user in terms of choosing the correct avatar size, or the application developer in terms of accommodating any huge images the user may wish to use.

Finally, to improve the social aspect of our application, we added the ability for the user to choose which friends they wanted to be able to contact, and gave them the option to block any other users who they did not wish to speak to any more.

Along the way, we have picked up some new features of SQL, such as UPDATE, SET, and IN, allowing us to manipulate existing rows in a database.

In the next chapter, we are going to cover packaging up applications into executables for different OSes. This will allow people to run them without installing Python. We will also touch upon several widgets which have not been utilized in any of our example applications, but that deserve a mention anyway.

11
Wrapping Up – Packaging Our Applications to Share

In this chapter, we are going to have a brief look at some of the widgets provided with Tkinter (and ttk) that we did not find a use for during our application development. We will go over very small samples of each and take a look at how each could be used in a real application.

Afterward, we are going to cover how we can ship our GUI applications to users without them needing to install Python or use the command line. Tools exist to pack Python applications into a single program for many desktop OSes, including Linux, Windows, and macOS.

In this chapter, we will cover the following topics:

- Unexplored widgets from Tkinter and ttk
- Packaging applications for Windows, Linux, and macOS

Let's begin with a look at a few widgets that we have not managed to make use of with our three example applications.

Unexplored widgets

Before we begin packaging up our application, let's have a quick look at some widgets which we have not seen yet. While reading about these widgets, have a think about how you could implement them in one of our existing applications.

The LabelFrame widget

The LabelFrame widget is included with your normal tkinter import and also has a ttk version. Its purpose is to write a label and draw a border around a group of widgets. The label can be either some static text or a reference to a Label widget.

To demonstrate a possible use of this widget, let's make a small script:

```
import tkinter as tk
import tkinter.ttk as ttk

win = tk.Tk()
name_frame = ttk.Frame(win)
address_frame = ttk.Frame(win)

name_label_frame = ttk.LabelFrame(name_frame, text="Name")
address_label = ttk.Label(win, text="Address")
address_label_frame = ttk.LabelFrame(address_frame,
labelwidget=address_label)
```

Our demonstration window will contain some information collection fields for the user's name and address. We will group these two pieces of information into their own LabelFrame widgets to give them a nice heading.

To define the text to show on the LabelFrame widget, we can either pass the text keyword argument, as we do with our name_label_frame, or we can pass a Label widget to the labelwidget argument (as seen for our address_label_frame):

```
first_name = ttk.Entry(name_label_frame)
last_name = ttk.Entry(name_label_frame)

first_name.pack(side=tk.TOP)
last_name.pack(side=tk.BOTTOM)

name_label_frame.pack(fill=tk.BOTH, expand=1)
name_frame.pack(side=tk.LEFT, fill=tk.BOTH, expand=1)
```

We begin with the name collection, which we do using two Entry widgets. These widgets are packed into the LabelFrame widget in the same way as they would be added to a regular Frame widget:

```
address_1 = ttk.Entry(address_label_frame)
address_2 = ttk.Entry(address_label_frame)
address_3 = ttk.Entry(address_label_frame)

address_1.pack(side=tk.TOP)
```

```
address_2.pack(side=tk.TOP)
address_3.pack(side=tk.TOP)

address_label_frame.pack(fill=tk.BOTH, expand=1)
address_frame.pack(side=tk.RIGHT, fill=tk.BOTH, expand=1)

win.mainloop()
```

We can then do the same thing with the `Entry` widget addresses, which are packed into our `address_label_frame`.

Give this file a run and you should see how `LabelFrame` looks:

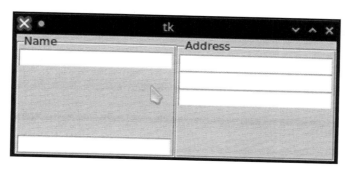

The Checkbutton and Radiobutton widgets

The `Checkbutton` and `Radiobutton` widgets allow a user to select an option by clicking to mark a box. A `Checkbutton` will allow the user to turn an option either on or off, whereas a `Radiobutton` is used to give the user a choice of one option from a group of multiple possibilities.

To get the values of each, a variable is passed to them via the `variable` keyword argument. With `Radiobutton` widgets, all possible options should be pointed to the same variable; then the user's chosen option can be obtained by querying this variable.

Let's have a look at the two in action:

```
import tkinter as tk

win = tk.Tk()

likes_python = tk.IntVar()
has_laptop = tk.IntVar()
```

```
c = tk.Checkbutton(win, variable=likes_python, text="Likes Python")
r1 = tk.Radiobutton(win, variable=has_laptop, text="Has Laptop", value=1)
r2 = tk.Radiobutton(win, variable=has_laptop, text="Does not have laptop",
value=0)
```

We create two variables – one representing whether the user likes Python and one for if they own a laptop.

The `likes_python` variable is then bound to a `Checkbutton` instance, along with the text `Likes Python`.

The `has_laptop` variable is assigned to two `Radiobutton` instances. One represents the user having a laptop and is assigned the value `1`. The other represents the user not having a laptop and is assigned the value `0`.

When the `Likes Python` button is not checked, the `IntVar` it is bound to will have the value `0`. When ticked, that will change to a `1`. This is the default behavior of the `Checkbutton` widget and does not need to be changed.

Likewise, if the user selects that they do not have a laptop, the value of the `has_laptop` `IntVar` will be `0`. If they instead select `Has Laptop`, its value will become `1`.

We can now finish off this demo by displaying the information and packing our widgets.

```
label1 = tk.Label(win, textvar=likes_python)
label2 = tk.Label(win, textvar=has_laptop)


c.pack()
r1.pack()
r2.pack()
label1.pack()
label2.pack()

win.mainloop()
```

We create two `Label` widgets, which are bound to our `IntVar` objects. This allows us to see the values change as we check and uncheck the buttons. All widgets are then packed and our window begins its main loop.

Give this demo file a run and see the results. Try clicking options and watching the text at the bottom of the window change in response:

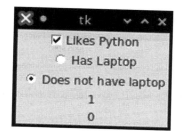

The OptionMenu and Combobox widgets

The OptionMenu and Combobox widgets are used to give the user the choice of one option from a group, much like a Radiobutton. They both display in a similar manner to a drop-down menu, or select menu, from HTML.

Whereas the OptionMenu widget only allows the user to choose an option that is in the menu, the Combobox widget essentially combines an Entry widget with the OptionMenu widget, allowing the user to type their own choice into the box as well.

We can have a look at these two widgets with a small piece of code:

```
import tkinter as tk
import tkinter.ttk as ttk

win = tk.Tk() '

options = ("low", "medium", "high")
om_chosen = tk.StringVar()
```

To prepare for these two widgets, we need a Tkinter variable to store the selection of the OptionMenu and a tuple of options which will be applied to each.

When instantiating the OptionMenu, the arguments will be the following:

- The parent widget (as usual)
- The variable in which to store the chosen answer
- The default answer
- The selectable options

In contrast, when instantiating a Combobox, we only need the parent widget, followed by the selectable options as a keyword argument named options. Since the Combobox is not linked to a Tkinter variable, we have to obtain its selection by calling the get method on the widget directly.

```
om = ttk.OptionMenu(win, om_chosen, "medium", *options)

cb = ttk.Combobox(win, values=options)

om.pack()
cb.pack()

win.mainloop()
```

Here, we create an OptionMenu, passing it the StringVar we made earlier, the string medium as the default value, and all possible options are supplied by unpacking the tuple options.

We then create a Combobox with just the parent widget and the options keyword argument.

Give this file a run and have a play with both widgets:

The Notebook widget

The Notebook widget is only available in ttk, rather than the regular Tkinter. The widget is used to create a tabbed interface for displaying multiple Frame widgets in one window. A small example will demonstrate this nicely:

```
import tkinter as tk
import tkinter.ttk as ttk

win = tk.Tk()
win.geometry("400x400")

n = ttk.Notebook(win)
frame_one = ttk.Frame(n)
frame_two = ttk.Frame(n)
```

```
label_one = ttk.Label(frame_one, text="We are in frame 1")
label_two = ttk.Label(frame_two, text="We are in frame 2")
```

We create an instance of the `Notebook` widget, then two `Frame` widgets to act as tabs.

Inside these two `Frame` widgets will be a `Label` widget which informs us which `Frame` we are seeing.

We now need to add these `Frame` widgets to our `Notebook`, which we do using the `add` method:

```
n.add(frame_one, text="Frame One")
n.add(frame_two, text="Frame Two")

n.pack(fill=tk.BOTH, expand=1)

label_one.pack(fill=tk.BOTH, expand=1)
label_two.pack(fill=tk.BOTH, expand=1)

win.mainloop()
```

Here, we add both of our `Frame` widgets to our `Notebook`, passing the `text` argument to control what will be written in the tab.

Since our `Frame` widgets are added to our `Notebook`, we don't need to use a geometry manager to display them, so we pack our `Label` widgets and `Notebook`, then fire off our window's main loop.

Run this code and you should see you have a window containing two different tabs. Click between them to see how each one contains a different `Frame`:

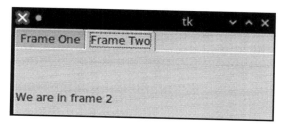

Those are all of the widgets of note which we didn't get to use in our example applications. If you would like to, have a think about how each could have been implemented in one of our applications.

For example, we could have used the `Notebook` widget to add file tabs to our text editor. If you are feeling adventurous, give this a go!

Now that we have covered these, it's time to have a look at how we can distribute our applications to other users who may want to install them.

Packaging applications

In order to easily share our applications with other users, we need an easy way for people to obtain and install them. Different operating systems will require different ways of accessing the needed libraries in order to run an application, and so the process for packaging them will likely vary slightly.

We will explore the world of Python application packaging using our text editor from chapters 5 - 7. Our goal will be to have it execute on three operating systems – Windows, Linux, and macOS. To package this application, it needs a name. I will be calling it `tkedit` for demonstration, but, if you have a better name, feel free to use that instead.

Before we can ship this file to work on all OSes, we need to adjust the folder structure. Recall that we were using local folders named `schemes` and `languages`, which lived inside the main folder for the editor. This will not translate when the application is packaged; so, we will need to hold our YAML files in the user's home directory. Let's get this change going.

Adjusting our text editor for portability

The main changes we will need to make will be in the `texteditor.py` file. Open up this file and add the following:

```
...
import os
from pathlib import Path
...
def __init__(self):
    ...
    self.config_dir = os.path.join(str(Path.home()), ".tkedit")
    self.default_scheme_path = os.path.join(self.config_dir,
                                'schemes/default.yaml')
    self.python_language_path = os.path.join(self.config_dir,
                                'languages/python.yaml')
    self.font_scheme_path = os.path.join(self.config_dir,
```

```
                            'schemes/font.yaml')
        self.create_config_directory_if_needed()
```

In order to access the user's home directory independent of the OS, we will use the `pathlib` module. The folder where we will be storing the user's YAML files will be called `.tkedit` and will live inside the user's home folder. To obtain the home folder, we can use `Path.home()`. This resulting folder is then joined to the `.tkedit` folder with `os.path.join`, and this is stored as our `config_dir` attribute.

Now that we have the folder stored, we can then construct paths inside of it where we will be storing our `schemes` and `languages` folders.

Once that is taken care of, we call a new method named `create_config_directory_if_needed`, which will take care of initializing these folders if they do not exist on the user's system:

```python
def create_config_directory_if_needed(self):
    if not os.path.exists(self.config_dir):
        os.mkdir(self.config_dir)
        os.mkdir(os.path.join(self.config_dir, 'schemes'))
        os.mkdir(os.path.join(self.config_dir, 'languages'))

    self.create_default_scheme_if_needed()
    self.create_font_scheme_if_needed()
    self.create_python_language_if_needed()
```

In this method, we use `os.path.exists` to check whether there is already a `.tkedit` folder in the user's home folder. If there is not, we use the `os.mkdir` method to create the directory, as well as the `schemes` and `languages` folders it needs to contain.

Since these folders may have just been created, we need to also put the default YAML files inside them if they aren't there already. We have three new methods for doing this:

```python
def create_default_scheme_if_needed(self):
    if not os.path.exists(self.default_scheme_path):
        yaml_file_contents = "background: 'lightgrey'\n" \
                        + "foreground: 'black'\n" \
                        + "text_background: 'white'\n" \
                        + "text_foreground: 'black'\n"

        with open(self.default_scheme_path, 'w') as yaml_file:
            yaml_file.write(yaml_file_contents)
```

In this first method, we check for the default scheme, which controls the color of our application and the `Text` widget inside it. If the file does not exist, we use a string to represent the default content and write this as the content of our `schemes/default.yaml` file:

```
def create_font_scheme_if_needed(self):
    if not os.path.exists(self.font_scheme_path):
        yaml_file_contents = "family: Ubuntu Mono\n" \
                            + "size: 14"

        with open(self.font_scheme_path, 'w') as yaml_file:
            yaml_file.write(yaml_file_contents)
```

This second method does much the same thing, but for our `schemes/font.yaml` file, which controls the editor's font family and size:

```
def create_python_language_if_needed(self):
    if not os.path.exists(self.python_language_path):
        yaml_file_contents = """
categories:
  keywords:
    color: orange
    ...
"""
        with open(self.python_language_path, 'w') as yaml_file:
            yaml_file.write(yaml_file_contents)
```

Our final new method does the same thing again for our `languages/python.yaml` file. I have omitted the content of this file for brevity; when following along, paste the content of the file in between the sets of speech marks.

You will notice that the indentation looks a little off here, which is because YAML is whitespace-sensitive. You may split each line as its own string for neatness, if you wish.

Now that our YAML files are taken care of, we need to replace all hardcoded references to them with the relevant attribute:

```
def __init__(self):
    ...
    self.load_scheme_file(self.default_scheme_path)
    self.configure_ttk_elements()

    self.font_size = 15
    self.font_family = "Ubuntu Mono"
    self.load_font_file(self.font_scheme_path)
    ...
```

```
        self.highlighter = Highlighter(self.text_area,
    self.python_language_path)

    def update_font(self):
        self.load_font_file(self.font_scheme_path)
        self.text_area.configure(font=(self.font_family, self.font_size))
```

We will also have to update our `fontchooser.py` and `colorchooser.py` files to use the attributes:

```
    ### fontchooser.py
    def save(self):
        font_family = self.font_list.get(self.font_list.curselection()[0])
        yaml_file_contents = f"family: {font_family}\n" \
                            + f"size: {self.size_input.get()}"

        with open(self.master.font_scheme_path, 'w') as file:
            file.write(yaml_file_contents)

        self.master.update_font()


    ### colorchooser.py
    def save(self):
        yaml_file_contents = f"background:
    '{self.chosen_background_color.get()}'\n" \
                            + f"foreground:
    '{self.chosen_foreground_color.get()}'\n" \
                            + f"text_background:
    '{self.chosen_text_background_color.get()}'\n" \
                            + f"text_foreground:
    '{self.chosen_text_foreground_color.get()}'\n"

        with open(self.master.default_scheme_path, "w") as yaml_file:
            yaml_file.write(yaml_file_contents)
        ...
```

With that, we are ready to package! We can now begin the steps necessary for packaging up our application.

Preparing to package with setup.py

When packaging an application, a special file called setup.py is required. This file will be read by the packaging tool and used to determine things such as which libraries to include, and which files should be run when the user executes the application.

Create a file named setup.py in your main text editor folder (which I have named tkedit) and add the following content:

```
#!/usr/bin/env python3

from distutils.core import setup

setup(
  name='tkedit',
  version='0.1',
  description='This is a python text editor with syntax highlighting',
  author='David Love',
  py_modules = [
    "colorchooser",
    "findwindow",
    "fontchooser",
    "highlighter",
    "linenumbers",
    "textarea",
    "texteditor",
    ],
    install_requires = [
        "PyYAML",
    ],
    entry_points = {
        "console_scripts": ["tkedit = texteditor:main"]
    }
)
```

To get our application building, we need to use a module designed to do that. Python comes with pip, which does a great job at handling this. Pip will use a module called distutils to prepare a package and we will need the setup function from its core module to do this.

After importing the `setup` function, we just need to call it, passing quite a few keyword arguments. These arguments represent the following:

- `name`: The application's name
- `version`: The application's version
- `description`: A short description of the application
- `author`: The author's name
- `py_modules`: The modules (Python files) which will be extracted from the current project
- `install_requires`: Any external libraries which need to be installed by `pip` to make the application usable
- `entry_points`: The commands which can be run once the package is installed, and what Python function they correspond to

For this example, the `entry_points` argument defines a command `tkedit` which should run the `main` function from the `texteditor` module. We don't have this function yet, so we need to quickly go back to our `texteditor.py` file and add it. Note that this function will need to be defined *outside* of the `TextEditor` class, just before the `if __name__ == "__main__"` block:

```
def main():
    mw = MainWindow()
    mw.mainloop()
```

With the setup file created, we are now one step closer to distributing our application. Let's now have a look at exactly how this will be done.

Installing our text editor

How to build and install a Python application is dependent on the OS which is being used to package it. Typically, each operating system only allows the application to be built for the same platform, meaning only Windows can create Windows `.exe` files, and so on. Pip, however, is able to run on all platforms, so can be used as a way of packaging once for any system.

For a user who will already have Python installed, we can distribute our applications as `pip` packages. This will work on all platforms, but requires the user to have the correct version of Python and pip already installed, and also to be able to use the command line.

Cross-platform using Pip

Our application is already set up to be distributed with pip. You can test this out yourself by opening a terminal window inside the root folder for your text editor and using the following commands:

```
$ python3 -m venv build-env
$ source build-env/bin/activate
$ pip install .
```

Provided that you are in the same directory as your setup.py file, pip should be able to parse this and install your text editor to your new virtual environment. You should now be able to run the tkedit command and be shown your text editor application!

If you wish to install the module globally, skip the creation of the virtual environment and just run sudo pip install .. This should install your text editor on your system so that it can be run from anywhere.

Whilst simple, the pip being used is a barrier to entry for any users who may not have Python installed or who are put off by using the command line. Let's have a look at how we can package our application into an executable file for each OS.

Windows

To package our text editor for Windows, we will need to use a module known as cx_freeze. This module is installed using pip via pip install cx_freeze.

To tell cx_freeze about our application, we will need to adjust our setup.py file:

```
from cx_Freeze import setup, Executable

import sys
base = 'Win32GUI' if sys.platform=='win32' else None

import os
PYTHON_INSTALL_DIR = os.path.dirname(os.path.dirname(os.__file__))
os.environ['TCL_LIBRARY'] = os.path.join(PYTHON_INSTALL_DIR, 'tcl',
'tcl8.6')
os.environ['TK_LIBRARY'] = os.path.join(PYTHON_INSTALL_DIR, 'tcl', 'tk8.6')

options = {
    'build_exe': {
        'include_files':[
            os.path.join(PYTHON_INSTALL_DIR, 'DLLs', 'tk86t.dll'),
```

```
            os.path.join(PYTHON_INSTALL_DIR, 'DLLs', 'tcl86t.dll'),
        ],
    },
}

executables = [
    Executable('tkedit.py', base=base)
]

setup(name='tkedit',
      version = '1.0',
      description = 'A tkinter text editor',
      options = options,
      executables = executables)
```

Instead of the setup function from `distutils`, we will be using the `cx_freeze` version. We import the `sys` module and use it to set a special variable as if we are on a 32 bit operating system.

Windows needs to know the location of the library of `tcl` and `tk` (which power Tkinter). To correctly form the paths to these files, we get the path to our Python installation, then join the necessary folders to it. These are set as environment variables, since `cx_freeze` will need to reference them during the build process.

When building the `.exe`, file, `cx_freeze` will also need to find the `.dll` files for `tk` and `tcl`. We create the paths to them inside a dictionary named `options`, under the `build_exe` and `include_files` keys.

With these libraries located, we now need to create an executable. We create an instance of the `Executable` class from `cx_freeze` and pass it a filename of `tkedit.py`, as well as the `base` which we defined earlier.

Once that is taken care of, we call the `setup` function as before, passing it our new `options` and `executables` variables.

Before we can run this, we need to create `tkedit.py`. Luckily, this is a very small file:

```
from texteditor import main

main()
```

Much like we had to allude to with Pip's version of the `setup.py` file, we need to call a function when the executable is run. This function will be the `main` function from our `texteditor.py` file.

In this file, we just import the function and run it. This allows `cx_freeze` to just run the `tkedit.py` file instead of parsing out the `main` function from our `texteditor.py` file.

With these two files taken care of, we can now build our application for windows. Open a command line in your root folder and run the following command:

```
python3 setup.py build
```

If everything has gone smoothly, you should see a lot of information about copying libraries, and then find that a folder named `build` has been added to your project.

Open up explorer and navigate to this folder. You should see another folder beginning with `exe-win32`. Head to that folder and you should see `tkedit.exe` sitting there. Run this file and check out your text editor!

Linux

Since Linux users will likely be familiar with command-line tools and most distributions will come with Python and `pip` installed already. Using `pip` is the recommended method for distributing your Python applications.

If you do not wish to use `pip`, there are many alternatives available, depending on the particular distribution the user is running.

For steps to create an `AppImage` binary, check out the official `AppImages` GitHub repository. There's a sample Python application available here: `https://github.com/AppImage/AppImages/blob/master/legacy/pythongtk3hello/Recipe`.

This sample contains the shell commands which need to be run in order to package your application as an `AppImage`. Before following the instructions, you will need a thumbnail image for you application (`tkedit.png` in our case) and a `.desktop` file to run it.

Here is an example `.desktop` file for our editor (`tkedit.desktop`):

```
[Desktop Entry]
Name=tkedit
Exec=tkedit
Icon=tkedit.png
Comment=A text editor with python syntax highlighting
```

You will need to create the icon, `tkedit.png`, yourself.

With these two files ready, you can then begin the process of creating an `AppImage` for your editor.

1. Download and source the helper functions from the `AppImages` repository:

```
$ wget -q https://github.com/AppImage/AppImages/raw/master/functions
.sh -O ./functions.sh
$ source ./functions.sh
```

2. Export variables which will be used throughout the script:

```
$ export APP=TKEDIT
$ export LOWERAPP=tkedit
```

3. Create the directory at which we will place our `AppImage`:

```
$ mkdir -p $APP/$APP.AppDir/
$ cd $APP/$APP.AppDir
```

4. Create a virtual environment named `usr` inside this folder:

```
$ python3 -m venv usr
$ source usr/bin/activate
```

5. Install our external dependency in this virtual environment:

```
$ pip install PyYAML
```

6. Copy your `python` modules into the `bin` directory of the virtual environment (ensure you have the `tkedit.py` file from the Windows section earlier):

```
$ cp *.py usr/bin/
```

7. Remove the file extension from `tkedit.py` and mark it as executable:

```
$ mv usr/bin/tkedit.py usr/bin/tkedit
$ chmod +x usr/bin/tkedit
```

8. Now, we can begin using the helper script functions to start doing the heavy lifting for us:

```
$ get_apprun
$ get_desktopintegration tkedit
```

9. You will be asked if you want to add the desktop entry to your system. This is up to you:

```
$ copy_deps; copy_deps; copy_deps;
$ delete_blacklisted
$ move_lib
```

10. You application will now need a version number, set as an environment variable:

```
$ export VERSION=1
```

11. We are now ready to package. A file named AppRun will have been created in your current directory. Run this file to test that the AppImage will work when executed:

```
$ ./AppRun
```

12. If all looks good, we are ready to package the AppImage:

```
$ cd ..
$ generate_appimage
```

13. After this command runs, you should have a new folder called out. Inside here should be a binary file called something like TKEDIT-01.glibc2.3.4-x86_64.AppImage. This is your binary file and can be run as follows:

```
./TKEDIT-01.glibc2.3.4-x86_64.AppImage
```

14. If your AppImage was created successfully, you can now give this file to other people so that they can run your editor!

macOS

When packaging for macOS, cx_freeze may work for you. However, there is another alternative named py2app, which we will take a look at now.

Ensure you have the tkedit.py file described in the Windows section earlier, then install py2app into our virtual environment using pip. We will need version 0.13, since later versions do not support Tkinter properly:

```
$ source env/bin/activate
$ pip install py2app==0.13
```

With `py2app` installed, you can go ahead and let it generate a `setup.py` file using its setup tools:

```
$ py2applet --make-setup tkedit.py
```

This should overwrite your `setup.py` file with a new one. We will need to add our `PyYAML` dependency to it, so it looks like so:

```
"""
This is a setup.py script generated by py2applet

Usage:
    python setup.py py2app
"""

from setuptools import setup

APP = ['tkedit.py']
DATA_FILES = []
OPTIONS = {'includes': ['PyYAML']}

setup(
    app=APP,
    data_files=DATA_FILES,
    options={'py2app': OPTIONS},
    setup_requires=['py2app'],
)
```

With this taken care of, we can now install our dependencies and then execute the `py2app` command:

```
$ pip install PyYAML
$ python3 setup.py py2app
```

This should create two new folders for you, named `build` and `dist`. Your binary will be in the `dist` folder. You can run it by referencing it from the terminal, a:

```
$ ./dist/tkedit.app/Contents/MacOS/tkedit
```

If your editor pops up, congratulations! You have now created a macOS binary.

That covers everything for building packaged binaries. You hopefully should now be ready to port over your Tkinter GUI applications to distribute to the rest of the world. Of course, the more complicated the application, the more steps will be involved in getting it packaged; so, some in-depth reading of packaging Python applications is recommended. The official guide can be found at `https://docs.python.org/3/distutils/setupscript.html`

Summary

In this chapter, we have looked at a few widgets which did not make their way into our example applications.

We saw that the `LabelFrame` widget allows us to surround a group of widgets with a heading, which can be either hardcoded or tied to a `Label` widget.

The `Checkbutton` and `Radiobutton` widgets were demonstrated, and we saw how to bind them to Tkinter's variables, such as `IntVar` objects, in order to return the user's choices.

We learned about the `OptionMenu` and `Combobox` widgets, which are used to make a choice from a list of pre-defined options. The `Combobox` acts as a combination of an `Entry` widget and an `OptionMenu` widget, also allowing the user to enter their own value if necessary.

If we want to have a tabbed interface, we have now looked at how the `Notebook` widget allows us to display multiple frames in a window using tabs and we can assign each one a label to display in its tab.

After covering those widgets, we moved on to learning how to create binary packages for our text editor project. After adjusting the application to store its configuration data in the user's home directory, we saw how to create a `setup.py` file, which allows the program to be installed with Python's package manager – `pip`.

The benefits and drawbacks of pip were mentioned and, then, we looked at packaging for each major desktop operating system independently. We used `cx_freeze` to create a `.exe` file for Windows, the `AppImage` suite to create a `.AppImage` file for Linux, and `py2app` to create a `.app` file for macOS.

That's it for *Tkinter GUI Programming by Example*. We have now built three working desktop applications and are able to share them with the rest of the world via packaging. I hope this book has shown you how easy it is to turn your simple Python scripts into full graphical applications or build a desktop application from the ground up. Go forth and create! Feel free to share your work with me over on GitHub, where I can be found at `https://github.com/Dvlv`. I look forward to hearing from you.

Other Books You May Enjoy

If you enjoyed this book, you may be interested in these other books by Packt:

Tkinter GUI Application Development Cookbook
Alejandro Rodas de Paz

ISBN: 978-1-78862-230-1

- Add widgets and handle user events
- Lay out widgets within windows using frames and the different geometry managers
- Configure widgets so that they have a customized appearance and behavior
- Improve the navigation of your apps with menus and dialogs
- Apply object-oriented programming techniques in Tkinter applications
- Use threads to achieve responsiveness and update the GUI
- Explore the capabilities of the canvas widget and the types of items that can be added to it
- Extend Tkinter applications with the TTK (themed Tkinter) module

Python GUI Programming Cookbook - Second Edition
Burkhard Meier

ISBN: 978-1-78712-945-0

- Create the GUI Form and add widgets
- Arrange the widgets using layout managers
- Use object-oriented programming to create GUIs
- Create Matplotlib charts
- Use threads and talking to networks
- Talk to a MySQL database via the GUI
- Perform unit-testing and internationalizing the GUI
- Extend the GUI with third-party graphical libraries
- Get to know the best practices to create GUIs

Leave a review - let other readers know what you think

Please share your thoughts on this book with others by leaving a review on the site that you bought it from. If you purchased the book from Amazon, please leave us an honest review on this book's Amazon page. This is vital so that other potential readers can see and use your unbiased opinion to make purchasing decisions, we can understand what our customers think about our products, and our authors can see your feedback on the title that they have worked with Packt to create. It will only take a few minutes of your time, but is valuable to other potential customers, our authors, and Packt. Thank you!

Index

Made in the USA
Middletown, DE
19 September 2018